The Legacy of
D'Arcy McNickle

American Indian Literature
and Critical Studies Series

Gerald Vizenor and Louis Owens,
General Editors

The Legacy of D'Arcy McNickle

Writer, Historian, Activist

Edited by
John Lloyd Purdy

University of Oklahoma Press
Norman and London

This book is published with the generous assistance of The McCasland Foundation, Duncan, Oklahoma.

Library of Congress Cataloging-in-Publication Data

The legacy of D'Arcy McNickle : writer, historian, activist / edited by John Lloyd Purdy.
     p. cm. — (American Indian literature and critical studies series ; v. 21)
  Includes bibliographical references (p.   ) and index.
  ISBN 0-8061-2806-2 (alk. paper)
  1. McNickle, D'Arcy, 1904–1977—Criticism and interpretation. 2. Indians of North America—Historiography. 3. Western stories—History and criticism. 4. West (U.S.) in literature. 5. Indians in literature. I. Purdy, John Lloyd. II. Series.
PS3525.A2844Z75 1996
813'.52—dc20   95-25863
                                                            CIP

Text design by Cathy Carney Imboden. Typeface is Palatino.

The Legacy of D'Arcy McNickle: Writer, Historian, Activist is Volume 21 in the American Indian Literature and Critical Studies Series.

The paper in this book meets the guidelines for permanence and durability of the Committee on Production Guidelines for Book Longevity of the Council on Library Resources, Inc. ∞

1 2 3 4 5 6 7 8 9 10

*This book is dedicated to
the memory of D'Arcy McNickle
and all those who have been moved
by the need to be heard.*

Contents

Introduction

April 12, 1932

> *Sanity is that fluidity of mind and personality which continues at all times, in all circumstances, aware of relationships—the individual's relation to other individuals, to his times, to his circumstances—and because of this awareness allows no walls to be built which will confine and restrict—crystallize— this fluidity, rendering it subject to categorical description; accordingly, opinions are expressed tentatively, beliefs are frankly stated in terms of motion, as are prejudices, faith is regarded as a constitutional bias, while knowledge is the one road that can be followed, and it only so long as it remains in the clear. As will be inferred, very few people can be called sane.*
>
> D'Arcy McNickle, *Personal Diary*

The words from D'Arcy McNickle's diary speak very clearly to an audience in the closing decade of the twentieth century, an era labeled "postmodern" or even "post-postmodern," yet they were written in a time that was clearly "modern," with all that the term implies. Today his words seem very prophetic, as though attuned with thought and literatures of the future, yet remarkably, the writer was completely removed from the influential circles of modernist innovators; he was an unknown visionary.

Why McNickle? No doubt McNickle asked himself this question numerous times throughout his life, but the answer for our purpose—to the question why we would wish to write a book about him—is simple: he is a prominent figure in twentieth-century Native American history who never achieved mainstream prominence. The general public, and even scholars, know little about him. His name is rarely mentioned in history books, although he had a hand in shaping policies and programs that dramatically affected contemporary Native American life and the ways historians address Native American history. In addition, his own writings not only reflect that history but also the issues, and the perceptions of issues, that became crucial to indigenous North American peoples. An exceptionally talented fiction writer, his innovations in that genre are now central to contemporary Native American written literatures. In short, his life and works are immensely interesting and worthy of careful study for they are clearly relevant to understanding interactions among all Americans, past, present, and future.

Condensing the essence of a life into a few words by way of introduction is not an easy task. A conventional biographical sketch of McNickle begins quite simply and predictably: "He was born near St. Ignatius, Montana, on January 18, 1904." This is fact, but only partially true when viewed from the distance of his future. McNickle was reborn several times throughout his life as he wrestled with who he was, who others wished him to be, and who he wanted to be. This fundamental model of human conflict and development, however, took an added dimension in McNickle's case.

It is tempting to simplify his dilemma by saying he faced the common dilemma of being torn between identifying as Native American or as mainstream American. While true to a degree, a reduction of this nature will not work here. McNickle faced many complex identity choices throughout his seventy-three years, as he first witnessed monumental changes in the affairs of Native America, and then helped shape them. Directly and indirectly, he faced the distinctly difficult challenges to self-identity that all indigenous peoples have encountered in the twentieth century, challenges that came about through the attractive power of "modern America" coupled with governmental dicta. His own attempts at self-awareness reflect similar efforts by many others who have confronted contentious, sometimes threatening or limiting forces. McNickle moved from a rural life-style to an urban and urbane one. He became an administrator, a bureaucrat, a political activist, an academic, a lover and father, and at every moment of his adult life, a writer. Studying the ways he integrated these lives into a coherent whole through his writings, to become what N. Scott Momaday termed "a man made of words," is a study of contemporary Native American written literature in all its complexity, layered visions, and voices.

In a recent workshop on Indian identity, Edward Castillo encapsulated Native American responses to European incursion into three simple, though traumatic, behaviors: fight, flee, and accommodate. McNickle's family followed this pattern, and he manifested the stage of accommodation. Nevertheless, "accommodation" is not always synonymous with assimilation, as the chapters in this book reveal. The degree to which, in their interactions, a person or culture adopts the characteristics of "the other" has always been a fundamental human issue, and it seems to have been a primary shaping influence in McNickle's life as well. The generational cycle one sees in the literatures of immigrant families in general is painfully apparent in McNickle's. The cycle begins with a generation closely tied to the old ways who leave, or are removed from, the Homeland. Their offspring, however, turn away from the parents' traditions in order to save their own children from cultural conflict in the new environment. Thus, a third generation is produced who must make a deliberate, atavistic leap back to the grandparents in order to satisfy a need to recover an identity that is tied to the traditions and places of the past. At the same time, this generation must learn to survive in a contemporary society sometimes hostile to "deviance" from a uniform identity. The theme that runs through McNickle's life and his works is pervasive in contemporary Indian written literature and experience: accommodations to change buffered by an urge to reaffirm and perpetuate traditions and values.

His was not the first generation to face sweeping change. His family came to the Flathead (Montana Salish) and Kootenai Reservation in northwest Montana after the failed Riel Rebellion in Saskatchewan. The lengthy conflict, like so many others throughout American history, was over the lands belonging to indigenous peoples, and therefore, it was also a contest over lifeways. The role McNickle's grandfather, Isidore Parenteau, played in the conflict is debated; however, in 1885 he lost his farm, home, and livestock and fled southward across the border with his family. It was into this family, dispossessed and supplanted by European immigrants from the East, that McNickle was born. His father was Anglo-Irish; his mother was listed as one-quarter Cree on the papers that record her adoption by the Salish people.

Although the degree to which his early environment shaped McNickle's perspective is also open to debate, his writings reveal a philosophy that is closely related to his home life as a child: existence is tentative, the future always in doubt. In such an atmosphere survival is all-important, but one must also determine its costs. The fact is, this is a recurrent concern for Native peoples and a recurrent thematic concern in their literature, but the degree to which McNickle's works reflect the survival of Native cultures is disputed. Adding to the interest, a study of his works raises issues that surface in many other texts and contexts.

Like many Native American children, McNickle attended a mission school, and then a federal boarding school, Chemawa, in Salem, Oregon. He wrote of his school experiences several times and in different contexts. In his first and last novels, *The Surrounded* (1936) and *Wind from an Enemy Sky* (1978), the protagonists share their less-than-fond memories of boarding school, but he also addresses schools in his historical writings, discussing them in the larger historical contexts of colonialism. In other words, a prominent element in his early life became a recurrent subject in his writings, in which he worked out in various ways its relation to his personal story and to the story of Native peoples in general. His blend of fictional characters and historical events is a skillfully drawn aspect of his work; the novels are situated within a complex network of historical events that he experienced directly.

His novels, however, are not solely concerned with the advent of colonialism and its detrimental effects, despite some critics' reliance upon this approach to them. McNickle's canon is not comprised of protest literature, although it effectively protests the course of events that culminated in his own experience. The power in his work lies in his extending "American history" to a point long before the incursion of the European and in the ways he integrates traditional verbal arts with a Native point of view to formulate a specific written poetics/aesthetics.

In *The Surrounded*, his protagonist's story can only be understood within the context of the longer history of his people. The tale begins long before the coming of Catholic priests to the valley of "sniél-emen," and to McNickle's credit it is conveyed through storytelling and personal revelation. In his second novel, *Runner in the Sun: A Story of Indian Maize*

(1954), he imagined the time that preceded the voyages of Columbus, which have come to symbolize the advent of European colonialism in the Americas. *Wind from an Enemy Sky*, published the year following his death, places the problems of his fictional "Little Elk" people not solely at the door of the whites, but also upon the inadequate early reactions of the people, themselves, to colonial policies. This expansive view permits a more comprehensive interpretation of his books, without allowing them or the issues they raise to be easily dismissed.

McNickle's "fluidity of mind and personality" afforded him perceptive insight and the facility to convince others of his observations. His "sane" understanding of issues and ability to craft revealing texts around them, in part, account for the attraction that his writings continue to hold for readers almost twenty years after his death. In fact, his popularity has increased dramatically during the last few years. *The Surrounded* was translated into Italian in 1992, and his other novels continue to engage new readers. Moreover, increasing critical attention has been directed to his works, much of it written by the contributors to this volume. This collection presents a cross section of the ways that the writings of Native American authors and poets can be interpreted. This has, in fact, been one determining factor in their inclusion in this volume.

The Legacy of D'Arcy McNickle: Writer, Historian, Activist is as much about how we, as readers and scholars, construct and value an author's text in relation to others, as it is about an individual named D'Arcy McNickle. These few essays afford an introduction. One of the strengths of contemporary written Native American or Amerindian or First Peoples or First Nations literatures is their wealth of evocative power. Our imaginations are not idle when we read McNickle's works, nor is our memory. At the close of his books, like Archilde in his first novel, we wonder at the force of the story, and then reflect and explore. We may search for the genesis of his narratives in the written texts of his times, as Birgit Hans does in her review of the histories and literary histories contemporary with the creation of *The Surrounded*, or like Dorothy Parker, who looks to the work of Joseph Campbell to provide a context for *Runner in the Sun*. We may, like Robert Gish, consider McNickle's texts in terms of the Western novel and Western conventions, popular in the 1930s, of hunters and heroes. Gish's style reflects his own works of fiction in its playful manipulation, in its stalking language that cuts back across our trails. We may also find ourselves wondering about the effects of federal Indian policies on McNickle's work, since he was intimately involved in those policies and writes about them extensively in his nonfiction prose, but Bill Brown, Philip Doss, Alanna Kathleen Brown, Lori Burlingame, and Jay Vest debate the degree to which McNickle deliberately drew upon tribal verbal arts and world views to create his novels. We may find—as in Robley Evans's provocative essay—challenges to reading *The Surrounded* as anything but a statement of dispossession. And finally, we may follow James Ruppert's lead and find it useful to employ contemporary discourse theory to sound the complexity of McNickle's vision.

These writers take diverse approaches to McNickle's texts to interpret his vision, his many voices, and his multiple points of view, but it would be futile to imagine we have put an end to the debates surrounding his life and works. Instead, we hope to encourage discussions of both so that new readers may be drawn into the depths and subtleties of D'Arcy McNickle's work and come to appreciate the general body of texts termed contemporary Native literatures. Critical theory seeks to resolve the mysterious dynamic we call literature; this volume merely celebrates its richness.

JOHN LLOYD PURDY

Bellingham, Washington

Part One

Origins and Words

Chapter One

D'Arcy McNickle:
An Annotated Bibliography of
His Published Articles
and Book Reviews
in a Biographical Context

Dorothy R. Parker

For forty years D'Arcy McNickle wrote about Native Americans. His novel, *The Surrounded*, published in 1936, was the first of a variety of publications that marked his distinguished career in Indian affairs. Two more novels, several short stories, a biography, three historical monographs, and numerous articles and book reviews all reveal the extent of his concerns. He is best known today for his novels, but his articles, examined in the context of his life, provide a more immediate and intimate insight into the development of his thinking.

D'Arcy McNickle (1904–1977) was one of a handful of people employed by the Bureau of Indian Affairs (BIA) under John Collier who continued to work for and write about Indian affairs for decades after the "Indian New Deal" of the 1930s and 1940s. McNickle, an enrolled member of the Flathead tribe of northwestern Montana, was hired under Collier's "Indian Civil Service" policy in 1936. At the time of his resignation from the bureau in 1952, he was head of the Tribal Organization Division. By that time, he had written his first historical monograph, a number of articles for the BIA's house organ, *Indians at Work*, and other articles as well.

After he left the bureau, McNickle established a health education and community development project among the Navajos at Crownpoint, New Mexico. This project, which lasted from 1953 to 1960, was funded through the National Congress of American Indians (NCAI), an organization he had helped establish in 1944. Although McNickle continued to write during this period, his lengthy report of the Crownpoint project was never published.

In 1961 McNickle chaired the steering committee of the American Indian Chicago Conference, under the auspices of the University of Chicago. He was also the primary author of the definitive statement issued by that conference, the "Declaration of Indian Purpose," which reflected the broad spectrum of Indian needs and goals at the time. From 1956 to 1967, he participated in and later directed a series of summer leadership training workshops for young Native American college students at the University of Colorado in Boulder.

In 1966, McNickle accepted an appointment as chair of the Department of Anthropology at the newly organized campus of the University of Saskatchewan in Regina, Canada. That same year he received an honorary doctorate in science from the University of Colorado for his work in applied anthropology. He remained in Canada until 1971. During those years he continued to write, producing a biography of Oliver La Farge, numerous book reviews for *The Nation* and other publications, and chapters for several books. Responding to renewed interest in Indian affairs during the 1960s, he also revised his earlier narrative histories.

By the time McNickle retired to Albuquerque in 1971, he was recognized as an elder leader in Indian affairs. His writing, teaching, and leadership had yielded a body of work that still speaks to those who are interested in and concerned about the country's Native American population. Two of McNickle's three novels deal creatively with the collision of Indian and white cultures; his first one, *The Surrounded*, is recognized as a forerunner of the modern "Indian renaissance."[1]

McNickle also wrote poetry and short stories, but he succeeded in publishing very little of his work. His short stories, both published and unpublished, have been collected in an annotated work by Birgit Hans. His only published poetry is found in early issues of *The Frontier*, the student literary publication of the University of Montana, which later changed its name to *The Frontier and Midland*.

McNickle's writing has three distinct audiences. The largest consists of those who have read his novels. *The Surrounded*, which postdates Mourning Dove's *Cogewea* by nine years, was one of the first novels published by a Native American author. Although both *Cogewea* and *The Surrounded* were set on the Flathead Reservation and both featured the life of a mixed blood, neither author was acquainted with or aware of the other. *Cogewea*, which has been republished recently by the University of Nebraska Press, is valued today primarily as an artifact. *The Surrounded*, however, is considered the first of a number of distinguished contemporary novels, including N. Scott Momaday's *House Made of Dawn*, Leslie Marmon Silko's *Ceremony*, and James Welch's *Winter in the Blood*, all of which, like *The Surrounded*, deal with the theme of the young mixed blood who returns to the reservation but is lost. McNickle's two other novels, *Runner in the Sun* (1954) and *Wind from an Enemy Sky* (1978), have received less critical attention than *The Surrounded*; all three have been reprinted recently by the University of New Mexico Press.

A second group of people interested in McNickle's work are cultural anthropologists. As a member of Collier's "Indian New Deal," McNickle observed and was sympathetic with the commissioner's attempts to enlist the help of anthropologists and other social scientists in redesigning the government's Indian policy. He was an eager student, and by the time his Crownpoint project ended in 1960, he was recognized as an authority in the field of cultural anthropology, although he was completely self-taught. His stature is evident in the fact that he was elected fellow in both the American Anthropological Association and the Society for Applied Anthropology. A number of his articles reveal his maturing insight into the relationship between personality and culture.

Historians of twentieth-century Indian affairs make up the third group of people who are interested in McNickle's work. Some of these historians are concerned with the overall development of Indian/white relationships, while others are more interested in Collier and the Indian Reorganization Act of 1934. McNickle's several narrative histories include *They Came Here First* (1949), *Indians and Other Americans*, in which he collaborated with Harold Fey (1959 and 1970), and *The Indian Tribes of the United States* (1962), revised and republished in 1973 as *Native American Tribalism*. McNickle used a broad brush to paint a picture of changing government policies and the remarkable adaptations Indians have made to those policies. Also of interest to historians is his *Indian Man: A Life of Oliver La Farge* (1971), which he admitted writing as much for a review of the history of the period as for the biography itself.

While McNickle's various books are important, it is the more ephemeral corpus of his articles that provides immediate insight into his thinking at any particular time. Although the articles are at times somewhat repetitious (he wrote about the same matters for a wide variety of publications), there are recurrent themes that provide an underlying unity.

McNickle's first job with the BIA bore the title of junior administrative assistant. It was a position created by Collier that allowed him to use McNickle as a "floater"; he could be assigned wherever there was a need. Collier first assigned him to update tribal roles and interpret the new constitutional structure that was the essential component of the Indian Reorganization Act. When he could be spared, he was loaned to Lloyd La Rouche, editor of *Indians at Work*, for various research and writing assignments. During his first two years with the bureau, McNickle wrote several brief articles, "Alaska-Getting Acquainted" (November 1936, 5–7), "Hill 57" (February 1937, 19–21), and "Maine" (October 1937, 15–18). These were straightforward expository accounts of the Native people in those areas and the bureau's efforts in their behalf. Of particular interest to McNickle was a place called "Hill 57," which was a community of "landless" Indians near Great Falls, Montana. These people were *Métis*, (the descendants of mixed blood French Canadians and Cree Indians), McNickle's own blood ancestry.[2] He described the bureau's attempt to acquire a land base for these people, an attempt that eventually failed when the local residents successfully fought the acquisition.

Indians at Work not only informed field workers about BIA activities across the country, it also contained an occasional book review, and in 1937 McNickle authored three of them. He reviewed Edwin Corle's *People of the Earth* in the issue of 1 July (47–48), Gregorio Lopez y Fuentes's *El Indio* in the 15 July-1 August issue (47–48), and Oliver La Farge's *The Enemy Gods* in the issue of 19 December (29–30). La Farge had enthusiastically reviewed *The Surrounded* the year before, and McNickle was, in turn, excited about *The Enemy Gods*. It was the story of a Navajo boy, reared by white missionaries, who gradually found his way back to the religion of his people. McNickle explained that the Indians' desire to worship was no different from that of other people, and the expression of that desire within their own culture was equally valid and deserved the same respect as any other religious practice. He would write repeatedly about the universality of the Native American experience.

McNickle's fervent praise of La Farge's book returned to haunt him later. By the late 1930s, Collier was under increasing attack from the right-wing American Indian Federation, most notably by an Iroquois woman, Alice Lee Jemison. Collier and Jemison faced each other during a congressional hearing in 1940, and Jemison flaunted McNickle's review as an example of the anti-Christian, procommunist bias of the BIA. McNickle was present at the hearing and was called upon to defend himself, which he did quite effectively. Collier also spoke on his behalf and probably saved McNickle's job.[3]

From his first days with the bureau, McNickle was an ardent supporter of Collier's program for the reform of federal Indian policy. Collier increasingly turned to McNickle for help in implementing this program, and, as a result, McNickle came to know it well. On the fourth anniversary of the Wheeler-Howard Act, which implemented that reform, McNickle wrote an article for *Indians at Work* entitled, "Four Years of Indian Reorganization" (July 1938, 4–11). Although it was hardly an objective assessment, this article was one of the first published evaluations of Collier's administration written from the inside.

The year of that article, 1938, marked the high point of congressional support for the Indian New Deal. After that, criticisms mounted from the far right. The debacle of stock reduction on the Navajo Reservation came to light, and Congress began to question the bureau's land acquisition policy and Collier's experiments in social engineering. In 1938, however, McNickle was still enthusiastic. He told his readers that the reorganization policy was leading to increased tribal self-determination by training tribal members in political and economic affairs. He cited events in Alabama, Arizona, Montana, New Mexico, and South Dakota to prove the effectiveness of land acquisition and various new education programs. Congress, he argued, must not reduce funding at this critical moment. The tribes must not be set adrift just as they were learning the rudiments of self-government. Many problems still existed, especially in dealing with heirship lands and law and order jurisdiction. While much had been accomplished, much still needed to be done.

McNickle contributed two additional book reviews to *Indians at Work* before its demise in 1945. One was of George C. Vaillant's *Indian Arts of North America* in July 1940 (27), the other of Julia B. McGillicuddy's biography of her father, *McGillicuddy, Agent,* in June 1941 (29–33). He also contributed a brief descriptive piece on Indian basketry in July 1940.

Of greater importance than his book reviews in reflecting his own opinions were four other articles in *Indians at Work* that revealed the direction of his growth in the field of cultural anthropology. McNickle had first become interested in linguistics when, working on *The Surrounded,* he encountered the problem of translating folk tales from an oral tradition into written English. In "What Do the Old Men Say," an article in *Indians at Work,* December 1941 (24–26), he addressed the fact that, among Indians, the old men who were traditional leaders had been quite literally robbed of their voice because they spoke no English. The BIA had failed to provide for translators who were sufficiently fluent in both languages, thus denying an effective voice for those traditional speakers. Young Native Americans who spoke English often were unable to understand their elders sufficiently to provide accurate translations. Perhaps the bureau preferred it that way.

Indians themselves, McNickle admitted, bore some of the responsibility for this condition by failing to teach the language to their children, but such instruction had become increasingly difficult as small children were removed from the family and sent to off-reservation boarding schools. The remedy was twofold. Indian parents should be encouraged to teach their language to children at home, and the BIA must begin to train some young people for the role of interpreter. The traditional wisdom must not be lost for the future.

In late 1941, just before the onset of World War II, the Bureau of Indian Affairs embarked on a joint program with the University of Chicago that became known as the Indian Education, Personality, and Administration Research Project. This project was Collier's most elaborate attempt to involve social scientists in the policy-making process. The so-called Indian Personality Study was designed to determine how Indian personality developed within the social context of the tribal community and what the cultural forces were that had kept Indian people Indian, despite all efforts of EuroAmericans to remake them into their own image.

In May 1942, as the project was getting under way, McNickle attended a training session in Santa Fe for those who could carry out the actual fieldwork, and he described the experience enthusiastically in "Toward Understanding" (May/June 1942, 4–7). Despite the distractions and dislocations of World War II, the fieldwork was completed on schedule, and a second meeting was held in Chicago in March 1943 to assemble the data and plan for its publication ("Science and the Future," May/June 1943, 43). Although the project eventually fell short of Collier's expectations, several important tribal studies emerged, produced by a committee on which McNickle and his wife both served.

McNickle wrote one more article for *Indians at Work*, "We Go on from Here" (November/December 1943, 14–21). This piece was longer than the others he had written for the bureau. It was a somewhat romantic, anecdotal exposition of Indian sensibilities that would be reflected in his later Native American histories. In it he defended the Indians' desire to maintain the reservations as their homes. Once again he expressed the idea that the Native American life experience was a universal one, only lived within a different cultural context. "Why should this be difficult to understand, this desire to live in the desert or the mountains, away from that which is not yours? To choose that which is your own and wrap it around you, hold it to you—surely this is a trait of our common humanity."

This was the same theme McNickle had used earlier in his review of La Farge's *The Enemy Gods*—the Indians' spiritual quest was not uniquely Indian, but rather an expression of a universal desire. The Native Americans' love for their homeland was also a trait common to everyone, not some savage aberration that marked the Indians as less than human. Nevertheless, whites had consistently viewed the Native "always through a culture [that was] not his, which he never claimed as his own, and which he ha[d] not yet desired as his own. All the difficulties we have with Indians trace to that, all the wrong things we do for Indians, trace to that." Nevertheless, McNickle concluded hopefully, "we are only at a place of beginning, and we go on from here." Collier, however, resigned in January 1945, and the ensuing fifteen years saw much that he had attempted undone by more "bad decisions and worse choices of policy."

McNickle published two other articles during his years with the BIA. In 1940 he addressed the fifth annual meeting of the Missouri Archeological Society, and his paper, "The American Indian Today," was published in the *Missouri Archaeologist* (Sept. 1940, 1–10). For this address, too, he used anecdotal material to describe and justify Collier's program. He assured his audience that the commissioner wanted neither "willy-nilly assimilation" nor "segregation behind reservation barriers." Instead, Collier's program was designed to assure tribal survival and increased tribal self-determination.

In 1943, *Scientific Monthly* (220–29) published McNickle's article, "Peyote and the Indian," which discussed the emotionally charged subject of peyote and the Native American Church. Here McNickle presented the last scientific information about the substance; he described its ceremonial use and stressed the incorporation of various Christian elements in the ritual of the Native American Church. Once again he insisted on the universality of the Indians' religious experience. The Indian, he wrote, "believes that the white man's God and his own are the same, but that each approaches him on his own or by his own road." The use of peyote, he explained, had made a significant social contribution by serving in a constructive way to restore unity to tribal people whose splintered social world was in danger of disintegration. Writing for a non-Native audience, he summarized his arguments by declaring that "most important of all is the social significance of the cult, which anthropologists can explain but the casual observer must miss." Whether or not peyote became a permanent element of Indian life, its use by Native Americans deserved valid social and religious considerations.

Collier's resignation in 1945 and Congress's subsequent determination to reduce the federal budget after the war paved the way for a reversal of federal Indian policy and a return to the pre-Collier concept of assimilation, with a stated goal of terminating government protection of tribal lands as speedily as possible. McNickle remained at the bureau, trying to help various tribes respond to pressures that by the 1950s would become almost intolerable. He was increasingly sensitive to the problem of communication between two disparate worlds, as was evident in his piece that appeared in *Common Ground* (71–76) in spring 1945. In "Afternoon on a Rock," he recalled a visit to the Hopi mesas in Arizona the previous summer. The Hopis had asked difficult questions about the whites' invasion of the Indians' land and the subsequent imposition of alien laws and customs, questions that disturbed the conscience of the visitors. When McNickle signed a contract with Lippincott for his historical monograph, *They Came Here First* (1949), he shortened this earlier article to use as the foreword for that book. Another essay published later in *Common Ground* (Summer 1949), "Golden Myth," was also incorporated into that book.

Another McNickle article, "Rescuing Sisseton," published in *The American Indian* (1947, 21–27), was a scathing indictment of past Indian policy as it affected just one tribe. It was written in response to a congressional bill that would restore the tribal land of the Sisseton Indians, a branch of the Santee Sioux in Minnesota. By 1945, these Indians had lost almost their entire land base and were living in conditions described by investigators as "one of the most disgraceful situations in America." McNickle argued in favor of the proposed legislation, and he used the situation as an object lesson for those who encouraged immediate termination. The future would be as grim for other tribes as it had been for the Sisseton should the others also be forced to undergo termination before they were adequately prepared for it. "For those who go on advocating the 'freeing' of Indians from the protective restrictions lying on their land- will they insist that every tribe of Indians live through the same experience in order to gain salvation?" he asked pointedly.

Nevertheless, termination reflected the public as well as the congressional will, and the process continued to escalate. Later, again in *The American Indian* (1949, 3–12), McNickle examined some of the underlying questions relating to termination in "Basis for a National Indian Policy." The United States government's relationship with its Native American peoples involved both a responsibility and an obligation. The government's responsibility related to righting past wrongs in usurping their lands and tribal autonomy, while its obligation originated in treaties that carried the weight of constitutional law and could not be abrogated unilaterally. The two, McNickle said, must not be confused. Native people could and should learn to adapt so that they themselves could assume responsibility for protection and maintaining tribal land and resources. The federal government, on the other hand, had long-standing obligations to assist in this development. McNickle then returned to an old Collier theme: Indian administration "must make increasing use of methods of the social sciences in resolving the basic problems of assisting the Indians to adjust their lives to the dominant culture." Although McNickle still believed that assimilation was both possible and inevitable, he insisted that it take place at a rate determined by the Indians themselves and not by government fiat.

Despite the rising tide of sentiment favoring termination, McNickle was not quite ready to give up on the ability of the federal government to develop a constructive policy. In response to President Harry Truman's Point Four Program of financial aid to Third World countries, McNickle suggested that such a program might also be effective among Native American tribes. In "U.S. Indian Affairs," *America Indigena* (October 1953), he presented the case for a domestic Point Four Program for Indians that would give them the deciding vote on how such aid would be spent. "It would cost money, rather staggering amounts of money at the outset," he wrote. "But it is to be questioned whether a decent alternative exists to such a program of investment, the success of which would pay back the United States many-fold in increased productivity of wealth and human adjustment." The various federal anti-poverty programs established among Indian tribes in the 1960s, which were administered by the Indians themselves, would show the practicality of McNickle's suggestion. They provided a training ground for self-administered programs such as the bureau itself had never attempted.

By the time he wrote that article, however, McNickle had taken a temporary leave of absence from the BIA, a leave that became permanent in 1954. He had become convinced that the government's termination policy was morally wrong and that the government per se was unable to develop and execute a constructive policy for Native American affairs.

Private agencies, he felt, provided greater flexibility, especially in their financial support, and in 1953 he launched a privately funded program in community development under the aegis of the National Congress of American Indians.

During this period of change in his professional life, McNickle wrote his second novel, *Runner in the Sun* (1954), and a long article on North American Indians for the fourteenth edition of the *Encyclopaedia Britannica*. The latter was a straightforward presentation based on his research in history, anthropology, and ethnography. This article, which included photographs and an extensive bibliography, was reprinted in updated editions of the encyclopedia into the 1960s and reached thousands of school children and other students.

Now freed from the constraints of being a BIA employee, McNickle could speak bluntly about the policy of termination being pursued by the federal government. In a series of articles published in the 1950s, he clarified his thinking. Through a variety of publications he reached an extensive audience; he even took to the airwaves. In February 1954, he participated in a University of Chicago Roundtable radio broadcast (no. 828, 21 February 1954). He challenged various private organizations, especially the American Anthropological Association, to join forces with NCAI to forestall congressional attempts to terminate federal responsibility for Native American tribal communities.

Later that year, in "A U.S. Indian Speaks" (*Americas*, 1954, 8–11), he presented his strongest case yet for cultural pluralism, defending in eloquent terms the Indians' apparent unwillingness to adopt the whites' life-style. The Indians, he pointed out, readily accepted guns and bullets, woven blankets and clothing, steel knives and iron pots, because these items improved life as they traditionally lived it. Becoming competitive and acquisitive, however, meant adopting values contrary to traditional Native American culture, and unless

Natives could be convinced that this was a good thing to do, they would refuse. Whites viewed this as either unreasonable stubbornness or innate stupidity, but the problem was with American ethnocentrism. "Rarely does it occur to any of us that *our* attitudes toward people, toward the physical universe, and toward the supernatural are not a universal characteristic of human nature," McNickle wrote. Native Americans were not yet convinced of the superiority of the whites' ways. The failure of the government to bring about the desired changes went deeper than the deficiencies of any individual or government bureau. "It has been a failure to understand the role of culture, a failure to see that culture shapes many of our ends," that left the majority unable to understand Native American resistance to assimilation.

McNickle's community development program in the 1950s among the Navajos at Crownpoint, New Mexico, reflected his desire to remove various impediments to change that had locked those people into a cycle of frustration and hopelessness. He believed that, once they were introduced to the technical advances available through white society, they would move toward adaptation and acculturation. As director of American Indian Development (AID), the program adjunct of NCAI, McNickle gathered together a core group of traditional Navajo leaders. They were first encouraged to identify the needs of the community, and then they worked toward solutions that were compatible with both their own and the outside culture. He described various aspects of that project in "Indian Crisis, U.S.A." (*Colby Junior College Bulletin*, April 1954, 11–14) and "The Indian in American Society" (*The Social Welfare Forum*, 1955, 68–77). In "The Healing Vision" (*Tomorrow*, 1956, 25–31) and "It Takes Two to Communicate" (*International Journal of Health Education*, July 1959), he discussed the health education program that was a vital part of the larger project.

McNickle's efforts to bring change to Navajo society by working with older, traditional leaders produced mixed results. Changes were occurring rapidly on the Navajo Reservation in the 1950s, and he was forced to accept the fact that the elders were losing the positions of leadership they had formerly enjoyed. They were being displaced by younger people who spoke English and were competitive for political power. These young people, educated in BIA or mission schools, had been taught to look down on their Native American heritage. They had been systematically denied information about their own history and traditions, and they had become marginal to both Native and white society. From 1956 to 1967, therefore, McNickle was involved with a six-week summer leadership training workshop designed explicitly to help Native American college students develop a positive image of their Indian identity and of themselves as tribal members. He described these workshops in both theoretical and practical terms in "The Sociocultural Setting of Indian Life" (*American Journal of Psychiatry*, August 1968, 115–19).

During the years of the Crownpoint Project, McNickle's income depended on contributions from various private institutions; to supplement this income he wrote a number of book reviews for the *American Anthropologist*. In volume 54 (1952) he reviewed Ruth Underhill's *Red Man's America: A History of Indians in the United States*; in volume 57 (1955) Peter J. Rahill's *The Catholic Indian Missions and Grant's Peace Policy*; in volume 59 (1957) David A. Baerreis's *The Indian in Modern America*; and in volume 65 (1963) Francis Paul Prucha's *American Indian Policy in the Formative Years: The Indian Trade and Intercourse Acts, 1790–1834*. These reviews reveal McNickle's sensitivity to the written language and his insight into other people's understanding of Indian affairs.

The government's termination policy continued throughout the 1950s, and McNickle continued to express his opposition to it. In "It's Almost Never Too Late" (*Christian Century*, 20 February 1957, 227–29), he harked back once again to Collier's appeal to the Indian Bureau: hire social scientists who know something about Indians to develop Indian policy! A bureaucrat who knows nothing about indigenous tribal people, whether an effective administrator or not, will be unable to work effectively with Native Americans. Dillon Myer, Indian commissioner for 1950 to 1953, had brought insensitive administrators into the Indian office. Myer had been director of the War Relocation Authority during World War II, and after the war had effectively closed the Japanese relocation centers and returned the occupants to American society. As commissioner, he viewed reservations in the same light as the relocation centers. According to McNickle, Myer had made a cynical decision to end the "Indian problem" by terminating the tribes, regardless of the consequences. For this purpose he hired professional administrators, rather than people who had been properly trained in human relations, as the situation demanded. By the time McNickle wrote this article, much damage had been done, and it was almost, but not quite, "too late" to halt the damage brought about by Myer's dogmatic decision making.

In two articles that followed within the year, McNickle reviewed the historical context of the contemporary scene. The articles were "Indian and European: Indian-White Relations from Discovery to 1887," in the *Annals of the American Academy* (May 1957, 1–11) and "The Indians of the United States," in *American Indigena* (March 1958). The *Annals* article was the lead-off feature in an issue devoted entirely to Indian affairs, and judging from the list of contributors to the issue, McNickle was becoming recognized as one of the nation's eminent authorities on Native American affairs.

His most powerful statement against termination was also written at this time. In "Process or Compulsion: The Search for a Policy of Administration in Indian Affairs" (*American Indigena*, July 1957, 261–70), he asserted that all Americans, not just Congress and the federal government, were responsible for the failure to develop a cohesive and humane Native American policy. Once again he reviewed the historical context. The original treaties had "plunged the United States without any master plan or forward looking, into a fiduciary role which ultimately resulted in the regulation of internal affairs in Indian tribes." As those regulations multiplied, often in response to demands from the public, the bureau failed to recognize the nature of the problem, which basically was to work constructively with the Native people and bring them into a functioning relationship with the rest of the population. Increased dependency, on the one hand, and autocratic paternalism, on the other, were the inevitable results. This was the ultimate failure of America's Indian policy. No administrative bureaucracy and no amount of money could create an effective policy unless and until the Native Americans themselves contributed toward the solution.

In this article, McNickle seems finally to have rejected the idea that assimilation was inevitable. He suggested instead that an accommodation of Native society to white society on an equal basis might be possible. "So long . . . as Indians adopt the ways of the white man only in part, they remain out of the general society," he wrote. "The problem becomes one of finding ways of increasing the area of adjustment . . . without destroying those parts of Indian life which are still functioning and which convey to the Indian a feeling of security in his own personality." An important principle was at stake here. How can the United States, as a political democracy, continue to reject people who are culturally non-conformist? McNickle asked. Policy must be directed toward the goal of accepting Native Americans as they are, as an integral part of American society, or it will continue to be frustrated in dealing with the long-festering "Indian problem."

But McNickle remained pessimistic about the government's ability, or its willingness, to act effectively. Nongovernment individuals and groups who were not constrained by the tyranny of annual budgets could produce more effective and longer-lasting results. In "Private Intervention" !*Human Organization*, 1961, 208–15), he discussed the historic role of private organizations in both the United States and Canada from the mid-nineteenth century to the present. He also used the occasion of the seventy-eighth annual meeting of the Indian Rights Association in April 1961 to tell his audience about the American Indian Chicago conference scheduled for June that year ("Indian Expectations," *Indian Truth*, June 1961, 1–6). Here, for the first time, Native Americans from all over the country, tribal and nontribal, gathered to discuss their common problems. McNickle himself chaired the steering committee for that conference and was the primary author of the "Declaration of Indian Purpose," a document that became the official statement of that conference.[4]

For the next several years, McNickle worked on larger literary projects. With Harold Fey he co-authored *Indians and Other Americans* (1959 and 1970). He wrote *Indian Tribes of the United States: Ethnic and Cultural Survival* (1962) and finished his report on the Crownpoint Project. Beginning in 1965, he also wrote a series of book reviews for *The Nation* on recently published Indian material. Among the books were Gene Weltfish's *The Lost Universe* and Ralph K. Andrist's *The Long Death: The Last Days of the Plains Indians*, reviewed in "The Goals of the Group" (27 September 1965); a reprint of Wane Dennis's *The Hopi Child* and Edgar Z. Friedenberg's *The Dignity of Youth and Other Atavisms*, in "Two Ways to Grow Up" (28 March 1966); Alvin M. Josephy's *The Nez Perce Indians and the Opening of the Northwest*, in "In Search of the White Man's Guidance" (25 April 1966); *Wilderness Kingdom: Indian Life in the Rocky Mountains, 1840–1847, the Journals and Painting of Nicholas Point, S.J.*, in "A Record of the Vanishing West" (25 December 1967); Frederick Dockstadter's *Indian Art in South America,* in "The Evidence of Their Lives" (22 July 1968); Alvin Josephy's *The Indian Heritage of America,* in "Looking Backward" (23 December 1968); and Alfonso Ortiz's *The Tewa World: Space, Time, Being and Becoming in a Pueblo Society* (27 April 1970).

McNickle also reviewed J. B. Jorgenson's *The Sun Dance Religion: Power for the Powerless* in the *New Mexico Historical Review* (April 1973); Wilcomb Washburn's *Red Man's Land, White Man's Law* in the *Journal of Ethnic Studies* (Spring 1973); and Margaret Szasz's *Education and the American Indian: The Road to Self-Determination, 1928–1973* in *The Historian* (May 1976).

McNickle wrote his last review for *The Nation,* "Interpreting Native America" (7 December 1974, 599–600) on William Brandon's *The Last Americans: The Indian in American Culture.* McNickle was particularly excited about this book, which examined the sweep of Indian/white relations from the perspective of conflicting cultural values. McNickle himself, having written extensively about Native American history, recognized two major problems in doing so: the lack of sources representing the Native American view and the difficulty of establishing a unifying theme in the face of tribal cultural diversity. He praised Brandon's meticulous efforts to reconstruct the context of the early narratives in order to gain insight into the Native rather than the white presence. Brandon had also dealt admirably with the second problem: he suggested that the unifying theme of all Native peoples was their attempt to live in spiritual harmony with the land. The European, on the other hand, wanted to acquire and control. According to Brandon, "the great reigning motive of life in the Old World was acquisition of wealth, property, business, the commerce of individual gain and ambition . . . and in this worldly welter religion was only one of many forces." For the Indian, religion encompassed all aspects of life. Summarizing the contrast, Brandon wrote that "the

Indian world was devoted to living, the European world to getting." Although the European accomplished the "getting" through use of superior technology, in all other aspects of life—in ethics, morality, justice, and wisdom—the Indian, according to Brandon, was his equal or superior. It is not surprising that McNickle was pleased with Brandon's effort; he had entertained similar ideas about Native Americans and the modern materialistic world for years.

McNickle wrote several other articles during the 1960s in response to current developments. In "The Indian Tests the Mainstream" (*The Nation*, 26 September 1966, 275–79), he voiced his disappointment over the 1965 firing of Indian Commissioner Philleo Nash, who had begun to rebuild the government's shattered relationship with Native people after the drive for termination was itself terminated. With Nash's firing, the federal government once again tried to impose its own pace on assimilation and refused to participate in a dialogue that might have provided an opportunity for Indians to have a voice in determining their own future. Native Americans, however, were beginning to realize the extent of their political leverage under the slogan "red power," as McNickle recognized when he referred to Nancy O. Laurie's depiction of an "Indian renaissance" that had appeared in the fall 1965 issue of *Mid-Continental Studies Journal*. Here indeed was an indication of change in Native American self-definition.[5] In such organizations as NCAI and the National Indian Youth Council, individuals were beginning to think of themselves as Native Americans as well as tribal members, and through this emerging Native identity they were talking, "in the language of politics." "It is obvious what must happen," McNickle explained. "The function of decision must be taken from the expert administrators and the wielders of power and put into the [Native] community where decisions belong."

In "The Dead Horse Walks Again" (*The Nation,* 25 December 1967, 677–78), McNickle pointed out that although termination as a policy had been discontinued, the BIA was apparently unable to free itself of the old habit of paternalism. Through the Indian Resources Development Act of 1967, it attempted once again to control the development of Indian assets by calling upon the credit resources of the private marketplace. "The Indians," McNickle dryly remarked, "are looking elsewhere" for economic assistance. They were not interested in continuing their old colonial status.

In view of McNickle's numerous contributions to *The Nation,* it is not surprising that Carey McWilliams, editor of that publication and an old friend of both McNickle and Collier, asked McNickle to write an obituary on the occasion of Collier's death in May 1968. McNickle had kept in touch with the former commissioner and had remained intensely loyal to him. He welcomed the opportunity to go on record once again in defense of Collier's vision. Collier, he asserted, "quite certainly rescued American Indians from the doom prepared for them by generations of stupidity and venality fostered by government policies and practices." In preserving the land base and culture of the Native communities, Collier had provided the ground from which adaptive and assimilative processes drew new growth. "A special debt [is] owed to John Collier," McNickle explained, "for having defined and explored the terms by which Indian people could survive" ("John Collier's Vision," *The Nation,* 3 June 1968, 718–19).

During most of the period from 1966 to 1971, McNickle was in Canada, at the University of Saskatchewan. In addition to his teaching and academic responsibilities as department chair, he continued to write. Among other things, he contributed the long second chapter for Eleanor Leacock and Nancy O. Lurie's *North American Indians in Historical Perspective,* which was published in 1970. This book was a collection of essays by a group of distinguished international scholars in the fields of Indian anthropology and history. McNickle's chapter, "Americans Called Indians," was a study in ethnohistory in which he stressed the changing environments and adaptive techniques of pre-Columbian Native Americans. McNickle deliberately and pointedly speculated on the direct connections between prehistoric peoples and present tribes. "The prehistory of the New World, or what we have been able to learn of it, is not disjoined from contemporary society," he wrote. "The history of any people at any point in time is a continuity, a process out of its own past." When in 1973 he substantially revised his earlier *Indian Tribes of the United States: Ethnic and Cultural Survival*, he renamed it *Native American Tribalism: Indian Survivals and Renewals*, once again stressing the tribal peoples' adaptability and continuity.

Another article McNickle wrote in the 1970s was entitled, "American Indians Who Never Were" and was published in *New University Thought* (Spring 1971, 24–29). Once again McNickle's work appeared with that of other leading Indian experts. This time he reminded his readers that "Indian" was a construct of the European mind, and that the images of Natives that had evolved over time reflected more the non-Natives' changing interpretations than the Native American reality. He appealed to anthropologists to look beyond the image of Indians frozen in the ethnographic present and search instead for the dynamics of change within Native societies.

McNickle was anticipating his retirement from academia, and by 1971 he had made several long-term commitments for extensive writing projects. Several authors had asked him to write chapters for their books of collected essays, and his next project was another long piece on Native American history, "The Clash of Cultures," published by the National Geographic Society in its beautifully illustrated volume, *The World of the American Indian* (1974, 311–49). Here was McNickle at his best, addressing a literate but nonprofessional audience, describing events from the period of first contact between Native Americans and Europeans until the end of the Indian wars in 1890. He wrote, as always, from the Indian point of view, discussing accommodation and conflict while being generous and understanding of both sides, but his writing was taking on a more pessimistic note. He suggested that, given the inherent differences between Native and white societies, conflicts between the two were almost inevitable.

In 1972, while he was working on the article for the National Geographic Society, McNickle was invited to a conference sponsored by the National Archives on sources for research in Native American history. In one session, Indian Commissioner Louis Bruce and historian Lawrence C. Kelly gave their respective opinions on the long-term impact of Collier and the Indian New Deal, and McNickle commented on their assessments. Once again he used the opportunity to defend Collier and to present an insider's view of events of that time. Despite the criticisms that had been leveled at Collier since 1945, he pointed out, it was worth noting how many of Collier's forward-looking policies had become standard practice. His initial use of social scientists had led to the offer of technical assistance to minority peoples worldwide; the personality studies had proven useful in ameliorating both administration and policy; bilingual texts and appropriate teaching materials were now widely used in Indian schools; Native American students were now taught their tribal history and encouraged to be proud of it; and Natives were increasingly consulted in matters that affected their lives. While Commissioner Bruce had not addressed the question of Collier's administration directly and McNickle had little to say about his presentation, he did question some of Kelly's statements. His remarks led to Kelly's subsequent articles about anthropologists and Collier's Indian reorganization program.[6] Proceedings of the 1972 conference, including the presentations of Bruce, Kelly, and McNickle, were later published in Jane Smith and Robert Kvasnicka's *Indian-White Relations: A Persistent Paradox* (1976, 251–57).

At about this time, McNickle wrote a two-part illustrated article, a light piece, for American Airlines to include in their in-flight publication, *The American Way*. Entitled "They Cast Long Shadows," the article consisted of half-page biographical sketches on Pontiac, Tecumseh, Geronimo, and others, and concluded with a list of such contemporaries as Vine Deloria, Jr., and N. Scott Momaday. This and other articles in the airline's series on Native Americans were compiled in a small volume called *Look to the Mountain Top* (19–28), published in 1972.

McNickle returned briefly to Canada in 1974 to address a symposium on "The Patterns of 'Amerindian' Identity," the proceedings of which were published with that title by les Presses de l'université Laval, Quebec, in 1976. Once again, in a paper entitled, "The Surfacing of Native Leadership" (7–17), he defended Collier's Indian New Deal, but here he admitted, for perhaps the first time in print, that Collier's vision was less than ideal. The true antagonist of Collier's reform, as McNickle phrased it, was the fact that Collier was a man of his time, whose thinking was shaped by the progressive reformers of the early twentieth century. "His mission as a man of reason was to create the opportunity [for the Indians to develop and use modern political devices] . . . and as a man of his class and generation he saw no reason why he should not speak for the Indian people, no reason why they should not be satisfied to have him speak." Despite some very real changes in government policy, the ethic of social intervention that motivated Collier in the 1930s functioned as a tradition from an earlier period. He was of necessity limited in what he could do: "He could not substitute his will and his vision for Indian will and vision." Only the Native Americans themselves could determine their own future.

One of McNickle's last projects was to write still another account of modern Indian-white relations, this time for the American Indian Policy Review Commission. It was published as part of *Captives Within a Free Society* in 1979 (Sec. I, 31–54). In "The Right to Choose: A Policy for the Future," McNickle reviewed the context of significant federal legislation passed since the 1920s, covering in greater detail some of the material he had written about earlier. Especially significant at this time was his discussion of the Office of Economic Opportunity, part of President Lyndon Johnson's War on Poverty that had a revolutionary impact on most tribal groups. The Office of Navajo Economic Opportunity (ONEO) operated on the Navajo Reservation in a manner strikingly similar to that of McNickle's Crownpoint Project of the 1950s. It offered help to Native American communities, as the Point Four Program had done as McNickle himself had suggested as early as 1951. His survey concluded by summing up recent advances Native American people had made in working together to achieve their common political goals.

McNickle did not live to see his last several efforts in print. He died suddenly of a heart attack in October 1977, before publication of his report for the Indian Policy Review Commission and two book chapters written for other compilations. Both of these chapters developed further his assessments of the Indian New Deal. "Anthropology and the Indian Reorganization Act" appeared in *The Uses of Anthropology*, edited by Walter Goldschmidt (1979, 51–60), and "The Indian New Deal as Mirror of the Future" was included in Ernest L. Schusky's compilation *Political Organization of Native North Americans* (1980, 107–19). Schusky dedicated his book to McNickle's memory. In both chapters, McNickle recalled the Collier years a "an aberration in time." While Collier was a reflection of early twentieth-century progressive idealism, the program that he envisioned for Native American self-determination was a program for the future. It had taken forty years for the federal government and the Native Americans themselves to catch up with Collier's vision of how they might reassert their autonomy as Native people.

McNickle had caught some of Collier's vision, and he, perhaps more than any other single person, had been able to carry that vision toward fruition. Yet, at the end, McNickle was pessimistic about Indian cultural survival. His third novel, *Wind from an Enemy Sky*, which was published post-humously in 1978, was a wrenching depiction of the insur-mountable obstacles suggested by William Brandon's observation that "the Indian world, the world of actual Indian communities, is under relentless siege still, as it has been ever since Europeans encountered it." The primary reason for the continued conflict was a basic cultural aliena-tion. The Native American and the Euroamerican still fol-lowed what he called different "maps of the mind," that led in diverging, not converging, directions. Mutual accom-modation, at least in his last novel, seemed increasingly unlikely.

Nevertheless, McNickle's presence and his writings helped shape the views of many of today's Native American leaders. It is, of course, impossible to assess with certainty the impact of his efforts to enhance both tribal and pantribal Indian identity through the American Indian Chicago Conference, his leadership training workshops, and the still-active National Congress of American Indians. Still, it seems fitting that D'Arcy McNickle is recognized today not only for his novels but increasingly for his vision of Native American identity. The Center for the History of the American Indian at the Newberry Library in Chicago, which he helped estab-lish, now bears his name, as does a new library at the Salish-Kootenay Community College on the Flathead Reservation in Montana. These two institutions are fitting tributes to his lifelong work on behalf of Native American people.

Part Two

The Surrounded:
The Construction of Vision
in McNickle's Best-Known Work

Chapter Two

Rethinking History:
A Context for *The Surrounded*

Birgit Hans

McNickle's single-minded goal in the late 1920s and early 1930s was to be a writer, an author of an American novel. To define "American" must have seemed an easy task to him at that point of his career when he was steeped in the Euroamerican accounts of American history and literary history; he had only to accept the "salesman's dream" and to blend completely into Euroamerican society. In accepting the Euroamerican history of his Native American people unconditionally though, he relinquished his hold on his Native heritage and became, for the time being, a mainstream American.

The early manuscript version of *The Surrounded*, now a part of the McNickle Collection at The Newberry Library, reflects McNickle's interest in American history and his unquestioning acceptance of it during that time. The manuscript is divided into three parts; the first and last ones are set in Montana while the middle one focuses on the protagonist's, Archilde's, experiences in Paris. Archilde spends much of his time in Paris sitting in the lounge of his hotel and reading a book on American history. In fact, it is Archilde's repeatedly voiced goal to join white mainstream society, the heritage of his Spanish father, and to leave his mother's Flathead heritage behind. Prior to his arrival in Paris, Archilde has attended a college in the East to, as his father called it in their first and last talk, "learn a few things" (Ms 103). By traveling east Archilde physically moves closer to Euroamerican culture and his education becomes of necessity less and less "tainted" with things Indian. The highpoint of his education is Paris, though, the city universally regarded as the center of European civilization. While McNickle acknowledged the refinement of Paris in this manuscript version, as well as in several of his short stories, he ultimately rejected that life for his characters because the superficiality of urban life in general stifles their relationship with the land and their basic American values.

How complete Archilde's acceptance of Euroamerican history is becomes evident in his trial at the end of the novel's manuscript version. The defense lawyer points out at the beginning of his speech that "right at this minute the defendant can beat him [the prosecutor] in any examination of history" (Ms 321) and "In his [Archilde's] home he has a library that won't be matched in many homes in this county" (Ms 322). Needless to say, the defense lawyer is speaking about Euroamerican history, and he sees the library as a measure of the civilizing process and its books, with their unchanging and unchangeable texts, are in direct opposition to the oral tradition of the Salish people. Archilde's assimilation is complete when the judge says after his trial "I commend you!" and he also commends Archilde's "stolid qualities that would, no doubt, make him a splendid citizen" (Ms 336). The final scene of the manuscript version reaffirms Archilde's assimilation; released from prison after the triumphantly concluded trial, he returns to his father's ranch. In contrast to earlier scenes in the manuscript version, Archilde has lost his close tie with the land and sees it in terms of fields, wheat, hay, and yield. Finally, he, who has been educated in the centers of American and French civilizations, has truly become a Euroamerican farmer with a firm sense of "his" culture's heritage.

The work of other early Native American novelists contains similar messages about the necessity of assimilation, for instance Mourning Dove's *Cogewea, the Half-Blood* (1927), John Joseph Mathews's *Sundown* (1934), and John Milton Oskison's short fiction (1920s). If McNickle had not revised the manuscript substantially, it would merely have reflected the popular Euroamerican views of the time and the Native American novels already published. It was McNickle's personal triumph that the final version of *The Surrounded* did not simply mirror populist perspectives.

McNickle wrote the manuscript version of his first novel before the federal policy of assimilation was officially reversed with the Indian Reorganization Act of 1934. At the time, Euroamerican historians were still busy justifying westward expansion and tribal genocide; the last massacres were still fresh in the public's mind, for instance, Wounded Knee (1890) and Sand Creek (1864), as was, from the Euroamerican perspective, the outrageous and inexplicable defeat of George Armstrong Custer at the Little Big Horn (1876). Very few historians were as outspoken as Theodore Roosevelt was in *The Winning of the West* (1886), but the sentiment he conveys would have been the same in the first decades of the twentieth century. Hofstadter describes Roosevelt's book and quotes from it in *The American Political Tradition* (1948) as "an epic of racial conflict in which he [Roosevelt] described 'the spread of the English-speaking peoples over the world's waste space' as 'the most striking feature of the world's history.' Only 'a warped, perverse, and silly morality' would condemn the American conquest of the West. 'Most fortunately, the hard, energetic, practical men who do the rough pioneer work of civilization in barbarous lands, are not prone to false sentimentality' " (212).[1] Roosevelt mentions three points here that recur again and again in the histories of the first decades of the twentieth century reviewed here: 1) Euroamericans did not really displace tribal peoples as the land was a vast empty space and its few inhabitants could barely be counted among human beings, 2) the pioneers' and farmers' deeds made them American heroes, and 3) tribal peoples were to disappear into the Euroamerican mainstream as the myths of the Melting Pot and of the Vanishing Indian had always predicted.

Setting the historical framework within which McNickle wrote, makes it possible to appreciate his development as a writer, to assess his early contributions (often indifferently received by the Euroamerican reading public), and to revise the written accounts of Native American-Euroamerican relations. In order to establish the historical framework that was familiar to and accepted by the Euroamerican readers of the first three decades of the twentieth century, representative American histories and literary histories were selected by their publication dates. They are books commonly available in libraries and secondhand bookstores. Among them are Leo Huberman's history, which was very popular during the Depression, and a history by Pulitzer Prize–winning historian John Truslow Adams.

That the United States was a vast empty space before the settlement by Euroamericans is implied in all the American histories written during the early decades of the twentieth century. For instance, Adams includes a population figure in *The Epic of America* (1931); only 500,000 Native peoples were living on the North American continent at the advent of the Europeans, he claims. This small number of people, the argument goes, certainly did not need the vast amount of land that they claimed as their own (401–402). In fact, that population estimate seems incredibly low today, when anthropologists consider eight million a more accruate estimate of the pre-contact Native population.

In histories and literary histories alike, Native peoples are usually mentioned only after discussing how Europeans established a foothold in the "New World." Leo Huberman, for instance, does not mention the aboriginal inhabitants until he is well into *We, the People* (1932): "Still another group of immigrants were brought against their will. When the early settlers found it practically impossible to make good slaves of the Indians they found here, because the red man was too proud to work under the lash, they turned to Africa, where Negroes could be obtained" (12).

In addition to simply dismissing Native aboriginal rights, Huberman sets up a contrast between Native peoples and those of African descent. Both groups were regarded as inferior by Euroamericans, inferior to a degree that makes exploitation seem the most natural and reasonable thing. Their very humanity is denied, since Euroamericans, according to Huberman, can simply dispose of them. In fact, they are not even regarded as very useful "objects," since they are "proud."

Adams dehumanizes the Native peoples as well in *The Epic of America* (1931); he states that there were a number of different tribes, but they share "general characteristics" and to look at them individually is entirely unnecessary: "Chatty and sociable in ordinary life among themselves, they held to a convention of extreme gravity on all public and ceremonial occasions. Their nervous systems were unstable and they were of a markedly hysterical make-up, peculiarly susceptible to suggestion. Cruel and revengeful, they could school themselves to stand pain as a matter of social convention, although when unsustained by that they were childishly lacking in self-control" (7). Adams mentions a number of stereotypes and prejudices here that have been perpetuated through the centuries, for instance, "Indians are stoic" and "Indians do not feel pain." The image is that of a child, but a malevolent child. Sadly, the historians were not lacking "scientific" support for their evaluation of Native peoples either. Sociologists and geographers provided them with the necessary proof.

In *The Character of Races* (1925), Ellsworth Huntington explains that the aboriginal peoples of America suffer from what he calls "Arctic hysteria," i.e., on their migration environmental influences deprived the Native peoples of "the alertness, curiosity, and inventive faculty which are so essential to progress" (72). Some progress may be achieved and, as he points out, has been achieved, but these stultifying traits are impossible to extinguish in the heredity of Native peoples. The American continent, then, was not only almost unpopulated but populated by a people locked into a lower evolutionary stage that made it impossible for them to make proper use of the land. Very few historians actually acknowledged aboriginal rights to the land and would have been reassured by Huntington that "the American Indian not only despises steady manual work, but is unfitted for it" (93). Huberman wrote in the same vein that the land was "valueless until people lived on it, until crops were produced, or animals killed for their fur" (11). Archilde clearly echoes this attitude in the manuscript version of *The Surrounded*. The manuscript version of the novel closes with him surveying the land that he has inherited from his father, seeing it merely in terms of crops and hay. There is none of the spiritual connectedness to the land that the Archilde of the published novel experiences and that has been a prominent theme in later Native American fiction.

The pioneers, then, those people who made the "proper" use of the land possible, play a very special role in these histories. They are always contrasted with the Native Americans they were displacing. Pioneers and settlers are, to quote Leo Huberman, "brave souls" and "determined courageous people" (20) while Native Americans, according to Edward Hale, are "savages," "enraged savages," and "savage foes," who engage in "predatory warfare." Hale is the only historian, however, to admit openly that his view of Indian-white contact and Native character has been formed by captivity narratives. In fact, he mentions Mary Rowlandson as a "historical" source.

While tribal peoples are seen as a disappearing people, (once perhaps noble, but now refusing to acknowledge the superiority of white civilization), the Euroamericans are shown to have actually overcome the temptations of the wilderness and established civilization in its most noble form. Huberman summarizes this inevitable progression from savagery to civilization in *We, the People* (1932), a very widely read history of America during the Depression:

> The pioneer had the difficult job of changing his old habits to fit into his new surroundings. The frontier line was "the melting point between savagery and civilization." The pioneer farmer had to give up his civilized ways and actually become, for a time, a savage. He took off his civilized clothing and put on the hunting shirt and the moccasin. He gave up his civilized home and lived in a log cabin. Before long, he plowed Indian fashion with a sharp stick and he planted Indian corn. He gave up the civilized way of fighting and shouted the war cry and scalped his enemy in true savage style. All these things he did, not because he wanted to, but because he had to in order to live. The wilderness forced these things; not to have fitted himself into this kind of life would have meant certain death. Little by little he transformed the wilderness, but in the meantime he had himself been transformed. He was a new person. Many of those qualities we think are typical of Americans in general were the result of this frontier life. (105)

In Huberman's mind the pioneer had to lower himself to the "savage" level of the tribal peoples living on the land that the pioneer was intent on claiming for himself. The lowering was made necessary by the pioneer's geographic isolation from his own "civilized" kind, and his lack of knowledge to survive in a basically hostile environment. Inherent in this passage, as well, is the irony that the Native peoples generously shared their knowledge, only to have that knowledge turned against them. What distinguishes the pioneer and Native peoples, according to Huberman, is that the former, once in possession of the knowledge necessary for physical survival, rises above the savage state, not only to rejoin civilization but to improve. For Huberman, the history of Native peoples shows that they are incapable of this development and will remain forever locked into the "savage" state. Since there is no potential for development, they must be forced to make room for those who can develop.

James Quayle Dealey paints a similar picture in *Sociology* (1909); he contrasts anthropological findings about aboriginal life on the North American continent with the Noble Savage image that the romantic European, especially the French, constructed in the eighteenth century:

> to-day some of the glamour has faded from those bright pictures of primitive man . . . a human being to be sure, but not sharply differentiated from his animal ancestry and subject to the conditions of that precarious life. He lived in the midst of dangerous animal competitors who loved the taste of human flesh; his half-starved body shivered in the cold rains and blasts of the winter or lay gorged and enervated by the riotous plenty and heat of the summer. His awakening intellect was multiplying his enemies by surrounding him with supernatural beings, malevolent and hostile. (44)

Dealey's characterization of aboriginal peoples makes only a perfunctory distinction between humans and animals; they both act purely on instinct, require instant self-gratification, are improvident, and are locked into the cycle by their primitive ideas of the supernatural.

McNickle's portrayal of Native culture in the early manuscript version can serve as an illustration of Dealey's ideas. While waiting for his trial, Archilde, for the first time, understands his ancestors:

> He stood arm in arm with his mother those days, breathing the unhealthy mist of a hundred generations before his day. Inhabitants of a bleak world into which the sunlight had not yet penetrated, these were his people. They gazed into the sky and scanned the earth, picking their food from under the rocks and in the meadows. They feared the passing shadow of a bird overhead, they stood in awe before a blasted tree, they worshipped the wind that howled at night. . . . They walked grim faced through life and passed out amidst a burst of waiting. When opposition and adversity overtook them and threatened death and starvation on the snowy flats of winter, they sat in a huddle before a sick fire and with blank eyes, awaited the hand to fall. (301–302)

But again, McNickle's character sees his ancestors' experiences in terms of the Euroamerican framework. There is no admiration for the fortitude and courage of Native peoples, no spiritual connectedness with them. This early Archilde would, undoubtedly, agree with Dealey that having remained locked into this cycle through centuries without signs of mental or physical development, the aboriginal peoples are replaced by the more aggressive, more "virile" pioneer farmer.

It is by no means the moral obligation of the settlers to educate "these backward stocks" (202), as Dealey calls them. He considers it altruism if they do. The elevation of aboriginal peoples to the level of civilization is a complicated process that requires the "superior stock" to lead the "inferior one" through the different levels. It is impossible to simply "substitute outright a higher for a lower civilization" (202). In order for Native peoples to become equals, then, the Euroamerican pioneer farmer is duty bound to force "civilization" on them, to become the dominant decision making "partner." To force tribal peoples to change is altruism, a noble pursuit.

James Truslow Adams, while agreeing with the basic assumptions made by Huberman and Dealey, adds another facet to the encounter of tribal peoples on the North American continent and Euroamerican pioneers and settlers: declining the moral obligation to raise the "backward stock," enables the exploitation of tribal peoples. In connection with the "Tecumseh conspiracy" Adams writes: "They [Tecumseh and his brother] urged that no further cessions of land be made, and preached against the use of strong drink. The land-hungry whites were alarmed. They saw their hopes dashed if the Indians should become moral, law-abiding, and insistent upon remaining on their lands" (142). Adams is clearly uneasy with the openly expressed goals of some whites, even calls them "land-hungry," but, in the end, considers westward expansion inevitable and justified. In summing up he says: "A continent which scarce sufficed to maintain a half million savages now supports nearly two hundred and fifty times that number of as active and industrious people as there are in the world" (401–402). Adjusting to the ethnocentric demands of the settlers does not guarantee equality or safety to Native peoples, and genocide, while deplorable, is justifiable.

Native peoples disappear from the American histories once the last Plains wars are fought and the last tribes are confined to reservations. Adams mentions them toward the end of *The Epic of America* (1931) but "rather for its own intrinsic interest than for its national importance" (396) to report on their satisfactory progress toward assimilation in a few sentences. Assimilation of tribal peoples is still the accepted goal; acculturation is not mentioned.

One issue that is not discussed in any of these histories of America is that of the ancestry of mixed blood children.

The colorful ethnic backgrounds of famous Euroamericans are always mentioned, but there is no mention of Native American–Euroamerican children. A popularly held belief was that the mixing of "racial stocks" could lead to a degeneration of the "superior stock." Ellsworth Huntington voices this notion in *The Character of Races* (1925); intermarriage is to the disadvantage of Euroamericans as "such dilution means a decrease in ability" (19). Edward Byron Reuter is even more outspoken about miscegenation in *Race Mixture* (1931):

> One school has occupied the position that racial stocks are somewhat grossly unequal in degree of native capacity for cultural achievement. They stand to each other in some sort of mental hierarchy. The existence of a superior racial group is a precondition to the appearance or even to the use and maintenance of complex forms of culture and social organization. Creative men can be produced only by a superior race. On the basis of this major premise, the argument runs to the effect that any intermixture of the unequally endowed stocks raises the capacity of one at the same time that it lowers that of the other. The net result of amalgamation is a decadence in racial stock and a corresponding decline in culture status. (6-7)

Marriages between Native Americans and Euroamericans, according to Huntington and Reuter, debase white civilization, and eventually, the Euroamericans will sink to the level of the "savages." This lowering is very different from the one described in Huberman. The pioneer had to become a "savage" to adapt to the unfamiliar physical surroundings, while maintaining the capacity ultimately to rise triumphantly above the savage state and rejoin, even improve, civilization. Lowering the superior stock by intermarriage, however, diminishes mental capacity and leads to degeneration of Euroamerican civilization which, in turn, becomes vulnerable to less desirable influences and more aggressive stocks.

According to Reuter, "The mixed blood's hysterical and insistent knocking at the white man's door is a familiar sound in every bi-racial situation" (209). The mixed blood then seeks to join the "superior" Euroamerican culture but is seldom successful because of Euroamerican ethnocentrism and racial fear. In short, although tribal peoples were still considered a rapidly vanishing people, they need to be assimilated culturally, but there should be little intermarriage.

Considering the attitudes of historians and sociologists during the first three decades of the twentieth century, the assimilationist nature of much early Native American fiction is not surprising. Even if Native American writers had managed to shake off the ethnocentric attitudes of Euroamericans that were very much a part of their daily lives, it is doubtful that a publisher could have been convinced to publish such a work. McNickle sent versions of *The Surrounded* (1936) to practically every publisher in New York City; not even the manuscript version, clearly in the established tradition and using the accepted version of American history as its framework, managed to snare a publisher. Each of the revisions that followed made publication less likely as it moved further and further away from the public taste, a taste that delighted in "the most picturesque, least complex situations of the 'blanket Indian' in the Southwest, or turning their faces towards the past" (La Farge 10). When Dodd and Mead finally took *The Surrounded* in 1935, the publisher demanded that McNickle share the risk. Needless to say, *The Surrounded* was not a financial success, despite its very positive reviews. Assimilation had been officially renounced with the Indian Reorganization Act of 1934; tribal cultures, it said, were valid and Native peoples had a right to their own cultures. However, public taste and deeply ingrained ethnocentric views of the Native American–Euroamerican relationship could not be wiped out by federal legislation. In fact, for the next thirty years very few fictions dealing with contemporary Native American life were published; only in 1969 did N. Scott Momaday's *House Made of Dawn* usher in what has been called the Native American Renaissance. By then, there were histories with very different versions of the Native American–Euroamerican encounter, some of them written by McNickle.

According to the literary historians of the early decades of the twentieth century, American literature definitely originated in Europe, more especially England, since the settlers had, according to the literary historians, no history to replace the one they had left behind. American literature was considered imitative and, at best, had modified to "meet changed condition" (Walter C. Bronson 7). A common refrain in the literary histories is that most worthwhile American writing "confesses to an English ancestry" (Thomas Higginson and Henry Walcott Boynton 2–3). As Henry A. Beers points out, American literature suffers from "decrepitude rather than youthfulness" (9). Life on the North American continent did not offer new themes or an awareness that people with a rich history and a firmly established oral literature had lived here for thousands of years.

Native peoples are generally ignored in discussions of the origin or form of American literature, except for Eva March Tappan's mention of John Eliot "whose Indian Bible is a part of literature, if not of American literature" (12). The statement, nevertheless, excludes Native peoples once and for all. Bronson points out that the lives of settlers in the seventeenth and eighteenth century provide appropriate material for the contemporary American writer of fiction (110) but does not mention the Native peoples they encountered. Higginson and Boynton believe that an American literature should express the American spirit, the spirit of the "moral greatness of the race" (Reuben Post Halleck 397), and not its "oddities and exceptions" (73). Native peoples and African

Americans are definitely considered "oddities and exceptions" by both Higginson and Boynton.

Literary historians, like historians, mention Native peoples as afterthoughts in their work. Of course, in dealing with the early colonial texts, Native peoples cannot be ignored; after all, writers like Bradford and Winthrop try to come to terms with the physical environment of the "New World" and the peoples that they encountered there. Literary historians, however, are more concerned with the accuracy of ethnographic detail than the literary quality of Indian portrayals. Walter Bronson, for instance, mentions Native Americans only as opponents of white settlers in *A Short History of American Literature* (1919): "The truth is, rather, that the Puritan sincerely endeavored to connect and educate these poor children of the forest; but when the red man became hostile, and the torch and tomahawk began their dreadful work, then the white man slew without mercy" (20–21). The same ethnocentric attitude previously encountered in the histories of America is evident here; Native peoples simply have to give way to a superior people and "destiny." Encounters with Native Americans may provide themes for an early American literature, but Native American cultures and oral traditions cannot replace the "civilized" European heritage of the settlers.

For the most part, Native Americans simply disappear from the literary histories for at least a hundred and fifty years after the colonial period. William Long, however, mentions them in connection with captivity tales in *American Literature* (1923), but again the accuracy of the portrayals of atrocities is more important to him than the descriptions' literary qualities. It is doubtful that he recognized their fictional and polemic nature. Most of the literary historians, among them Fred Lewis Pattee, Eva March Tappan, and Thomas Dickinson, continue this obsession with "truth" into the nineteenth century. They discuss Francis Parkman's and

W. H. Prescott's works on Native Americans as "histories" without explaning why these "historians" were included among the works of American writers of fiction in the first place.

In discussing individual American writers, literary historians cannot completely ignore those writers who did use "Indian" themes or reduce the portrayal of Native peoples and their life to ethnographic detail. It is surprising how little space is given to the Indian theme though. In fact, Walter Bronson mentions merely the "ugly realism" of Indian warfare (101) in his discussion of Charles Brockden Brown's *Edgar Huntley*, and none of the literary historians pays much, if any, attention to Henry Wadsworth Longfellow's *Hiawatha*. Fred Lewis Pattee is the only one to quote from the author's preface to explain the research Longfellow had done for the epic poem; he concludes that Longfellow is the "only poet who has succeeded in extracting any real poetry from the Indian" (269). In their literary history, Thomas Wentworth Higginson and Henry Walcott Boynton only mention Longfellow's using "material belonging peculiarly to America" (142), and Eva March Tappan gives merely the name of the poem (71). Philip Freneau is granted the distinction by Pattee of being the first to have used a Native American theme; at the same time Pattee explains why Freneau was able to strike such a "poetic note": "But as he [the Indian] had vanished from his old hunting-grounds the romantic mist that is wont to involve a fading race, no matter how ugly, had begun to enfold him" (101). Earlier in *A History of American Literature* (1896) Pattee refers to Eliot's Bible as "the most valuable relic of a vanished race" (34). Even though Pattee considers Native Americans extinct, he still feels uneasy about the "poetic note" and the mythologizing of these dead people. His reference to "ugly" is puzzling and seems to imply that Native peoples were physically inferior; however, that does not fit in with Freneau's decriptions that Pattee mentioned earlier. Pattee's later discussion of John Greenleaf Whittier makes clear that he is referring to cultural inferiority. He criticizes Whittier's use of the Native American materials, which the poet considered "a rich mine of poetry and romance in the history and traditions of the Indians,—a delusion that was widespread during the early years of the century" (335). There is simply impatience with those who want to break the established patterns, but no reflection of the quality of their literary work.

The test case, though, is the treatment of James Fenimore Cooper by these literary historians. Cooper's fictions fall into three generally accepted categories: novels about the sea, political novels, and historical novels, many of which have dominant Native American themes. The sheer volume of the novels with Native American themes makes it difficult to overlook them. Eva March Tappan, however, actually manages not to mention Indian characters at all while lauding Cooper's "best" character Natty Bumppo (37) in *A Short History of America's Literature*. Thomas Wentworth Higginson and Henry Walcott Boynton claim in *A Reader's History of American Literature* that Cooper was a literary success in Europe, because he, like Mrs. Stowe, appealed to the readers' curiosity about a race "practically forgotten" (129). In their discussion of *The Prairie* they deal with Cooper's use of landscape in this work but not with the Indian characters; they echo the American historians of their time, claiming the "utter vacancy of human life" (236) as the Prairie's most striking characteristic. Fred Lewis Pattee, predictably, has little to say about Cooper's novels with Indian themes in *A History of American Literature* and only mentions the accuracy of the Indian materials included, a sentiment that is echoed by Thomas Dickinson in *The Making of American Literature*. Henry Beers, on the other hand, calls Cooper's Indian characters "individual and vital" and credits him with creating the "Indian of literature" (105) in *An Outline Sketch of American Literature*. A short list of Native characters follows: "Hardly less individual and vital were the various types of Indian character, in Chingachgook, Uncas, Hist, and the Huron warriors" (107), but, a few sentences later, Beers refuses to give his opinion of James Fenimore Cooper's literary merit. Perhaps his answer is the final sentence of the paragraph that discusses Cooper's "Indian" novels that relegates the writer's fiction to "boy" fiction.

In general then, the literary histories follow the pattern of American histories. Those American writers who use Indian themes and draw on Native American poetic expressions are ignored or, at least, that part of their creative work is ignored. Certainly, Indian themes cannot replace the noble themes of the Euroamericans' European heritage.

Daniel Brinton's *Aboriginal Authors and Their Productions* (1883) and Thomas Dickinson's *The Making of American Literature* (1932) must be considered separately; they make up a singular group of their own by acknowledging that there was literary expression before the advent of the settlers. In fact, Dickinson refers to it as a "great body of Indian imaginative work" (26). While Brinton emphasizes the contemporary achievements of Native peoples of Mexico, he mentions the "linguistic and literary ability" (13) of earlier peoples:

> Nor are these narratives repeated in a slipshod, negligent style. The hearers permit no such carelessness. They are sticklers for nicety of expression; for clear and well turned periods; for vivid and accurate descriptions; for flowing and sonorous sentences. As a rule their languages lend themselves readily to these demands. It is a singular error, due wholly to ignorance of the subject, to maintain that the American tongues are cramped in their vocabularies, or that their syntax does not permit them to define a more delicate relationship of ideas. Nor is it less a mistake to assert, as has been done repeatedly, and even by authorities of eminence in our own day, that they are not capable of supplying the expressions of abstract reasoning. (10–11)

Brinton denies the ethnocentric assumptions of the nineteenth century that were to endure many decades into the twentieth century: that Native peoples remained on such a low evolutionary level that they had no imagination, no artistic sense. Native Americans have an oral literature, sometimes even a written literature, that could rival that of Euroamericans. Oral transmission is not seen as a liability here, but as something that inspired the artist. It is not surprising that Brinton's work is not mentioned by the other historians of American literature, with the exception of Dickinson.

Dickinson draws on Brinton for his information and adds a section, "Indian Legends and Poems" (26–27), to the otherwise conventional structure and content of his literary history. He acknowledges repeatedly the existence of oral literature preceding the coming of the Europeans, in the beginning of his book, but he seems to feel ambivalent about it. He states "that the first American book was not made by white men. It was made by American aborigines on birchbark plates, and is called the *Walam Olum*, 'The Red Score' " (26). He is careful, however, not to comment on the quality of the "great body of Indian imaginative work" (26) and pays little attention to Euroamerican writers attempting to make literary use of these materials in their work. Dickinson, like the other literary historians included here, is concerned with the ethnographic and historical accuracy of Indian portrayals and the descriptions of Native American–Euroamerican relationships, and like others, he saw the frontier devoid of Native peoples. Ultimately, his comment on precolonial literature excludes the Native peoples' imaginative expressions from a place in American literature: "Pre-Colonial literature [A.D. 1000–1607] is one of two general types, records of voyages of exploration and poems and legends composed in Indian tongues. Strictly speaking, of course, neither of these can be counted American literature. The record of voyages were not written on this side of the Atlantic, and few of them were in English. The Indian poems were not written down at all until many years later" (20). It is not the Native languages that make Indian literature remain outside American literature; Dickinson includes works written in German, French, and Yiddish in his literary history. Indian literature is set apart solely by its oral nature, which Dickinson, unlike Brinton, does not regard as an extra dimension of the creative expression. He holds that literacy had been a distinguishing characteristic of the colonists as early as the Pilgrims. Libraries were established on the Western frontier as soon as possible. Eliot translated the Bible into an Indian language for Indian converts to *read*. Of course, literacy is a requirement for civilizing Native peoples. Ultimately, Dickinson's literary history is not as different and innovative as it seemed at first.

McNickle had been trained in the Euroamerican view of history and literature at the University of Montana, Oxford University, the University of Grenoble, and Columbia University. His journals show that he was an insatiable reader and, during his residence in New York City, he seems to have been a steady visitor of the public library. He regularly read the newspaper and enjoyed concerts and plays. It is not surprising that he had internalized Euroamerican history and literature and that they provided the framework for his earliest writings. If he had indeed managed to publish the still extant manuscript of *The Surrounded*, it might have brought him the yearned for commercial success. Unlike *The Surrounded*, it would have appealed to the taste of the Euroamerican reading public.

By 1932 McNickle's journal shows loss of faith in that Euroamerican framework, though, and growing awareness that he had lost something important: "instinct, right or wrong, cannot be abandoned without seriously impairing integrity, out of which rise self-possession, confidence and the very ability to act and think" (Diary, 11 August 1932). He no longer accepted the American vision that only "the 'smart,' the supersalesmen, had any chance or any right to survive" (Diary, 11 August 1932). Revisions of the manuscript version of *The Surrounded* discarded more and more of the Euroamerican framework, until it finally became the story of the clash of two equally valid cultures. The assimilationist message of the manuscript version was completely abandoned. *The Surrounded* is also the first attempt to find a new form for writing the history of Native peoples. Native voices are not as strong as they are in the works of later writers, but McNickle struggles to include tribal history and oral literature. *The Surrounded* started to create a new framework that later Native American writers continued to expand and define.

Chapter Three

Elements of
Traditional Oral Narrative
in *The Surrounded*

Phillip E. Doss

Fundamentals of the Orality/Literacy Opposition

Tracing the contrasting elements of the oral and literate traditions begins in the nineteenth century, when scientific and scholarly attention was focused on the evolution of species, their proliferation and differentiation. Concomitantly, an interest also developed in charting the seemingly limitless diversity of human social organization. The latter half of the twentieth century, however, is characterized by both an intellectual and emotional concern with the *extinction* of animal species, stressing the absolute finality of the loss and its consequences as the loss of possibilities in the lives of those who remain. The more recent concern is with charting the paths of retreat, often into isolated pockets of resistance, of traditions, cultures, and lifeways. D'Arcy McNickle argues most powerfully in *The Surrounded* that retreat, in some cases, actually constitutes a survival technique, since Native American traditional cultures remain strong. Neither attempts at extirpation nor programs of assimilation have eradicated them. McNickle's intent in all his works (but particularly in *The Surrounded* and *They Came Here First*) was to show that it is the adaptability of Native American traditions in the face of physical, cultural, and intellectual opposition that has prevented those traditions from being completely supplanted by Western European social organizations. Survival for any tradition depends upon expression. McNickle shows in *The Surrounded* how an oral tradition can find expression in a print medium.

At the heart of most dialogue about the opposition between literacy and orality is a more fundamental opposition in which one or the other is imbued with moral overtones. In addition to serving as a form of communication, the medium of expression appropriates semantic content from the culture that employs it, and distinct cognitive processes may be associated with particular media of expression. Moreover, certain consistencies and consequences are evident between a people's way of life and/or philosophy of life and their dominant medium of expression. For example, the colonial atrocities committed by Western European nations were not only engendered by the written contracts that enabled them, but also by the philosophy of life that made the contracts a possible reality. Similarly, the positive good that the Native American derives from the oral medium is that, in terms of lifeway, oral expression requires proximity and community.

Following this line of thought, the collective cultural psyche is recognized as overlaid on language and, by extension, on the medium of expression. Michel Foucault notes that expression in language "manifests and translates the fundamental will of those who speak it" (290).[1] Foucault argues that for the Western (literate) tradition an awareness of the dynamics of this expressive process comes to life in the nineteenth century, contemporaneous with the West's rediscovery of language as paradoxically fundamental and immensely complex, and understanding that the written word is only a minimal expression. In Native American oral traditions the recognition of language as a manifestation of will (though in a more pragmatic, less philosophical manner) occurred much earlier than the nineteenth century, in part because the lurching development of manuscript/print literacy did not intervene to mask the expressive capabilities of language.[2] With the extralinguistic nuances of expression available to an individual speaker, disambiguation is rather easily accomplished, particularly since the participants in communication events are always proximate. It is possible to achieve disambiguation in a print medium as well, but it often occurs at the expense of immense detail, all of which must be apprehended linearly and subjected to the (linear) cognitive processes of apprehension. The set of references necessary for disambiguation is rarely immediately available in a connotative field in a literate tradition. Marshall McLuhan argues in *The Gutenberg Galaxy* that linear apprehension relies on the visual and that this reliance creates an imbalance in the senses, an imbalance that affects cognition: "The notion of moving steadily along on single planes of narrative awareness is totally alien to the nature of language and of consciousness. But it is highly consistent with the nature of the printed word" (244). The "space" in which one communicates in an oral tradition is not planar but multidimensional, filled with the cultural reference points that constitute tradition. The mysterious wilderness that in print exists in the space between expression and meaning is easily avoided in an oral tradition (if the speaker finds such avoidance desirable) not only by means of extralinguistic expressive tools but also by reference to a cohesive cultural tradition. It is as if a speaker in an oral tradition always has at ready disposal the means to speak from the heart of the matter, to express, in Foucault's terms, a "fundamental will."

Native American literacy does not, for the most part, arise from within Native American groups, but has been introduced to them from without. Partially for this reason, literacy *qua* expression has never completely supplanted orality in Native American traditions. Literate expression simply does not allow an easy approach to pure form (in the form/content complement), something oral expression does allow.[3] It is an understanding of this expressive capability that allows N. Scott Momaday to argue that in "the Native American oral tradition expression, rather than communication, is often first in importance" ("The Native Voice," 7). The significance of expression derives from the fact that the spoken word (including all the semantic variables that constitute its meaning) nearly embodies the tradition to which and in which the performer speaks. These are compelling arguments for the close association of orality and Native American lifeways, and one might even be tempted to argue that Native American lifeways *require* orality. McNickle's wholesale belief in Native American adaptability suggests, however, that he might have viewed literacy as just one more Western European obstacle, or one more tool: "Indian society did not disappear by assimilating to the dominant white culture, as predicted [by governmental institutions], but assimilated to themselves bits and pieces of the surrounding cultural environment" (*They Came Here First*, 283). The questions of whether distinctly different cognitive processes are called upon for oral and printed media, whether the fundamental will of a people can be expressed in *only* one medium, and whether the medium in some way determines that will are explored in *The Surrounded*. Working within a literate framework, McNickle uses stories, aphorisms, ceremonies, and celebrations, all of which partake of an oral medium of expression. Rather than revealing a conflict between literacy and orality, he demonstrates that literacy, far from supplanting orality, is merely inadequate to the task of maintaining Native American traditions. In the process of delivering his exposition of the positive values of Salish culture, he shows that there is a reciprocity between the necessary condition of orality and the necessary conditions of the Salish tradition. His emphasis throughout *The Surrounded* is not on the medium of expression but on the nature of the culture that is expressed.

John Foley notes that contact with literacy engenders for oral expression the loss of a certain purity: "it does not follow that tradition, even oral tradition, ends with the poet's or culture's first draught of literacy. What does end, unambiguously, is the oral tradition in its Ur-form, together with the possibility of recording the oral text in its Ur-form. What continues, just as unambiguously . . . is some vestige of orality and some vestige of tradition" (*Traditional Oral Epic* 5). One supposes that the only thing McNickle might object to here is Foley's characterization of the continued tradition as vestigial, since the word implies a loss of effectiveness.[4]

It was just McNickle's point that Native American traditions are efficacious, that in fact the reason they survived was precisely because they provided lifeways that *sustained life*. In *The Surrounded* there is moral efficiency in the whip, beyond its ability merely to cover the fault (206), and a type of social and psychological efficacy in the "minute observances" from which Archilde's mother derives such satisfaction as she prepares Narcisse for the Dance (215). Modeste's cure for Mike's fears is effective. The thong by which Mike leads Modeste to the Dance (213) works overtly at the community level as a symbolic device to conduct the past into the future and simultaneously, at the individual level, to connect Mike to the tradition of the community. The responsibility that the thong represents reestablishes for Mike the connectedness that the religion of the school at St. Xavier had severed. McNickle is rarely overtly didactic, though these examples demonstrate that he was concerned with maintaining a specific tradition. Certain elements of Salish culture McNickle judges superior in promoting human and environmental harmony, but beyond that concern,

McNickle demonstrates that Native Americans are themselves capable of sustaining the well-being of the individuals in their community. He uses the devices available to him from an oral tradition as well as devices of the modern literate tradition. Like Foley, McNickle argues that an oral tradition can absorb the impact of literacy without the culture itself dissolving into the one that introduces the new medium of expression.

Memory or Politics?

Walter Ong argues that "without writing, human consciousness cannot achieve its fuller potentials" (*Orality and Literacy*, 14–15). Momaday similarly argues that the oral tradition is a stage in the evolution of myth and legend. The "mature condition" of that evolution is literature ("The Man Made of Words," 105). Momaday goes on to note that the commentary voices (those sections printed on the recto pages) in *The Way to Rainy Mountain* "*validate* the oral tradition" (107) by placing it in a discursive context [emphasis added]. These views raise the question, is there a determinant relationship between medium of expression and consciousness, and by extension, between medium of expression and cultural values? The answer is not yet clear, and the issue is confounded by the inescapable fact that oral traditions are subject to the limitations of human memory. Though medium of expression certainly conditions consciousness, particularly in regard to the semantic units used to represent the phenomenal environment, it is doubtful that the cultural values carried in oral traditions are *determined* by the means of their expression.

Throughout *The Muse Learns to Write* Eric Havelock reminds that oral traditions are prompted in every expression by the necessity to remember, and that the maintenance of an oral tradition is subject in every expression to the limitations imposed by memory.[5] For Havelock this explains an oral society's predisposition to ritual and ceremony because, codified to a greater degree than other oral forms, they avoid the transmogrifications to which oral transmission is susceptible (70 ff.).[6] The systematic nature of ceremony constitutes a logic that may indeed be arbitrary and even contrary to the logic of scientific empiricism, yet the logic of ceremony serves by virtue of its internal order to preserve itself. Washington Matthews notes that there are vocables in many Navajo ceremonies to which the *hatali* (singers) can attribute no semantic value (Bierhorst, 269). Their value is ordinal, i.e., is solely a function of their place in the order of the ceremony.[7] The best example of such internal logic in *The Surrounded* occurs when Archilde's mother is preparing her grandson Narcisse for the Dance: "She took up folded garments of beaded buckskin and placed them on her grandchild in a kind of devotional act that derived satisfaction from minute observances; in a matter so simple, the least part has its significance or it is all meaningless" (215).[8] The lesson here is that one should not discount the value of ceremony because its logic is arbitrary or merely internal, or because it is fundamentally an efficient mnemonic device. McNickle, instead, intends us to look to that which the ceremony calls into consciousness.

The Surrounded is about remembering. Archilde's return home is motivated by his need to recharge his memory. The first chapter ends: "he would always keep the memory of these things" (14). Archilde's mother's memory "begins" with the missionaries (21). "The Story of Flint" engenders "a spark of gay remembrance in [Archilde's] mind" (66). And the summer Dance rekindles life-sustaining memories for the old men: "In weeks following [the Dance], the old men tried to go on living on the memories which had come alive then" (233). The act of remembering in these instances is not an empty exercise. Rather than providing escape from a valueless present into the past, remembering serves to bring the past, *and the cultural values that originated there, into the present.* Havelock notes that maintaining the oral tradition is accomplished by a close association of generations (4). McNickle would add, however, oral tradition cultures maintain an intricate network of relationships, one portion of which is the close association of generations, but that this network in its entirety transmits cultural values. When Momaday says that the elements of an oral tradition are "always but one generation removed from extinction" ("Native Voice," 12), his emphasis, as McNickle's would be, is upon the tenuousness of the tradition, not upon its orality.² It is the loss of the culture, which is logically prior to its means of expression, that is to be feared.

José Limón is aware of the confusion that arises from conflating orality and the traditions that are orally transmitted. For Limón there are dangers in viewing the verbal arts as "incipient" forms of literature, dangers that are political as well as intellectual and aesthetic (127). Because orality is prior historically to literacy, Limón argues, it is often characterized as somehow "lesser," in keeping with the evolutionary bias of most critics and academic commentators. By association, the cultures in which orality is a significant medium of expression are also viewed as lesser.[10] Limón writes from experiences with Hispanic literature and folklore, both of which have significant traditions of political resistance.[11] In general, however, Native American orality contains very few examples of political resistance to the established Native culture.[12] As is evident in the *oral*-derived sections of *The Surrounded*, it stays focused upon maintaining the cultural values of the group in which it operates. Political resistance is much more evident in works of Native American print literature, such as *The Surrounded*, Momaday's *House Made of Dawn*, Louise Erdrich's *Love Medicine*, and Leslie Silko's *Ceremony*. Each of these works utilizes elements of orality, however subtly or overtly, to express resistance.

Although confrontation between cultures is certainly an overriding theme throughout *The Surrounded* and, as the title indicates, the ending is bleak, Archilde's recognition of the positive values of his Native American heritage is also a theme. The feast, more than any other event in the narrative, reimmerses Archilde in Salish culture, and it does so *via* traditional stories. If we superimpose the heroic framework of the Western novel (separation-initiation-return) upon *The Surrounded*, the feast represents return, though with a curious irony.[13] In the Western framework the hero acquires new knowledge in the initiation phase, but in *The Surrounded* the new knowledge ironically takes the form of recognizing old knowledge and of participating in tradition. John Purdy has commented upon the in medias res beginning of *The Surrounded* (40). The technique in this instance leads the reader to believe that the separation and initiation phases of the hero's journey have already taken place, and gives the reader to expect expository flashbacks to provide the information necessary to fill in the plot. To a certain extent McNickle fulfills these expectations, episodically, by recounting Archilde's history prior to his return. With the feast scene, however, McNickle conflates the initiation and return phases of this heroic journey framework. The drama of the story is heightened precisely when the reader realizes that the development of Archilde's character has not already taken place, but is still in process. A crucial event, which the reader expects to have occurred in the past, occurs in the present. When the heroic return does occur, it is not the return of an individual (which is a necessary and sometimes sufficient condition of heroism in the Western tradition) but of a member of an integrated community. Individuality is not renounced so much as subsumed in the communality of the group.

Archilde's first mention of the feast is derogatory: "You gorged yourself on meat until you felt sick, and a lot of old people told tiresome stories" (4). As the event unfolds, and stories are told, Archilde's attitude begins to change. "The Story of Flint" brings Archilde pleasant memories, which, besides the comments on the landscape of Sniél-emen, is the first positive comment in the book about Salish culture. Whitey's story, "The Thing That Was to Make Life Easy" (66), causes Archilde to reflect: "A story like that he realized, was full of meaning" (69). Finally, the story told by Modeste is specifically for Archilde. Though the story's explicit import is to verify Archilde's judgment that "those old days are dead and won't come again" (70), its ironic effect upon Archilde is to remove that assurance. It does so by reminding him that the Salish were once a "mighty race" (70), and that they have fallen to their present condition not because of any weakness or evil inherent in their culture, but because of extrinsic forces. It is this story, which Archilde has heard many times but to which he has never truly listened, that turns him once again toward his people. Archilde tells us later, at the point when Modeste explains his decision to once again employ the whip, though he has promised the Jesuits not to, that "nothing was ever done without telling a story" (210–11). The connection between storytelling and decision making illustrates that the social context that permits and promotes storytelling also permits and promotes the examination (and celebration) of self, specifically the self as it relates to the tribal group. One can see how group solidarity promoted by storytelling might be converted to political solidarity, as Limón notes has been the case for Hispanic culture.

Connotation

Alan Dundes's valuable distinctions among "text, texture and context" illuminate the source of communicative power in oral tradition because they outline the many variables that attend an oral communication event. Many of these variables escape analysis because they simply are not isolable entities; they depend for their existence upon sets of relationships that only obtain at the time the communication event occurs. Their ephemerality does not affect their communicative power, however. For example, "The Story of Flint" is the type of story that "grandmothers tell to grandchildren" (66). It therefore lacks denotative significance for the adult intellect; but we see by its effect upon Archilde that its connotative power (unlike the story told by Modeste, in which there was "meaning") derives not from its content but from the circumstances of its telling and retelling, from what Dundes would call its "context." The stories that speak to Archilde have meaning for him not merely because they are stories, but because they are stories that are imbricated in Salish culture.

Foley notes that connotation works in oral tradition by bringing to immediacy cultural associations: "Traditional referentiality . . . entails the invoking of a context that is enormously larger and more echoic than the text or work itself, that brings the lifeblood of generations of poems and performances to the individual performance or text" (*Immanent Art*, 7). This is not fundamentally different *per se* from the referentiality of literate traditions. Any student who has traced allusions in *The Waste Land* knows that Eliot was speaking out of the Western literate tradition, albeit Eliot's individualized version; and even the campaign of E. D. Hirsch, Jr., for "cultural literacy" was based upon the notion of shared spheres of reference. In a literate tradition however, one cannot logically assume a uniform field through which connotation can reverberate, because the nature of the document allows (and perhaps promotes) encounter with individuals of disparate experience. This difference between literate and oral referentiality lies partially in the fact that most cultures for which primary orality is the basic communication medium are necessarily close-knit, at least by present standards of nationhood.[14] The very nature of orality, which requires a present speaker and present auditor, demands that it be so. Orality simply requires proximity.

It is this closeness that makes oral tradition "echoic"; the similarity of individual experience within a cohesive cultural context makes connotation possible, and powerful.[15] In *The Surrounded*, for example, Archilde may speak indirectly to Mike (272) when he is dealing with Mike's fear of the "evil one," because Archilde can be certain that his general experience has been the same as Mike's. These qualities of oral tradition also permit a dialogue of aphorisms (which are formulaic and thus excellent mnemonic devices). When Archilde returns from his morning hunt without venison his mother says to him: "A young man waits for a better shot and hits nothing. An old man makes the best of it and gets his meat." He answers in like style: "When the smoke clears away the women are still talking" (122).

Orality and the Modern Literacy of D'Arcy McNickle

A diametrical difference between oral and literate concepts of textuality is reflected in a passage from Wolfgang Iser's *The Implied Reader*: "Reading reflects the structure of experience to the extent that we must suspend the ideas and attitudes that shape our own personality before we can experience the unfamiliar world of the literary text" (291). Iser sees each literary text as a potential implement for remaking the individual who encounters it. The oral text, however, because it is an expression of a unified tradition, is generally more concerned with reaffirming the individual who encounters it (perhaps only a less radical form of remaking).[16] In a section of *They Came Here First* McNickle quotes from Pueblo law: "To hold membership and rights in this pueblo, the member must do his community duties. The duties are known to everyone. Everyone is responsible for doing them" (61). Later in the same work McNickle makes the point that Pueblo law is "customary rather than written" (233). The duties are not set down in writing, since being a member of the community and knowing the laws of the community are correlative experiences. The oral text of the law presumes the life experience that gives rise to it. The result is a body of law flexible enough to adjudicate fairly individual situations and rigid enough to maintain a stable relationship between the individual and the community. McNickle notes that provisions written into the Civil Rights Act of 1968 threatened the survival of the Pueblo code simply because the federal law did not (as no written law could) take into account all of the variables inherent in Pueblo tradition, and it was Pueblo tradition that embodied Pueblo law.

One of the primary movements in the plot of *The Surrounded* is toward Archilde's reintegration into the Salish community. At the same time the plot moves inexorably toward confrontation between Native American and while cultures. One senses the former movement primarily through a juxtaposition of episodes, which are presented not so much with any particular regard for Aristotelian necessity as for the total effect they will produce by story's end. Herein lies not only the didactic subtlety to which LaFarge indirectly refers (quoted in Towner, 299), but the operative logic of orality as well. Purdy notes that "McNickle's success in revising his novel came when he employed the strategies and motifs of the verbal arts" (22). These strategies result in a logic of the whole, which is connotative in nature. Conclusions, if they are drawn at all, must be drawn from premises presented in casual, often capricious fashion, rather than in the straightforward fashion of linear logic. Only in its entirety is the form systematic. Purdy also notes McNickle's awareness of Euroamerican narrative conventions. The most Aristotelian of these is a concern for plot and the all-important action that impels the plot toward a conclusion. McNickle's artistry resides in his ability to balance these two plot movements, confrontation and reintegration, each exercised with reference to a different communication medium.

One of the most notable characteristics of oral narrative is repetition. It serves as a mnemonic device, creates rhythm, and in some ceremonies it has an incantatory effect, but in a prose work such as *The Surrounded* the function of repetition is more allusive than incantatory mnemonic. The tacit rules of the literate framework, and particularly of the novel genre, require that the repetitions that do occur (and that must occur to create rhythm in the work) must be connotative within the work itself. Because the novel form enables an author to create a world *in toto*, divorced from the constraints of relationships to the empirical world (cf. Iser, 278–79), it makes itself susceptible, more than any other literary form, to application of the concept of organic unity. In the literate medium, however, the reiterations that create rhythm and thereby create the illusion of unity are conceptual rather than acoustic. Northrup Frye calls this the "semantic rhythm of sense, or what is usually felt to be the prose rhythm" (*Anatomy of Criticism* 263). Even if acoustic repetitions should occur in the literate prose narrative form, they are categorized as poetic, subtle violations of the novel genre; at most they become an element of a particular author's style. What are functions of mnemonic necessity in an oral medium become stylistic devices in a literate medium.

McNickle does indeed employ thematic repetition as a narrative device in *The Surrounded*. One of the most obvious themes is failed communication. Failures occur by honest misunderstanding, as a result of the recalcitrance of the parties, or simply because the parties speak different languages. Examples include the dialogue between Max and Father Grepilloux (37–38); the dialogue between Max and Archilde in regard to his Indian habits (24–25); and the exchanges between Max and George Moser, and Max and the other ranchers at Moser's store (28). In a broader frame, the reconciliation of Max and Catharine is blocked by miscommunication.[17] Throughout the book obvious thematic repetitions are created in the opposition between the "new ways" and the "old ways," between fish hooks and spears (13). Both of these themes rise into and fall from prominence to create a rhythm of tension throughout the novel.

The Work and Its Time

In the tradition of discoveries that dislodge authors and works from historical obscurity, the works and the days of D'Arcy McNickle are, at last, receiving long-overdue critical attention. *The Surrounded*, as an object of dialogue today is scrutinized by a postmodern poststructuralist world. The world from which we extract it, and the audience for whom it was composed, was Modernist and Structuralist. *The Surrounded* was first published in 1936, the year Faulkner's *Absalom, Absalom!* and Margaret Mitchell's *Gone With the Wind* were published. Like Mitchell's book, *The Surrounded* speaks from the "margin" (part of its current appeal and extra-aesthetic value). It represents a world apprehended from a social, political, and psychological perspective that is different from the mainstream perspective of the United States in the 1930s. Like Faulkner's work, *The Surrounded* speaks in a style and uses literary devices that are, for the most part, Modernist.[18] Further, like Faulkner's work, it offers bold insights into the sociological and psychological nature of racial conflict, relevant thematic material for our day.

The Surrounded also speaks to us at this particular moment because it utilizes elements of separate and fundamentally different communication media, orality and literacy. The elements of these media usually blend roughly, if they blend at all, but in *The Surrounded* a reciprocity between them is established, wherein the presence of one helps define the other. Today, the relationships between literacy and electronic media are under consideration, and the technical aspects of *The Surrounded* gain added significance. McNickle's two communication media do not conflict, but complement, within a work of literacy, and in which an older form is not residual but operative and integral within the new one.

For all these reasons, interest in McNickle's work, *The Surrounded* particularly, is more than overdue, it is also timely. McNickle could not have known, as he fashioned the juxtaposition of oral and literate elements in *The Surrounded*, that his work would serve as evidence for cognitive possibilities beyond literacy and into an electronic age.

Chapter Four

The Surrounded:
Listening Between the Lines
of Inherited Stories

William Brown

The chemistry between "inherited stories," which are primarily oral stories, and the Native American fiction in which they appear is the subject of ongoing inquiry.[1] The interaction of these two elements (or to use Mikhail Bakhtin's term, "utterances"),[2] however, can teach us about a variety of subjects and is part of a larger context that is both literary and social. The essential natures of written and oral stories are made apparent by juxtaposing them against each other, and we learn more about the bridges and walls between cultural viewpoints that give expression through one form or the other.

One of the four included narratives in *The Surrounded* tells of "Coyote and Flint."[3] As McNickle tells us in his opening "Note," he found the story in Helen Sanders's book, *Trails Through Western Woods*. He alters this version when including it in the novel. As John Purdy demonstrates in his study of McNickle's three novels, variable insights are gained from comparative study of the two versions. However, additional insights can result from an alternate approach, and these can have a profound influence on our reading of the novel as a whole.[4]

Our method for comparative text analysis stems from the ethnographic practice of interlinear translations and the ethnopoetic recognition of verse tendencies in oral narrative.[5] To demonstrate the method, McNickle's version of "Coyote and Flint" is divided into numbered lines, and the Sanders version comes between the lines, in smaller print. McNickle's version was divided first and the Sanders arrangement based on it, with the intention of finding semantic units that enable and enhance comparison. The intent is not necessarily to approximate oral performance—even though one can occasionally imagine pauses in the storyteller's delivery—nor to establish a consistent system of line division applicable to other prose oral narratives.[6] Most often the lines represent a single idea or action. Sometimes two or more closely related items appear in a line. Using ideas and actions to determine arrangement more clearly highlights differences; it improves our view of material that McNickle adds or discards. At the same time, it gives some sense of his attention to rhythms in the presentation. Finally, when Sanders has longer sections mildly related to a McNickle line, her sections appear in the right margin, and the quotation marks remain in order to show paragraphing in the prose versions.

"Coyote and Flint"

(1) "In the long ago
"In the old times
(2) the animals had tribes just like men.
the animals had tribes just like the Indians.
(3) Coyote had his own tribe
The Coyote had his tipi.
(4) and this was one of the mightiest.

(5) Now he was hungry
He was hungry
(6) and all his people were hungry.

(7) They had nothing to eat.
 and had nothing to eat.
(8) He sat in his tepee and pulled his blanket close.

(9) " 'If I just had something to put on my arrow,' he said.

(10) "It was like this. He has nothing to put on his arrow.

(11) He had just bark
 He had bark to shoot his arrow with
(12) and you can see that would not go through a buffalo.
 and the arrow did not go through the deer.
(13) When he shot something with the bark it just bounced
off and the buffalo said 'Now I will eat that fly if he doesn't
go away.'

(14) "And Coyote had nothing to eat.
 He was that way a long time   when he heard there was Flint coming
 on the road that gave a piece of flint to

                          the Fox and he could shoot a
                          deer and kill it, but the Coyote
                          did not know that and used the
                          bark. They did not give the
                          Coyote anything. They only
                          gave some to the Fox.

(15) Next day he went to see Fox,

(16) and Fox was cooking a piece of meat on a stick.
 Next day the Fox put a piece of meat on the end of a stick and
(17) He was holding it to the fire.
 took it to the fire. The Fox had the piece of meat cooking there
(18) Coyote sat down and watched the meat getting cooked.
 and the Coyote was looking at the meat
(19) And he smelled the hot fat.

(20) And he got very hungry.

(21) Then when it was all cooked
 and when it was cooked

(22) Coyote jumped and grabbed the meat

the Coyote jumped and got the piece of meat

(23) and put it in his mouth all at once.

and took a bite

(24) But when he bit

(25) there was something hard in it.

(26) And it was the Flint.

and in it was the flint, and he bit the flint and asked why they did not tell him how to kill a deer with flint.

(27) " 'Now why didn't you tell me you had the Flint?' Coyote asked.

" 'Why didn't you tell me?' the Coyote asked his friend, the Fox.

(28) 'When did the Flint go along here?'

'When did the Flint go by here?'

(29) "Fox said it was three days now since the Flint went by.

"The Fox said three days it went by here.

(30) "Then Coyote took his blanket and his things and started after the Flint.

"The Coyote took his blanket and his things and started after the Flint

(31) When he had walked all day

and kept on his track all day and evening

(32) he said, 'Here is where the Flint camped.'

and said, 'Here is where the Flint camped,'

(33) Then he slept.

and he stayed there all night himself,

(34) Another day he traveled

and next day he travelled to where the Flint camped,

(35) and then he said, 'The Flint made his bed here.'

and he said, 'Here is where the Flint camped last night,'

(36) And he slept in that place.

and he stayed there,

(37) Then he walked the next day

and the next day he went farther and found where the Flint camped

(38) and at night he said, 'The Flint started from here this morning,'

and he said, 'The Flint started from here this morning.'

(39) and so he slept again.

(40) Next morning he got up early and walked fast
He followed the track next morning and went not very far,

(41) and there he saw the Flint going along the road.
and he saw the Flint going on the road,

(42) Coyote went out that way and then went faster and got ahead of the Flint and waited.
and he went 'way out that way and went ahead of the Flint and stayed there for the Flint to come.

(43) And when the Flint came
When the Flint met him there

(44) Coyote said: " 'So here you are.
the Coyote told him:

(45) Come here now and I will fight you.'
" 'Come here. Now, I want to have a fight with you today.'

(46) "And the Flint said, "All right. We will fight.'
"And the Flint said: " 'Come on. We will fight.'

(47) "Then they were fighting and going this way and that way
"The Flint went to him

(48) and Coyote took what he had in his hand—it was a war club—and he hit the Flint very hard and the Flint broke all to pieces.
and the Coyote took the thing he had in his hand and struck him three or four times and the Flint broke all to pieces

(49) " 'Hoh! said Coyote. 'It is done.'

(50) And he put the pieces in his blanket and put it on his shoulder and started back.
and the Coyote had his blanket there and put the pieces in the blanket and after they were through fighting and he had the pieces of flint in his blanket he packed the flint on his back and went

(51) And he said to his people

(52) 'Just put some flint on the point of your arrows

(53) and we will kill buffalo.'

(54) Then he went to all the tribes

    to all the tribes

(55) and gave them flint

    and gave them some flint

(56) and after that they did not have to starve.

    and said: " 'Here is some flint for you to kill deer and things with.'
    "And he went to another tribe
    and did the same thing and to
    other tribes and did the same
    until he came to Flint Creek
    and then from that time they
    used the flint to put in their
    arrows and kill deer and elk."

(57) "That is the story of Flint."

    "That is the story of the Flint."

Purdy describes the "dramatic, vocal quality" McNickle gives the narrative (54). Through shorter sentences, second person and other devices, McNickle gives "the telling a vigor, a life . . . more closely representative of an actual storytelling event" (54). The interlinear presentation allows one to appreciate McNickle's methods and concerns. For example, Purdy concludes that "the result [of Sanders's many compound sentences] is a quality suggestive of a hasty, childlike narrative" (53), and that McNickle "opts for short, simple sentences" (54). While this conclusion is true in most cases, it is worth noting the exceptions, for McNickle judiciously rearranges. He does not completely undo these compound sentences. In line 42, he preserves the string of clauses joined by "and." His addition of the adverb "faster" suggests his preservation may represent Coyote's quicker pace. Additionally, while shortening sentences, McNickle retains the "and" more often than not. The new effect, as Purdy claims, does encourage silence and visualization of the action; at the same time, the retained "and" undercuts that effect, perhaps to offset the influence of a written form. As Purdy suggests,

McNickle has tried to approximate actual storytelling experiences more closely, but one must also recognize the oral elements already in Sanders's version.

With his observations about Zuni narratives, Tedlock injects another element for consideration. In the opening essay of *The Spoken Word*, he notes that "Zuni narrators, like many others, frequently keep a story in motion by combining strings of clauses into long sentences and by joining these sentences with parallelism" (38). Despite faults sometimes ascribed to the Sanders book generally and her version of this story specifically, some of her style may have come from the version transmitted to her.[7] Conversely, a marked similarity is evident between McNickle's version and Ruth Benedict's translation of a Zuni passage.[8] Both Benedict and McNickle make predominant use of short sentences. In the 1930s both were also writing and reading ethnographic accounts of native narratives. Although as Purdy pointed out, McNickle wants to approximate the oral story event (i.e., keep it "authentic"), his style was also likely influenced by some ethnographic tendencies of the time.

Lines 30 to 39 present another informative point of comparison. Coyote follows close on the heels of Flint for three days. Sanders, perhaps reflecting the version translated to her, expresses the three days' events with occasional repetition. Tedlock illustrates types of repetition people sometimes consider primitive stylistic elements (*Spoken Word* 51–53). He cites examples of "parallelism," where similar or identical phrases or clauses keep narrative momentum through a series of links. Although Sanders's version does not incorporate parallelism, it does use repetition. Sanders repeats the phrases "next day" and "where the Flint camped." McNickle, however, chooses to vary the phrasing of repeated ideas. He uses "another day" and "next day," and he varies phrasing around the clause, "he slept." On the second night of Coyote's travels, McNickle augments his own phrasing by having Coyote sleep "in that place;" Sanders simply repeats her adverb, "there," showing no sense of movement or progression. Native verbal art has many examples of "simple" repetition of words or phrases, but other locations in Sanders's version suggest that rather than remaining absolutely true to the story given her,[9] she may have treated its language as Tedlock says the early ethnographers, like Benedict, treated parallelisms: "as not worthy of preserving in print" (38).

The tendency to dismiss Native verbal art, or parts of it, is quite evident throughout Sanders's book. Purdy implies this by raising the possibility that "she purposely manipulated the material" in order to place "a hasty, childlike narrative against . . . her own formal, flowery prose" (53–54). The language she uses to describe the people whose stories she recounts also reveals her attitude toward Native Americans. In referring to their visits to the ram's horn tree,[10] she writes that "the poor children of the woods play truant, nevertheless, and wander back through the cycle of centuries to do honor to the old, sweet object of their devotion in the primitive, pagan way" (33). Later she notes that "the Indians, impressionable and fanciful as children, feel the weird spell [of Waters of the Forgiven (St. Mary's Lake)]" (77). While wondering about the missionaries' "success," she concludes "the Indians were probably in their racial infancy when the maturer ranks marched in. . . . It would seem that with them it is a case of arrested development" (148). If there could be any further doubt about her attitude, she also uses the epithet "we, the superior race" (141).

It comes as little surprise, then, to find listless moments in Sanders's stylistic (in)decisions, moments that McNickle has carefully reworked to add force and liveliness. For example, McNickle invests Coyote with more obvious motivation and more character. He is hungrier and more desperate in the later version.[11] Therefore, when the meat "was all cooked / Coyote jumped and *grabbed* the meat," whereas in Sanders he simply "got the meat," even though he jumped there, also. Sanders's Coyote then "took a bite," while McNickle's "put it in his mouth all at once." Earlier in Sanders, in the margin of line 14, she includes an awkwardly worded explanation of how Fox acquired Flint. McNickle does away with the entire explanation, perhaps because he knows how much Fox and Coyote travel and visit with each other in Salish stories generally. To say that Coyote "went to see Fox" suffices. He also resolves the explanation's unclear final reference to "they." In his version, McNickle uses just the one character of Flint. The tendency to dismiss can also, given these other moments, account for Sanders's use of "there" in the three-day sequence in lines 30 to 39. McNickle enlivens this section, as well, by economizing in the first case and varying in the second. At the same time, though, McNickle may be trying to vary repetitions for a reading public less willing to encounter "authentic" Native styles of narration.[12] He shows similar attention when in line 34 he omits the phrase, "to where the Flint camped." Its appearance in Sanders's next line may encourage him to see it as unnecessary repetition. Finally, in line 50, McNickle elimi-nates the repetition of references to the blanket. He sees the first and last references obviated by the middle one. Two impulses operate simultaneously in McNickle's version: to provide dramatic and stylistic variety for the novel's intended audience (primarily non-Indian) and to lend greater care and vitality to the numerous careless, listless passages in his model.[13]

Bakhtin's theory of utterance sheds light on our discussion.[14] Bakhtin claims that each utterance has meaning partially through its relationship to previous utterances addressing the same object (in this case, "Coyote and Flint"), and his theory can help define the struggle seen in this novel. McNickle has received a version of a Salish story. His utterance expresses itself through links to Sanders's utterance *and* to oral tellings. In these terms McNickle, in composing his utterance, listens to relationships between Sanders and the oral source(s).[15] He attempts to understand the "scenario" of discourse between these two.[16] In fact, he does this *because* Sanders does not. "The one doing the understanding," Bakhtin says, "takes on the role of listener. But to play this part, he or she must also understand clearly the position of the other participants" (Todorov 47). Meaning ("theme" for Bakhtin) of an utterance derives from several contexts, one of which is evaluative. The utterance is expressed by its subjects (i.e., speakers) successfully when this and other contexts are shared. When speakers occupy different "evaluative horizons," meaning is missed. Sanders's judgmental comments cited above suggest she and her interlocutor have something other than effective utterance.

McNickle's version reflects an understanding of this misconnection. More to the point, McNickle, while claiming Sanders's tale as "authentic,"[17] tries through literary tools at his disposal to actualize an utterance heard by Sanders but not yet listened to.[18] The novel itself, as does his ethnological writing, increases the chances of a shared evaluative horizon for the reader and the people whose narratives McNickle includes. In this sense, McNickle tries to be true(r) to the story, and his attempt suggests that a novel(ist) can give to, as well as receive from, an inherited story. This returning and consequent reciprocity corresponds not only to Bakhtin's ideas on dialogue, but also to the give-and-take in physical performances as well as themes of oral storytelling.[19]

Put another way, the relationship illustrates Bakhtin's description of the meeting between quoting and quoted discourse. In such a conjunction, the quoting utterance can treat the quoted one either linearly, "which consists in the creation of clear and external contours for the discourse of the other, which is itself at the same time poorly individualized internally," or pictorially, in which "the context of the author attempts to break up the compactness and closure of the other's discourse, to absorb it, to erase its borders."[20] Sanders's stylistic listlessness in the story and cultural judgment in the book align her treatment of oral sources more with linear tendencies, whereas McNickle's treatment of Sanders tends toward the pictorial. While both styles aim to contain the other's discourse, the pictorial style necessarily alters the surrounding discourse through internalization. Faced with Sanders's externalizing approach, McNickle in his recasting tries to erase some of its borders, for example, in his granting more personality to Coyote. This character has more substance and importance for him than for Sanders.[21] In particular, McNickle's Coyote shows greater desperation. He pulls "his blanket close" because of hunger and weakness (line 8), he is ridiculed by the buffalo for his inability to kill large game (line 13), and he smells "the hot fat" while watching Fox cook the meat he (Coyote) so urgently wants (line 19). At each of these moments in the story, Sanders either briefly describes Coyote's emotional state or says nothing.[22]

The Surrounded has four included narratives. Three— including "Coyote and Flint"—are told at a special feast Catharine holds for her son, Archilde, after his return from the city. The other narrative, however, comes first in the novel and is told to Archilde's father, Max, by the priest, Father Grepilloux. The priest says he has heard several versions. He also refers to this story, the story of Big Paul, as "the history of a very different affair" (52). Interestingly, the narrative matches in length the one told by Modeste about "the coming of the Blackrobes," which is twice the length of the other two told the night of the feast. Why, then, in most of the writing about this novel is the story passed over? Perhaps because it is less "authentic" than the other three, coming as it does from the priest's pen (he has written what he considers an "accurate" account) and not from a Salish character in a tribal setting.[23]

As it happens our interlinear analysis also illuminates links between McNickle's rewriting "Coyote and Flint" and his composing "Big Paul," and it opens another dimension of the discussion, interaction between oral stories and the novel. A central theme of the Big Paul story emerges in the patterns of McNickle's rewriting and that association provides new "angles of vision" on the novel.[24]

Father Grepilloux reads his account of Big Paul (to Max) as he has written it, without interruption or editorial. He takes great care in narrating the events. Several times he strikes a cautionary note like "Evidently," "My informant tells me" or "My witness tells me." Referring to one set of details, he claims, "I have been told this by a man who was living in the mining camp at the time" (56). Perhaps the gravity of this story prompts the emphasis on accuracy. Or perhaps, because he receives pieces of this story secondhand he shows more caution, for in the earlier passages from his daybook he recounts his own arrival in the valley and qualifies his statements less often. Whatever the reasons, his caution becomes relevant when he tells how "the trouble began" (53) with Big Paul and how it ended. Big Paul's father, Nine-Pipe, also called the Judge because of his wisdom and peace making, is killed by a white man.[25] That murder sets off revenge killings and intratribal tensions. Right from the start the story contains examples of people's dismissing others without listening. Even though the white men are guests in the Judge's tipi for storytelling during an autumn buffalo hunt, one of them accuses him of lying. Apparently drunk, this white man continues to the point of insulting his host. Nine-Pipe seeks no revenge, but some unknown person does by killing the offender later the same night. According to Turner-High, slander was listed among the Flathead as a "chief public crime" alongside wife stealing, murder, and theft (46). This makes all the worse the behavior against such a respected elder.[26] Grepilloux, in *his* cautious telling, seems to absorb the Judge's penchant for truth.

The white man's friends then stab the Judge in retaliation. Grepilloux's commentary on that act captures the spirit of the whole Big Paul episode, as well as McNickle's rewriting of Sanders and his composition of the novel. The priest responds that "In their stupidity, they never asked themselves whether the old man could have committed that murder. If they had questioned him before they took his life, he would have been shocked by what had taken place, and I have no doubt that he would have impoverished himself, in order to make amends" (54). This same manner of action—inattentive to facts but convinced of cause—occurs twice more in the story, first with white miners who "overrode a village of Kootenay Indians, who had nothing whatever to do with the affair" (55). The second time, a group of Big Paul's people, led by his younger brother, "*without stopping to ask a single question* fell upon him [Big Paul] and stabbed him to death" (58; emphasis added). Despite the story's occasional coincidence, the inability of characters to consider and inquire is incontestable. In fact, the story ends with the silencing of Big Paul's voice, the voice of clear-minded struggle. He eschews a quick, inattentive approach; instead, he shows courage—emotional and intellectual, as well as the physical brand of his brothers—in expressing his assessment of the new realities, as complicated as they may seem to his people. The story, at one level, places his thoughtful responses against (and ultimately at the mercy of) the hasty, childlike actions of the others. This tragic silencing is balanced, in Grepilloux's eyes, by his belief that "Of course . . . they [Big Paul's people] have God" (59).

The priest's final comment on "Big Paul" shows the reader of the novel that acknowledging and understanding another's utterance does not come easily. Even when he works at synthesizing versions of a distinctive story into an "accurate" account of people who fail to listen, that same priest cannot learn the inherent lesson well enough to adjust his own response.[27] Further evidence of his inability arises from comparisons between his version of the Jesuits' arrival and Max's. The latter raises questions the priest had not considered. Modeste's version of the Blackrobes' coming reinforces our suspicion that Grepilloux's arrival story (dis)misses important components.

During the intratribal tensions after the white man's and Nine-Pipe's deaths, "Big Paul remind them [those who wanted to follow the 'ancient custom . . . primitive law' (Grepilloux's words) of avenging the murder] that times were changed" (54). This reminder characterizes the substance of the novel's other three included narratives. At Catherine's feast, an old woman tells of Coyote's discovering flint on behalf of his tribe. Bringing flint to his people changes their hunting capabilities. Next, an old man named Whitey tells of "The Thing That Was to Make Life Easy," an iron axe. Here again, substantial change enters tribal life. Finally, Modeste tells of two significant changes: guns and priests. In the first case, he tells how guns increased killing and, among other things, made the ancient custom of revenge harder to enact. In the second, he tells of the people's consequently desperate attempts to regain their former power by inviting the Blackrobes.[28]

"Big Paul" connects with the last story told at the feast, which runs into the most recent past. The story of Big Paul also provides several valuable links within the novel. It reminds us, for example, of something Old Grandma says in Silko's *Ceremony*: "It seems *like I already heard these stories before* . . . only thing is, the names sound different" (260; emphasis added). Each of the successive included narratives addresses how people handle change. Realizing a thematic similarity helps one appreciate the link between stories told now and then, or in Bakhtin's language, between an utterance and a predecessor. They both can continue to help us learn, if we listen to them. If we pay attention to the old stories *and* the new ones, we are more likely to see—and are better equipped to handle—change.

Archilde, too, needs these tools. After Modeste ends *his* story, the last of the four included narratives, the novel's narrator tells that "He [Archilde] had heard the story many times, but he had not listened. It had tired him. Now he saw that it had happened and it left him feeling weak. It destroyed his stiffness toward the old people. He sat and thought about it and the flames shot upward and made light on the circle of black pines."[29] Since his return to the reservation from Portland, Archilde has grown to share more of the evaluative horizon with Modeste and the other elder Salish storytellers. For a variety of reasons—his maturity, a renewed vision of his family's troubles, a greater sense of his own and his people's desperation—he places more value on the experiences of Coyote and the other characters than he did before. McNickle helps all readers do the same with respect to Sanders's version of "Coyote and Flint." He counteracts the dismissal evident in her book and Archilde's earlier tendencies.

Because Archilde has listened to (and not simply heard) Modeste's story, he has grown into someone slightly different. He has changed through the story. The feast episode ends, however, with a reminder that change on a larger scale takes widespread effort. Archilde's Spanish father is lying in the house trying to sleep. He wonders "why couldn't just one of his sons have the sense and the courage to make himself a new way of life" (75). He does not know, somewhat reminiscent of ignorances in "Big Paul," that his son has in an unspectacular-yet-meaningful way, made himself new.[30] Listening is an act of making, and stands distinct from the activity of hearing reflected in the final words of Max's wondering in this episode: "What were they [the voices of the storytellers at the feast next to his house] saying? Why didn't they talk to him?" Why, indeed?

Bakhtin claims that "meaning always answers some questions" (Todorov 54). Expression of the meaning occurs partially through a double-voicing effect in the questions. Our analysis makes more audible the double-voicing in the narrator's questions about Max. He has "some stiffness, some pride" toward his wife's Salish culture that weakens too late in his life and the life of his family. McNickle tries to weaken such stiffness in his readers, while acknowledging (and reflecting in his literary strategies) the struggle. His novel and its thematic workings forecast later novelists' attempts to amplify inherited stories in formal ways. If, as Bakhtin suggests the novel is still becoming, (15), *The Surrounded* shows a stage in that evolution. It tells part of the story of distinctive Native voices emerging[31] from this earth[32] to meet the novel.[33] For criticism, both of Native and non-Native works, faithfulness to the story of this meeting is an important consideration, as is McNickle's instruction on how to listen. For all the impossibility of understanding depicted in this novel, he still, as author and activist, has shown belief in the struggle. That belief gives a valuable model for all criticism.

Chapter Five

Lost in Translation: McNickle's Tragic Speaking

Robert Evans

When Modeste, in McNickle's *The Surrounded*, ends the story of his people's decline with the transliterated Indian phrase, "Ies choopminzin" (I stop talking to you), one of the very few in McNickle's novels, we readers are startled into recognizing that the myths told at his mother's feast for Archilde have been "translated" into English, the master language of the novel itself (74). The old people's stories of Flint and of "The Thing That Was to Make Life Easy" insert the legendary with its referral to mythic time into the historic present of the novel's discourse, as though the myths provide some meaningful analogy for the half-breed's returning from the white world. In fact, the tales do begin to awaken feelings in Archilde that lead him to identify with his tribal heritage and their success arouses readers' expectations of a reconciliation of traditional and modern concepts of Native American identity figured in this young man who "might be the promise of the new day—" (97). After all, we would like to believe in some kind of human connectedness transcending time and cultural differences, "a fundamental unity underlying the facets of experience."[1]

What such fantasy about McNickle's affirmation of universals leads to, however, is the discovery that Archilde's return to his mother's world destroys him, and to our realization that the novel is not written in a Native language, Salish for instance. Archilde thinks in English, and the novelist has told his story of the boy's inevitable fall using the generic conventions of English literature. Modeste's history and the "translated" myths only confirm the hegemony of the master language, the "universal" tongue for the Native American novelist. The fragment of Modeste's original speech with its fateful pun hides a subtext reflecting the problem of "translating" Indian identity through Western fiction. In fact, Modeste *has* stopped talking to us.

When the narrator of *Wind from an Enemy Sky* says that "How to translate from one man's life to another's—that is difficult" (26), he establishes the topos of translation at the center of McNickle's novels, and of his life as a mixed blood anthropologist, scholar, and novelist. Like other Native American writers McNickle was aware of language as a political weapon in the warfare between Indians and whites where not only control of the land but also determination of Native identity is at stake. Translation itself is a difficult task: "the words men speak never pass from one language to another without some loss of flavor and ultimate meaning" (*Wind*, 2). As Chief Seattle may have said to Governor Stevens, "we are two distinct races with separate origins and separate destinies. There is little in common between us."[2] It is the differences among human beings, between Natives and whites, that English speaking seeks to erase. If we look, for instance, at any speech by reservation-founding Governor Isaac Stevens, we hear a language that is universalist and condescending (however conscious the speaker may have been of this) in its address to the Natives as "children," its simplistic legalisms, and its complete dismissal of Native cultural identity in favor of white definition.[3] Its essential rhetorical premise is assimilation by analogy: Bull puts the same concept metaphorically when he says that whites do not want Bull's grandson, Antoine, to become a "man like one of us, a man with brown skin, speaking our language. . . the white man means, 'You'll be a strong man when you become a white man' " (*Wind*, 93). Typically, in their responses to such government proposals, tribal leaders emphasized their unwillingness to give up the country of their origin for a reservation life with other tribes who were not like them: to give up, in other words, their Native identities.[4]

In such frontier confrontations where the master language erased differences, the role of the translator, of someone who served as an often faceless and impersonal mediator between cultures because of an ability to speak both languages (or more), was crucial but usually elided in historical accounts.[5] Translation, as Paul de Man points out in writing about texts, is always a case of substitution, continuous displacement that moves away from the original text or speech, "an errancy of language which never reaches its mark, which is always displaced in relation to what it meant to reach,"(92). Providing an inadequate formulation of the original, nevertheless, the translator or interpreter in the act of mediation becomes the instrument by which intercourse between Native and white cultures succeeds, and fails. In American frontier history this go-between provides a metaphor for the master language's reductive universalizing of non-English speakers as inferior, dispossessed of their tribal "difference" by being forced to speak the language of power or be silent. In turn, it is the successful interpreter who, by translating the government requirements and his people's accession to them, guarantees the destruction of the tribal world that English speaking redefines. If the translator is also a Native American, translation is an act of self-erasure that parallels the disintegration of tribal identity.

The language of treaty making, of turning Indians into whites, represents the effort to domesticate what is different or strange, that is, to make the culturally-different "Red Man" one of the mainstream. For McNickle, the issue of language is not just one of failed communication, the theme Louis Owens identifies as basic to the novels (280). It is that words in translation cannot convey the "flavor and ultimate meaning" of the culture that lives in the imaginations and emotions of the people. Like other important Native American novelists, McNickle figures cultural conflict in the "mixed blood" who has learned the master language and so has inevitably become foreign, apart; his Native tongue no longer has power except to immerse him in a dying tribal past. When Archilde is thinking about the old people telling stories, the narrator uses free indirect discourse to displace him: "Archilde with his impertinent new ways of thinking would be forgotten"(*Surrounded* 64). "Thinking" means not just the boy's own English-ed thoughts but also the modern white world he believes at this point in the novel has replaced whatever had been Indian. Translators are the "hinge" figures of historical submission and dominance, in theory moving their people toward a synthesis of Indian and white, but actually directing them to loss of tribal identity that their own learning of English prefigures.

Alfonso Ortiz points out that themes and figures borrowed from the Orient, in Western fiction, represent novelists' efforts to describe identity through what he calls "an engagement with alterity." That is, "Every attempt to establish the domestic or native requires a confrontation with what is 'foreign' or alien" (1). This condition holds true, as well, for western fiction using Indian material, and may help explain why McNickle's two contemporary novels are more interesting than his second work, *Runner in the Sun*, set entirely in a precontact world. In the major novels the narrative tensions are generated by confrontations between two historic ideas of identity. McNickle lodges Indian self-definition in the tribal community and the past, a mythic world of timeless stability in which the old stories can be told over and over. They still seem to have emotional and imaginative meaning to the old or to those who can recover them. They require a living culture, however, as a context. Unlike Silko, McNickle suggests that this mythic world view cannot be "translated" into the modern world without destroying its "speakers": the differences between cultures is too great. There is no language, Indian or white, that can achieve that transference.

In *The Surrounded* (1936), the mixed blood Archilde enacts the "errancy of language" within himself; the destructive effects of white power stand revealed in both speech and its complement, silence. Both expose Archilde to his crossed identity and further his destruction. In *Wind from an Enemy Sky* (1978), McNickle develops more politically delineated contrasts between the tribal, Indian world and the mythically dead white world. Here he moves to a narrative structure based on ideological confrontations requiring interpreters in the historic frontier sense; their roles in seeking or representing communication are inevitably destructive of their people, not just an individual. For McNickle there is no language that can defend the Native speaker against the master language certainly not that language itself.

In *The Surrounded* differences are generational as well as cultural: the older generations evolved certain mythologies about the valley's frontier world, but for them have been substituted history and silence. The Spaniard, Max, once in love with this land, has cross-married but cannot "understand" his Native wife, though he can speak her tongue. In a typical narrative suspension, McNickle does not tell us why Max has been isolated from his world, until late in the novel. His friend, Father Grepilloux, also "discovered" the valley and has retired there to write its history, culminating in the account of Big Paul with its record of conflict and the breakdown of Indian conceptions of justice and honor. Father Grepilloux, like Governor Stevens, thinks of the Indians as "children" whose doings are primitive and childlike, equating sins with sticks (52). He admits that the Indians have lost a way of life, "and with it their pride, their dignity, their strength." "Of course . . . they have God," he adds, an irony since the Church is identified with their alienation.

The novel's initial pages give us history, a discursive representation of the domestication of the Indians and their natural world by outsiders whose lives have atrophied or are dying. Father Grepilloux sees Archilde as a figure from the younger generation who seems to have a future: he "is standing there where the road divides. He belongs to a new time" (108). Archilde's "story" will be placed against that of Big Paul, who had tried to represent Indian values in the frontier and been destroyed. The problem here, however, is that neither Max nor Father Grepilloux thinks of the boy as "Indian" but as a foreigner to be assimilated into the successful white world, leaving the valley, studying music abroad. Paradoxically, what is regenerated in Archilde is exactly what is Indian and "strange" in the white sense. While the boy comes to share his mother's silences and to work his father's ranch, McNickle nevertheless makes the atavism of the Indian past dominant in Archilde's imaginative development. Initially with both parents he is silent, telling "silent" lies, protecting himself: "When you came home to your Indian mother you had to remember that it was a different world" (3). But the silences shared with Catharine enable feelings to develop that might be deflected through words. Catharine's own silence hides her growing sense of alienation from the modern world, keeping her inner Indian nature intact, reserved from the present and her life as a Christian.

Her silence speaks to Archilde, as do the tribal myths told at his mother's feast for him, myths that translate past into present feeling and counter the dead weight of history. Initially, sitting with his mother's people, he develops "the deeper feeling" of "impatience, irritation, an uneasy feeling in the stomach"(62). He cannot eat the traditional fatty meat; he does not want the Indian definition of who he is: he literally cannot take it in: the old days are "gone, dead. So don't tell me what I ought to do to be like that" (63). As the stories of Flint and the thing that was to make life easy are told, he begins to feel closer to his people; recovering the past imaginatively makes him feel both revived and then "weakened." After Modeste's history of the coming of the missionaries and the loss of tribal power, Archilde "felt something die within him. Some stiffness, some pride, went weak before the old man's bitter simple words" (74). He relives in himself his tribe's mythic sense of identity, and its loss, a proleptic reversal of Silko's use of myth in *Ceremony* where the old metaphors give Tayo new life. For Archilde, imaginative identification with the ancestral world will be both renovating and destructive.

Hunting with his mother, Archilde can also accept the natural world of his homeland; its mountains are a "strange country," (120) undomesticated by either myth or history. When Catharine kills the game warden, however, the mythic world with its attractiveness for Archilde collides with the modern, and Archilde cannot translate with words from one to the other. The elliptical phrasing of his speech analogizes his incomprehension. Already caught in petty lies to his mother and brother about shooting a deer, he tries to explain his Indian view of the game laws. The situation grows "baffling" and when Louis is shot and Archilde tries to explain, he has to stop: "You're wrong! It's a mistake—" but "explaining was useless. It only added to the stupid confusion" (127). The narrator's use of indirect discourse includes the reader in the uncertainty here. Like Archilde, we do not see the final action; like him, we miss the old woman's attack: "he could not explain how his mother had been able to move without being seen or heard. That was inexplicable" (127–28).

Catharine's violence, of course, can be read as the expression of her suppressed Indian nature, the atavistic element that has led her on a last hunt, and, afterwards, to seek the old way of punishing her guilt. At this point in the narrative, her son's partial reporting of what he sees and his inability to "translate" either Indian or white world for the other keeps the murder from being explained. What has happened remains strange, a black hole in the white's version of causality, represented in the narrative itself. The shutting down of verbal faculties in Archilde also signals his own fatal involvement in Catharine's mythic world. She can go into the past: "the whip had covered the fault" (206–11); Archilde, between generations and cultures, can only become the past's inarticulate victim. The sheriff is after him; Max dismisses what has happened when his son tells him, a reinforcement of the historical disconnectedness of the two worlds. As Catharine withdraws into the Indian world and death, she speaks only her Native tongue and refuses church ritual. Archilde, confronted by Father Jerome, cannot use words to explain himself or his mother, who has gone beyond his ability to understand, in any case. McNickle uses the referentless third person to suggest the split between the boy's feelings and his ability to express them: "One should not feel compelled to answer such a thrust, and yet that was just what one did feel. And the worst of it was that one fumbled in answering" (64). As speaker for the past, Archilde can only fail: "It was not that he feared speaking his own mind, but he saw the uselessness of it. The priest would have his way—and let him! It was empty. It meant nothing."

The novel's second killing scene is inevitable because Archilde's own mental world no longer has any connection with reality. Sheriff Quigley is killed by a crudely-westernized woman, Elise, who has none of Catharine's feelings of guilt and none of her emotional loyalty to ancient tribal values. Archilde's last moments watching Elise and the sheriff mark him as victim in a sequence of actions for which he has not been responsible. His speech fails: "Then—, Archilde could not pronounce the words. . . . saying so meant that he was delivering himself into the hands of powers greater than he" (293). Even if he did *not* speak, this surrender would happen; silently extending his hands to be shackled is, of course, the ironic conclusion to his promised future in the modern world. Fittingly, his identity is merged in the universalizing metaphors of the master language: "you and all your kind. . . you people never learn that you can't run away" (296–97).

In *The Surrounded*, McNickle's representational strategy locates cultural conflict as an interiorized struggle within the mediating figure. In *Wind from an Enemy Sky*, he moves the conflict into a more specifically political arena, where Native and white confrontations are rigidly schematized and conducted at the public level. Here Indian dispossession, the white effort to domesticate the strange, is attempted through a series of translators; this novel's heavily politicized world requires mediators who can "talk" with the other but who bring destruction to both sides and to the ideal of cultural exchange and respect for difference. While presenting a far more intensive representation of the Indian vision in this last novel than in *The Surrounded*, McNickle represents the connections between private and public language as fatally inadequate for an entire society, not only for single figures like Archilde.

Organized as a series of councils and debates, *Wind* idealizes the Little Elk world as closed, self-sustaining, still a community living in its mythic past. In consequence, however, Bull's people have not developed the language and the necessary political sensibility for dealing with the white's pragmatic, opportunistic reality. There are no disused farming tools lying around their front yards, as in the earlier novel, the signs of Indian inflexibility and passive resistance to assimilation. On the other hand, McNickle's use of more exclusive cultural symbols—the medicine bundle, Feather Boy, and the dam—suggests the inevitable failure of such idealized isolation. The dam's disruption of the tribe's holy places is balanced by the medicine bundle's return, with its affirmation of the Little Elks' symbolic relationship to their world. Both dam and icon require interpretation for those on the other side.

For whites, the dam is the instrument for domestication, as Adam Pell puts it, providing water for farmlands forced on the Indians "for their own good." Here is history as apologia, self-justification offered for the exercise of power. The Indian response to the dam McNickle makes specifically inadequate in the historical sense if metaphorically "right": Bull shouts and shoots at it, both actions futile responses to the foreign. Bull's shouts are also about his own rejection of the master language that builds dams: he does not want to believe the white's words can make things happen and subvert Indian identity (13). As with Catharine, the identification of not speaking English with preservation of the mythic past puts Bull on the defensive and leads to violence. The generational connection is clearer here, however: Bull's confrontation with the dam is tied in with his grandson Antoine's dancing in the still-sacred midsummer festival (3–4), a living ceremony for him as it is not for Archilde in *The Surrounded*.

Antoine is one of the novel's translators, perhaps, one day, a leader. Unlike Archilde, however, he is a cultural and ideological Indian, with all his heritage learned in school, with no interior conflict to complicate his speaking to either side. Bull's remarks to him make a concise public demarcation between speakers: "you will remember what happened today. . . . The white man makes us forget our holy places. He makes us small" (9). As James Ruppert points out, Antoine is left to one side in the story, as though he were an unconsidered solution for the future (130), but the absolute character of Bull's language also tells us about his essential inflexibility.

To reinforce this position McNickle establishes a meto-
nymic sequence of translators whose speech or silence seem
to promise recognition of the other, but whose representations finally must fail. There are well-intentioned figures on
the white side, like Pell or the agent, Rafferty, whose inability
to speak the Native language enacts his inadequacy as
mediator. How to deal with the Indian mind was not in the
instructions he had been given, and he recognizes he had
not been "listening" to the Indians, a recognition that comes
too late (38–39). Consequently the actual translators are all
from the Native side, throwing into relief McNickle's vision
of this "Indian mind."

In this novel Catharine's place has been taken by Bull's
elder brother, the translator Henry Jim, who gave up tribal
identity, learned English, and moved into a modern house
on the sectioned prairie. Henry Jim's Indian-ness has been
compromised, in consequence, and also his ability to translate ideas into actions: his departure from origins in language
and land use have not led to his people's assimilation or
"advancement." He and Bull represent an initial split between beliefs whose healing seems to forecast future unity.
Henry Jim, however, has been rendered homeless in a
spiritual sense: it is he who gave away Feather Boy, as though
by destroying the tribe's symbolic center he could move them
into a present symbolized by the dam. Delegated to speak
for his people, he paradoxically contributes to their being
silenced. Henry Jim wants, thirty years later, to believe that
talking—reconciliation through discourse—will translate history back into myth, rejuvenate the tribe spiritually. He
thinks that the Old People were right who said that "today
talks in yesterday's voice" (28). McNickle aligns Henry Jim
with another old man, the outsider Two Sleeps. Nearly blind
but a visionary, he translates his dream world into the present, however ineffectively. He believes in the ancient dream
of the tribe's acting together as unified by blood: "even a

strong wind from an enemy sky had to respect their power" (197). His dream is treated, finally, as ambiguous fantasy. Given the realities of the power struggle between Indians and whites, Two Sleeps cannot truly foresee.

His is the language of feeling, of visionary insight, operable only in the context of a mythic community. Far more than in *The Surrounded*, McNickle pretends to a transliterated Native speech more metaphoric than that of the whites. The older generation, like Henry Jim and Two Sleeps, signal their reliance upon symbol reading to connect their people and the world. When Two Sleeps speaks about the brothers' reconciliation, using the metaphor of being like "lost children" (20), this is not the condescending "my children" of Governor Stevens but the expression of recoverable love and equality. When Bull is asked to think about reconciliation with the whites, his language draws from metaphoric resources that bring the legendary past into the present—for him: "A man and woman fit to each other after they live together a long time—that is the way a stream fits itself to the earth. They have no secret from each other. A stream has its life" (24). Even the representation of the dam in Little Elk is expressed metaphorically: Adam Pell becomes the man who "killed" the water (169). Pell has only the descriptive language of history available to him, speech that is empty of respect for the world as the Little Elks understand it: "We didn't stop the water or kill it—we put it out on the land, to make the land rich, Indian land as well as white man's. . . .' The enormity of the misapprehension swept over his mind and silenced him" (169). Behind his "misapprehension" and failure of speech lies the political issue of assimilation that "silences" the Other by denying (here, ignoring) difference.

McNickle also directs our attention to the otherness of the Indian mind through the metaphor of "singing," a poetic connection with the earth not available to whites. Henry Jim "sings" his way into his brother's camp, for instance (15), but more importantly, he hears history as a "song," a metaphoric translation of Native American history that leads from Henry Jim's own past into present time and the dominance of the white's view of the world (29–31). He wants to believe that he can secure the return of Feather Boy, that this time his mediation will work, in this case, to reverse the process of tribal loss: "this time, certainly, we will have help" (31–32). There is no answering poetic mode from the other side, and Henry Jim's song is an ironic affirmation of the Indians' distance from political confrontation: "the song was again on his breath. Telling of a time when the plover cried" (32). The song is not translatable. They sing to keep Henry Jim alive, but no one translates what they sing for the whites, who hear the song as one more sign (like Pock Face's shooting of the dam worker) of the Indians' irrational and irreconcilable difference. This metaphoric recasting of history has the effect of withdrawing the Little Elks into the legendary, even as they struggle to come to terms with their history-become-story.

As Henry Jim begins to die, "to go with the singing," his next-generation alternate as interpreter appears, the tribal police chief, The Boy, who has been given power as well as language by the whites. His various names—The Boy, Richard Marks, Son Child, Coffee Lip—suggest his ambiguous position between cultures as each tries to define his identity. The Boy says he liked learning English, but he likes "to hear the old people talk too" (81). He knows when to be silent. When he does speak, it is in the polite, formulaic rhythms of tribal speech, with an important difference: he does not himself speak with the metaphoric tongue of the Little Elks.[6] Usually he is said to be translating for the whites like Rafferty, the discursive historical language of confrontation, as in Bull's historical summing up (84–85).

McNickle carefully keeps The Boy at a distance from the reader, representing his thoughts initially only as someone detachedly observing others: Indians arriving for a meeting are recorded from his point of view, without comment. At the end, he "seemed to speak from a great distance" (85). The Boy can therefore seem the perfect impersonal translator rather than "interpreter," if we take the word to mean someone who explains meanings, not just relays information. His appropriately laconic statements, however, have the effect of exposing responses in others. When he says of the white's version of justice, "That is the law they follow," Bull delivers a speech reinscribing his faith in Indian values as opposed to the whites: " 'What kind of law is that? Did we have such a law? When a man hurt somebody in camp, we went to that man and asked him what he was going to do about it. If he did nothing, after we gave him a chance, we threw him away. He never came back. But only a mean man would refuse to do something for the family he hurt. That was a good law, and we still have it' "(89). The Boy does not comment on this speech and its relevance for the moral issue that divides Indian and white. The agent, he says, "sent me here to tell you how it is" (89). We are left, as readers, to evaluate the humanity in Bull's tribal reasoning—and its potentially fatal distance from the white world's concept of justice. The Boy can thus seem sympathetic to his own people. Bull comes to respect him, agreeing with Two Sleeps, not always the most realistic of visionaries, that this tribal policeman "talks like one of us. . . . we are one people here together"(92). The Boy has really said very little, and it is this same laconic directness, just this side of saying nothing at all, that leads Rafferty to accept him as interpretor for his people of the kind the agent wants. Watching The Boy build a fire, he sees him, wrongly, as more than just a translator: "He will know how to decide. Not only for me and my way, but for all these people" (125). A frighteningly impassive "still center," The Boy is read as each wishes.

Though often silenced in the narrative and present only as someone supposedly translating for others, this translator is subversively articulate. In spite of his protest that "I never left my people" (91), his gun power is from the whites, after all. Chapters ten and eleven show him in two different settings, first interpreting for Rafferty with a delegation of Indians, and then gradually gaining the confidence of the Indians imprisoned in the schoolhouse basement. Here The Boy reveals the inevitable duplicity of the "one between" as he leads Bull and the others to trust Rafferty: "He wants to be good to Indians—he says that? That's how it is. He says that" (87). When challenged, The Boy says he is not working for the sheriff but for the agent, and denies that he has become like the whites, "always angry, always shouting. Have I become like that, when I carry a piece of paper and have to take a man to jail?" (91). He is attempting to erase his actual empowerment, a gesture continued in his denial that he has just heard Pock Face confess to the murder of the dam worker: "My friends, I never left my people. What happened in the canyon is not my affair. Since a white man was killed, it is not my affair. I heard nothing in this room" (90–91).

The Boy is not a cunning Iago. He is a well-intentioned intermediary who is not fully aware of the implications of his position. His denial can be read as a mark of his Indianness; he wishes to emphasize an issue of more importance to the tribe, Henry Jim's request that Feather Boy be brought back. His speech even turns metaphoric in describing the dying man: "The grass is singing for him. It troubles my mind" (91). Nor is there any Archilde-like verbal fumbliness in his speech. His representation of the issue of the killing as demanding silence only reinforces the Indians' unwillingness to confront the white's concept of justice. In seeking to achieve some kind of accommodation, The Boy becomes the instrument of fate. He suppresses his knowledge of the murder before Rafferty's questions (121), thereby perpetuating a tactic of evasion and conciliation that traps everyone.

Answering Rafferty, he says, "I think they better forget about the man who got shot. Nobody ever find out anything" (122). Though presented by a speaker more in control of voice and audience than is Archilde, what is not said again sets up a tragic conclusion.

It is The Boy who brings word that a final meeting is wanted, and he who says Pell has brought a "gift" for the Little Elks, though we know this announcement represents another misreading by everyone concerned. At the meeting, Pell cannot be stopped from telling in his confessional truthfulness the incriminating history of what happened to Feather Boy, balancing the comparable confession by Pock Face. Both have "killed" through misunderstanding the other side's culture symbol. Pock Face has killed a man; Pell has "killed" the water. For the white, this is the language of metaphor; for the Indian it is reality. Significantly, The Boy does not translate Pell's apology, that it was an "accident" (254); no one is listening. More clearly than in *The Surrounded*, the final violence enacts the failure of translation. Bull says, "It is no good talking to these men. This is all they understand," (55) shooting both Pell and Rafferty. He is shot in turn by The Boy whose altered nature as the embodiment and enforcer of white institutionalized power is exposed: "Brother! I have to do this," he says, in a perfect concluding allusion mingling respect, coercion, and fatality. The rhetorical stance is Indian; the meaning is white.

Ruppert sees this conclusion as a cleansing one, sweeping away old misunderstandings to prepare the Little Elks for a future led by the boy, Antoine. To the contrary, however, Antoine does not express "appreciation of the need for unity in change," nor does either novel really support what McNickle is interpreted as saying in a letter: that non-Western peoples will survive (in this example, the Eskimo) because they are "adaptable," not preordained to remain their historic selves (128). If McNickle's fiction can be read for its prognosis, however, "cultural identity and self-definition" are crucial to that survival, the source and sign of difference. In *Wind from an Enemy Sky* the dam remains; Feather Boy is dusty history. There will be no need for translators with Bull and Henry Jim gone. Only novelists will be around to record the cry of the plover.

McNickle's writing of this tribal history in the conqueror's language—English, not "Little Elk" (or Salish)—enacts that fate. We forget, when we speak about a people's "remaining themselves," that even though they have adapted to the modern world, what makes a culture Eskimo or Apache or Salish is its language, the language in which its members think of themselves. Language is originating and self-affirming, and this power does not come in translation. The tragedy expressed in this work is not just in the deaths of the characters for being who they are, but the loss of a whole culture figured in Archilde and The Boy who have achieved that unenviable state Georg Lukacs calls "transcendental homeless."

McNickle's own life participates in this ambiguous metaphor of the translator whose failure, in his case, lies in his success. Like Charles Eastman and other Native Americans who took up the language of power to serve their people, to bring them into the modern world, McNickle can be read as a homeless mediator. His writings, as acts of translation, turn the Native into a linguistic construct at yet a further remove from the "true" being who can never be known through English, save in some transition toward us and away from origins. Just as histories of Indian-white relations represent misreadings on both sides, McNickle's novels, in the language and genre of the conquerors, signal the triumph of the ruling culture, inadequate representations of what have become only fictional Indians. They have become "texts" to be "read."

Chapter Six

Irony of Consent:
Hunting and Heroism in
D'Arcy McNickle's
The Surrounded

Robert F. Gish

*The hunter does not just come and go, working hard in valleys
and on cliffs, urging on his dogs; rather, in the last analysis,
he kills. The hunter is a death dealer.*
  —*Ortega y Gasset,* Meditations on Hunting

*I should not wonder if your worship were surprised at this
appearance of mine, for it is both novel and out of the common.
But you will cease to be so when I tell you, as I now do, that
I am a knight*
            Of that breed that, the people say,
                  After adventures ride.
  —*Cervantes,* Don Quixote

The basic theme of D'Arcy McNickle's *The Surrounded* is
engulfment. The novel's title announces this, as does its epi-
graph: "THEY CALLED THAT PLACE *Sniél-emen* (MOUN-
TAINS OF THE SURROUNDED) BECAUSE THERE THEY
HAD BEEN SET UPON AND DESTROYED." But surrounding the obviousness of the book's title and its announced

theme of engulfment is much subtlety of technique, much stratification and compounding of ironies associated with engulfment, of conquest and subjugation, and of hunting and heroism.

Although a general reading of *The Surrounded* seems to lead to straightforward observations about a "simple," even formulaic book (especially if *The Surrounded* is read as a Western novel), the text has many ironic patterns dealing with the act and metaphor of the hunt and with what may be called the "irony of consent" in the interaction of hunters and hunted, especially as hunters become hunted. The notion of "irony of consent" in the context of hunting, and its use as a theme in *The Surrounded*, focuses on the causality and conclusion of forces that lead to the object of the hunt's yielding to the hunter. More precisely, the dynamics of *The Surrounded* lead (through his consent) to Archilde Leon's surrender and capture.

The metaphor of the hunt is far-reaching. In a certain sense all of life is as easily considered a hunt as it is a stage, or a race. Beyond any facile clichés, however, there is much artistic process and "conceit" in McNickle's drawing out of the metaphor, extending it as he does beyond characterization and plotting until readers, too, are placed in the position of "hunter/hero." That is to say, reading *The Surrounded* necessitates special "hunts," and special notice by the reader of "the Hunt": (1) hunts of animals serve as particular incidents in the story; the larger implications of the manhunt for Louis as horse thief; and the contradiction of the at-once-known and unidentified killer of the game warden, Dan Smith; and (2), the "hunts" attendant to racial and ethnic conflict, of Anglo-European, and white American encroachments on the Salish. The presence of hunting and the hunt operates then as both process and subject.

The idea of the prey, either escaping or being wounded or killed, sets up diverse plot possibilities, especially in the context of Native/white relations. The fatalistic ending of the published book and its emphasis on Archilde's acquiescence or resignation, is a reading that is subject to question. It is a reading that tends to reinforce the "myth" of the vanquished and vanishing American Indian and the destruction or "assimilation" of Native peoples. McNickle ambivalently promotes this assumption in his advancement of more than one plot. Archilde is hunted and captured, does extend his hands, and in his surrender offers a degree of consent. Catharine, however bleak and disappointing her old age, does "return to the blanket," and the Salish people do renounce Catholicism. Such ambivalence is made more intriguing, albeit problematic, in earlier versions of the novel, the versions McNickle called "The Hungry Generations." In earlier drafts, Archilde is triumphant and "successful" in the Anglo-European and "American Dream" of upward socioeconomic mobility—personified by his father, Max Leon—and brings in a bountiful harvest of hay. In the context of the "plotting of parents" the ironies of consent and rejection extend circles of engulfment. What are the techniques and patterns for characters involved directly in these actions and what are the implications for the reader as participant/voyeur? The process is conditioned by forces and formulas as much archetypal as stereotypical.

The juxtapositions in theme and technique surrounding the success or failure of the hunt, between hunting strategies planned and reversed, work so that the prescribed roles of dominance and victimization reverse themselves in ways simultaneously predictable and startling. The role reversals are predictable given certain classic and modern, hero/anti-hero premises of fate in the traditionally "tragic" sense, and in the plots of escape and pursuit in the contexts evolved by the western novel. Yet, the reversals may surprise us, given the mixing of such traditional forms with the reflexivity and recursiveness of modernism, of naturalism tending toward nihilism. By the novel's end, the pursuers Dan Smith and Dave Quigley are both dead and Archilde is surrounded and captured. The cost has been high, and the hunters have been "hunted" by the hunted.

Both traditional and innovative techniques contribute to the pervasive sense of irony in the book. Archilde is cast as a "tragic hero," but acquiescence, consent, and victimization are present to such an exasperating degree that the reader might see the novel's protagonist as anti-hero and coward. The reader is engulfed in a double view of Archilde as at once universal and local, cosmic and regional, the "dealer of death," and hunter become hunted.

Archilde is, as heir to his kingly father's, Max Leon's, realm, one of the Darwinian "fit." Archilde is capable of prevailing over the weaker and less fortunate. He is the person most capable of changing the circumstances of the Salish, his mother's people. His responsibility extends to the innocent and less fortunate: his widowed sister, Agnes; his nephews, Mike and Narcisse; his aging and failing mother, Catharine; his renegade, black-sheep brother, Louis; the blind-seer, and tribal elder, Modeste, now weakened, dispossessed, and trivialized by "tourism"; and the wild reckless "flapper," Elise La Rose.

On the positive side, Archilde is potentially a "lion prince" (lion-named "childe," knight quester, young heir apparent) in search of and momentarily attaining his birthright, his father's legacy. His father, Max Leon (lion-hearted) is landed gentry. Equally, however, Archilde is heir to his mother's once glorious Native American heritage (glorious before the coming of Catholicism when crimes were resolved by "the whip covering the fault"). In both respects, Archilde adopts the role of fiddler returned from the urban "music" of Portland to the more bucolic melodies of home. In Oregon, and once again home in Montana, Archilde follows his search for self, which takes the form of a hunter after happiness. Like the archetypal searcher, Don Quixote, this "Knight of the Lions," is heroic in his mock-heroism as a hunter of captive lions. Archilde's happiness and his success are dashed. His character is more in keeping with Quixote's other identity: the Knight of the Sad Countenance. Moreover, like the archetypal Big Paul of the interpolated story that Father Grepilloux tells Max Leon, Archilde's future is bleak, doomed, and hopeless, surrounded by the ironies that confront a person of mixed blood. As a "marginal" person, he consents to the inevitable but universal predicament of being born to die. The figure of Big Paul is clearly an encompassing, almost eponymic, manifestation and analog of Archilde. The betrayal of Big Paul is a poignant instance of the heroic sacrificial figure who is hunted down and made to pay the ultimate price—not just for himself but for his kind.

Catharine's "legacy" to Archilde is juxtaposed with Max Leon's materialistic endowment. In her role as mother, she bestows life (Archilde's birth), but she deals death to the game warden, Dan Smith. Intended as protective, the murder was nevertheless to revenge Smith's (both justified and unwarranted) shooting of Louis. Catharine also gives Archilde a greater appreciation of the traditional Salish ways. Her own character as woman-wife-mother and as obedient follower of Christ (first believing, then rebellious and doubting) contains ample ironies of consent. Ultimately, Archilde "inherits" the guilt of his group and assumes responsibility for the crimes of father, mother, and brother. He takes on the legendary role of scapegoat/victim to mirror the story of Big Paul.

His lineage works directly to victimize Archilde, to do him in, but not without his own spoken words and silences, lies and confessions. What results is a chain of exasperating reconciliations with inevitable doom in a simultaneously courageous and cowardly season at home, with actions surrounded by non-actions. He functions (like Quixote, Oedipus, and Hamlet) within the contours of the classic, tragic hero.

Like countless persecuted and prosecuted, shot or hanged western heroes turned cowardly or villainous (from *The Virginian* to *Lonesome Dove*), Archilde is captive to the scripting of his parentage and of himself, captive to his destiny which could have been (but not really) otherwise.

It is part of this controlling "irony of consent," of hunter ironically somehow agreeing to become hunted, that controls the plot and also enables those with the least chance of prevailing in the novel, those with the slightest possibility of escaping—that is, Archilde's mother, Catharine, and his "loveless lover," Elise—to strike out in violent resistance to captivity and engulfment. They try to save (but they trap) Archilde, and are undone by larger extensions of the "societal hunt" of social Darwinism, by white man's "laws."

The central hunting scene that focuses the many ironies of consent in the novel is the fateful deer hunting trip Archilde takes with Catharine into the mountains of the "Surrounded." It is an important scene on several levels: for the multiple ironies it establishes, and for the patterns and rhythms of the architectonic and thematic elements of the novel as a story of engulfment.

Archilde consents to the outing, an invitation to doom extended by Catharine, and he enters into the hunt, mainly, as a way of connecting more fully with his Native heritage. His decision to go is also in response to his developing empathies for his mother and for the old people and their ways. It is the deer hunt—remnant of an ancient ritual, tribal values surrounding food, masculinity, personality, and volition—and the confusing turns it takes (especially after Louis's arrival) that McNickle uses to dramatize the very essence of Archilde's hunt for himself. He is "hunting hard" for his identity (past and present, real and "storied") as much as for deer.

Here too McNickle artfully advances the controlling theme of engulfment in several more abstract ways: (1) by having the confusions and reversals of lies as truth and truth as lies illustrate how language itself serves as an engulfment for Archilde; (2) by linking assumptions of the hunter as hero with assumptions about gender—about manliness and femininity, about traits of decisiveness, assertiveness, and aggression; (3) by juxtaposing tribal and individual pressures to conform. Underlying it all are the implications of death and destruction, hunting and hunted, set forth in the archetypes of Cain and Able and the variations of sibling rivalry played out in *The Surrounded* yet again.

As autumn advances into October, the season moves Archilde progressively toward his destiny, and he grows closer to Catharine. He plays his violin daily and his outlook improves at the same time that the plot builds to the murder and subsequent events that will implicate him inextricably. Catharine is insistent in her direct and indirect requests to go hunting. She indicates that it will be her last hunt—one last hunt before age (and depression) engulf her. Archilde consents, but reluctantly: "Finally he relented and said he would take her hunting. He knew he should not do it. He had a feeling about it which he could not explain. But that wasn't enough to withstand his mother's desire" (115).

When the first snow is due the notion of its descent works imagistically to underscore Catharine's age and her approaching death, as well as Archilde's cold fate. All of the emphasis on Catharine's weakening condition serves to make her hatchet-wielding murder of Smith all the more shocking— to Archilde and to the reader. McNickle simultaneously tightens the suspense and heightens the sense of impending disaster and death. Events are beyond control of the mother's volition and son's reluctant indulgence of her wish. Fate speaks with the paternalistic pronouncement, "Here is a piece of foolishness! This should not be" (115).

Once underway into the mountains, Archilde imagines himself riding back in time and conjures the feelings of ancient hunters. Game is scarce, the mountains are empty, and he is forced to ride farther in search of deer. "Archilde and his mother had to ride on and on, trying to go backward in time rather than onward in mountain fastness" (116).

In step with the ironies engulfing Max's pronouncement, Archilde's time travel, the surrounding mountains, and the plot itself, the first "game" to break cover is not a deer—rather it is Sheriff Quigley. He is in the mountains on the trail of Louis and the horses he has stolen. (Archilde will soon attempt to foil his brother—the horse thief in the role of a horse hunter who saves an old decrepit mare by delivering her to her death, in effect, "stealing" her life away.): "Then unexpectedly game broke cover—unexpected and not quite pleasant. Archilde riding along in advance, looked up suddenly when he saw a horse and rider standing in the trail. For a moment he did not recognize the intruder. Finally he knew him without doubt, and felt chilled" (117). Archilde recognizes Quigley as a stylized character, the Western sheriff. Ironically, Archilde identifies with him: "He [Quigley] sat his horse, an imperturbable rock of flesh. . . . He was a sheriff out of the Old West. He knew the type—he had read of those hard-riding quick-shooting dispensers of peace, he had heard stories about them—and he was intent on being all of them in himself. He had made the part his own" (117). Archilde's irony of consent is identifying with Quigley, for how the sheriff perceives his prescripted self is fortuitous: here is a man playing a role larger than life, in a sense similar to Big Paul, a man out of a legendary time and place appearing simply in order to hunt down Archilde and his brother.

As Quigley defines himself, through the narrator's perceptions and indirectly through Archilde's, he is a hunter of a higher order than a mere deer hunter. Archilde hunts desperately for himself in the person and role of Sheriff, even though he (Archilde) is now the "game," standing in the trail before him. Archilde's is a patterned "knowing," a realization and recognition which reoccurs—especially when Archilde spots real game, a fine buck majestically drinking water.

When Archilde actually does spot the game, he refuses to consent to programmed expectations to kill it. He decides, conversely, to spare it, and by suggestion, himself, maybe even Quigley, the embodiment of Western law. Archilde's "buck fever" is a curious, double-sided irony of consent, however. Quigley would have killed the buck unthinkingly, as would Louis, as would Catharine. This is inferred from her adage in response to Archilde's "failure" as a hunter: "A young man waits for a better shot and hits nothing. An old man makes the best of it and gets his meat" (122). Moreover, Archilde's stray, benevolently-guided shot (and miss) of the buck, signals Dan Smith, and, as he tracks the sound of the shot, the hunt of Archilde starts to form.

Archilde considers his decision, rationalizes it perhaps, through "stories of the hunt" similar to stories he knows about sheriffs. He attempts to place himself as a character in a story within larger stories of the hunt, both immediate and more metaphorical: "The sheriff enjoyed mentioning things that, like death, made people uncomfortably aware of life's threats" (118). Quigley, it is sensed by Archilde and the reader, will also hunt Archilde. The man first seen as "game" by Archilde will metamorphose into a cosmic enforcer, a grim reaper with badge and gun.

A day after Quigley rides on into the mountains relentlessly to hunt first for Louis, and then for Dan Smith's body (and, ultimately for Archilde), Archilde locates the game he and Catharine seek. He finds tracks (in keeping with the scripts of hunter-hero), and infers where the deer will be: "They come in the early morning, no doubt. In the afternoon they're on the ridges, he said of the deer" (118).

Louis, however, intrudes on the peaceful camp established by Archilde and Catharine, and the ancient Cain/Abel rivalries surface again. Louis discounts news of Quigley's pursuit, and when Archilde rejects Catharine's request that the brothers hunt together, a new phase of competition begins. Which brother will claim title to best hunter, take the trophy deer, win the approval of Catharine (who is interested more in food than a successful hunt)?

When he encounters the buck, Archilde is overcome in his appreciation of its beauty and presence. Deliberately, he aims off target and misses, but Louis shoots a deer. It is a doe, and a yearling at that, a much lesser kill, according to heroic codes of the hunt. These codes, at once aboriginal and chivalric, govern the hunt as well as the initiation rites that confirm the transition to adulthood. The test of courage and heroism involves killing more competitive, challenging game.

Archilde's decision not to kill, once he has the buck easily in his sights, is finally presented somewhat ambivalently as a matter of poetic, even philosophic perception:

> An inexplicable thing happened to him. He could not shoot. He looked in wonder at the thin-legged, nervous creatures. They had filed down the trail and stood knee deep in water. When they lifted their heads from drinking their black muzzles dripped.
>
> Hunting stories had always excited him, giving him a feeling that he would like to be envied for his good shooting and his hunting sense. But it was clear that he had not understood himself, he had not understood about killing. The excitement was in matching one's wits against animal cunning. The excitement was increased when a man kept himself from starving by his hunting skill. But lying in wait and killing, when no one's living depended on it, there was not excitement in that. Now he understood it. (121)

Here two crucial ironies of consent and justice develop. Were he less the thinker and more the man of action (like Louis), the hunt, the meat, and other satisfactions of success would be his. By sparing the deer he becomes both less and more heroic. He faces, however, the disapproval of his mother and the increased ridicule of his brother, and so, Archilde lies.

Not a heroic thing to do. Smith's, Archilde's, Louis's, and Catharine's fates are sealed by the illogic of Archilde's presumably logical premises.

This first hunt establishes the major pattern of the hunt as dramatic incident, and in its reverberations of larger themes of hunter and hunted with the ironies of reversed stations and destiny, as fate works its way, inviting "consents" even when not willfully offered. Beyond the episode of the deer hunt, and its motives and consequences, are other significant incidents of the hunt.

The action of the hunter who refuses to kill is played against a later scene in which Archilde, with worthy but misguided benevolence, chases down a lame and starving mare. His desire to save the horse results in the necessity to shoot her. And although the scene is presented against broader contexts and suggestions of knighthood, of Archilde, the novice knight (childe) mounted on a more majestic white mare, sallying forth like Quixote in the service of idealism and the good name of Dulcinea, the events and setting are soon reversed.

By chapter's end Archilde projects a surreal inversion of the potential hunter hero with a beautiful buck and the bounty of a legitimate, admirable kill/trophy. Consider McNickle's brief description of the bucolic setting become badland if not macabre wasteland. The once and potential lion prince, a childe, "of that breed that, the people say,/After adventures ride" (Cervantes, 565), leads the stalking horse of death: "The sun had set and in the evening light a rider on a strong white horse led an unprotesting skeleton on a rope. It was grotesque" (241).

The decision to shoot the mare, an irony of consent that reverses the heroic image points unmistakably to Archilde's doom. For imagery and symbol, the scene of the mare serves as a correlative of many recursive and reflexive ironies, and gives evidence to McNickle's masterful sense of novelistic form. The mare is not only associated, most obviously, with Catharine and Elise (at this point anticipated but not reflexive), but also with Louis, Dan Smith, Max Leon, and Sheriff Quigley (whose fate, too, is to be shot and "surrounded" while "surrounding"). Finally, the mare is associated with Mike and Narcisse and, ultimiately, with Archilde by the expansive but closed ending of the novel.

The narrator's description—"It's grotesque"—of Archilde and the skeleton mare echoes Max Leon's pronouncement of Catharine's foolish wish to hunt. The phrase is repeated again by agent Parker, as Joe La Ronde closes in to shackle Archilde: "It's too damn bad you people never learn that you can't run away. It's pathetic" (296–297).

The overall significance of the horse shooting scene played against the deer hunting scene becomes all the more apparent when placed in the context of the many scenes in which horses play a key part. The hunts and horses are not just a part of the Montana/Western ambiance and fictive formulas and subtexts that inform *The Surrounded* as horse opera and chivalric romance, they are the machinery that drives the plot. Horses, throughout the novel, reinforce and undercut Archilde's "heroism."

Had Archilde paid more attention, sooner, to his puzzlement about details—such as his allowing Elise to take him, on the lam, into the mountains, to his lack of feeling for her "in his blood," his soul-felt knowing that Quigley was "a kind of last foe," the curiosity of Quigley's suddenly walking into camp without his horse when he and La Ronde brought their hunt for Archilde into the mountains—had Archilde paid attention to Elise's placing a presumably empty coffee pot back on the fire, had he been attentive to these things, his fate might not have been sealed as one of the eternally "surrounded."

One quintessential passage reveals the degree to which Archilde's "heroism" as a hunter has utterly reversed and the depths of despair to which the ironies of consenting to his situation have led him, the passage in which he turns his gun on the pathetic mare: "Before the night ended he had to shoot her. . . . Finally, in a rage that was partly resentment at the unfairness of the whole episode and partly interrupted sleep, he went out to her, placed his rifle against her head, and blasted her into eternity" (242). Archilde, "in a confusion of feeling" sits down, now a decidedly foolish and grotesque "hunter," to guard the "worthless carcass" throughout the rest of the night. His early potential as a hunter-hero and brave benefactor and the nobility of his Leon/lion lineage fade into the darkness. As readers, our own slim hope for Archilde rests there in the mountains with "our child"—but he is as dead as the sorrowful prize and prey by his side.

McNickle's artistry in *The Surrounded* is more sophisticated and profound than facile or preliminary judgments suggest. By no means is this novel a formula Western or an "Indian love song." Much of this artistry resides in McNickle's utilization of the patterns and rhythms, the themes, myths, and legends, the stories and the dreams of the hunt in the human psyche. McNickle's achievement in *The Surrounded* resides, most especially, in his adaptation of the heroism and villainy of the hunter/hunted and its eternally ironic interdependency. McNickle's artistry hauntingly, surrounds us all.

Part Three

Runner in the Sun:
Mythologies of the Times

Chapter Seven

D'Arcy McNickle's
Runner in the Sun:
Content and Context

Dorothy R. Parker

D'Arcy McNickle's second novel, *Runner in the Sun: A Story of Indian Maize*, which is the most recently reprinted of his three fictional works, is the least known, and it has received very little critical attention. This is in part because it was written for young adult readers and soon allowed to go out of print.[1] A few who reviewed it when it was first published in 1954 praised it as both "history and mystery," an "unusually illuminating, rather serious tale," with "much authentic data about Southwestern cliff dwellers," conveyed with "the feeling of a tribal legend."[2] The reviews, however, offered no clue to the story behind the story and why it was so different from his other work.

A brief summary of McNickle's three novels will illustrate the point. His first novel, *The Surrounded*, published in 1936 when he was thirty-two years old, was largely autobiographical.[3] It was the story of a young mixed blood Indian boy, Archilde, from the barely disguised reservation town of St. Xavier, Montana. Archilde, who intends to leave the reservation for good, returns home to say goodbye to his Indian mother, but even as he struggles to break away into the white world, he finds that he is drawn to the traditions of his mother's people and the older generation she represents. As the story ends, he is surrounded by both the old tribal traditions and the whites' institutions, and is unable to free himself.

In his third novel, *Wind from an Enemy Sky*, published posthumously in 1978, McNickle again writes about a young boy, Antoine, who returns to his traditional family after attending an off-reservation federal boarding school for several years.[4] As in *The Surrounded*, the story is set in a vaguely described valley in the mountains of the Northwest. Antoine comes home just as the Little Elk people are attempting to recover their most sacred medicine bundle, Feather Boy, which had been given away many years earlier and is now in a New York museum. The modern world is encroaching on his people's land, and they believe that Feather Boy must be restored to them if they are to survive. As in the earlier novel, Antoine learns the traditional wisdom of his elders while the modern world closes in. The story unfolds as a tragedy, and at the end the author laments that "no meadow larks sang, and the world fell apart."[5] Neither *The Surrounded* nor *Wind from An Enemy Sky* offers much hope for the survival of traditional Native American life.

Runner in the Sun, published midway between these two novels, is quite unlike the other two in that it affirms the possibilities of the future. While the hero of this story, Salt, is also a young Native boy, the story is set in the pre-Columbian Southwest, and Salt lives in a cliff dwelling such as those occupied by the Anasazi people at Mesa Verde or Canyon de Chelly. As the chief protagonist, Salt confronts the evil powers that are arrayed against his people. To protect him, the leaders of the powerful Turquoise Clan, who have recently initiated him into adulthood, relieve him of his turquoise amulet, the symbol of that initiation. Attempting to regain his status, Salt embarks on a journey to unknown lands. He overcomes a series of obstacles and rescues a young woman, Quail, who returns with him to his village. Together they bring new seed corn and new life to his people. The situational conflict in the story evolves from tensions within the village rather than from any intrusive outside element.

McNickle incorporated various motifs from Native American mythologies to locate Salt in the Anasazi world, in a time and place that might be recognizable to his young readers. The development of the hero in *Runner in the Sun*, however, closely resembles that of the mythic hero described by Joseph Campbell in *The Hero With a Thousand Faces* suggesting more than a coincidental relationship between that work, published in 1949, and McNickle's novel, which was first published in 1954. While McNickle's papers do not mention Campbell, his personal library contained most of Campbell's publications, and McNickle was obviously familiar with them.[6] He used various thematic materials from the Native American mythology he knew so well, and then adapted the story to Campbell's interpretation of the universal hero myth.

The initial inspiration for *Runner in the Sun* is found in McNickle's first historical monograph, *They Came Here First*, which also was published in 1949. As he described the early occupants of the Southwest in that work, he noted that the Kayenta people of northern Arizona had a long history of peaceful relations with those living immediately to the south. "Except for a ten-mile strip running the length of this boundary in which some intermingling occurred, the two peoples remained separate," he wrote of them. "This continued, according to the archaeological record, for six hundred years, from A.D. 700 to A.D. 1300. No defense works were built along that international boundary. The archaeologists have uncovered no fire-blackened walls, no arrow-pierced skulls."[7] This long period of peaceful coexistence intrigued him, and in his Foreword to *Runner in the Sun*, he repeated the theme. "Scientists digging into old village sites tell us of tribes living side by side for hundreds of years without warfare. The myths and legends of the many tribes are not battle stories, but convey instead a feeling for the dignity of man and reverence for all of nature."[8] This would be the theme of the new novel.

Publication of *They Came Here First* was followed by a long article about the Indians of North America that appeared in the fourteenth edition (and several editions thereafter) of the *Encyclopaedia Britannica* in 1954. Less interpretive than his earlier work, this article required extensive anthropological and ethnographic research of precontact Native Americans, which augmented his already considerable firsthand knowledge of the subject. He was still working on this project when he agreed to write an Indian story for Holt, Rinehart and Winston's "Land of the Free" series for young adults.

By 1952, his new novel was well underway. It is not surprising, in view of the earlier projects, that he chose to set the story in the canyon country of the Southwest. As the reviewers noted, the details of the setting are authentic, although the location of the village itself is somewhat ambiguous. A map sketched by the well-known Apache artist Alan Houser, who also did the delightful line drawings for the book, places the village in Chaco Canyon, which in fact has no cliff dwellings that resemble Salt's home.[9]

With a Southwest setting thus established, McNickle turned to familiar Navajo mythology for thematic material. His interest in Native stories, evident earlier in his use of Salish folk material in *The Surrounded*, had expanded considerably since 1936. He was familiar with the work of most of the anthropologists and linguists who had spent time in the Southwest, and he knew of the transcriptions of Navajo mythology made by Washington Matthews for the Bureau of American Ethnology in the 1880s and 1890s. Thus he was able to draw from familiar folk tales and myths for specific motifs. He also began to play with possible titles, and several options that appear on a hand-written manuscript at the Newberry Library such as "Journey into the Sky," "The Boy Who Stole the Sun," and "Call to the Kiva" (which he later used as a chapter heading) suggest his interest in creating a new myth.[10] Well-known themes such as the vision quest, the reciprocity of opposites, and the restoration of balance and harmony delineate the characters and provide action as the story progresses.

The first and most obvious motif McNickle used is that of the vision quest. Venturing into the unknown, Salt overcomes a series of obstacles and returns with gifts that provide his people access to sources of power and wisdom. This theme of the returning hero appears almost universally in world mythology and is a common element in Native American folklore. Katherine Spencer, in her perceptive analysis of Navajo chantways, describes the importance of the ritual knowledge and ceremony that is made available to the people through the hero's return: "The power that the hero gains in his supernatural contacts," she explains, "is knowledge of the appropriate ceremonial equipment and ritual actions. . . . The compulsion of the proper word and act to bring divine aid is a cornerstone of Navajo religion."[11] Along with new seed corn, Salt brings a new ceremonial, the Red Corn Dance, thus providing a classic example of such a quest. Such ceremonies and ritual actions are performed to maintain or restore harmony.

The concept of balance or harmony among opposing elements of the created world is still another theme that often appears in Navajo mythology. This concept is essential to an understanding of Navajo cosmology. Father sun and mother earth, birthing and dying, life and death, summer and winter, day and night, male and female, active and passive, right and left, elder and younger, wet and dry, war and peace—these opposites, appearing in various guises throughout the literature, emphasize the reciprocity inherent in the universe.[12]

The most obvious pairing of opposites in McNickle's story is the conflict between good and evil. The peaceful Village of the White Rocks, where the Turquoise Clan has traditionally provided leadership, is threatened by Salt's innocent violation of tradition: he has planted his corn in a forbidden area. Salt's actions provide an opportunity for the evil Dark Dealer, leader of the opposing Spider Clan, to attack the people of the Turquoise Clan. His victory, however, is short-lived. In the final scene describing Salt's triumphant return from his journey, Dark Dealer also returns. He is neither banished nor killed, but forgiven and accepted back into the village, which is thus restored to its earlier wholeness. Reconciliation has taken place and harmony has been restored, although the possibility of future disruption is not eliminated. Paul Zolbrod explains the significance of this precarious balance between opposites. He maintains that "in Navajo tradition, . . . tension is likely to be sustained, not resolved; or else resolution is more tentative so that one force remains uneasily balanced against another with disorder constantly threatening."[13] While McNickle tells his readers that the gift of the ancient cliff-dwellers is the gift of reconciliation, harmony, and peace, the potential for evil is allowed to remain in the village as reciprocal and complementary to good.

McNickle makes further use of this traditional striving for balance between opposites by representing Salt and his clan brother, Star Climber, as mythic twins. As Salt moves from youth to adulthood, he challenges tradition with innovation and chooses the accompanying risk over the security of the status quo. Star Climber, who fears that Salt's punishment might be extended to himself, tries to avoid any suspicion that he participated in Salt's transgression. "What may happen to me," he asks, "for have I not been his friend since we were children together? But if they ask me, I shall say I know nothing, and whatever it is, I don't approve. I cannot be blamed."[14] As prominent personae in Navajo mythology, twins often represent pairs of opposites such as older and younger, active and passive, or risk-taker and tradition-bound. Salt and Star Climber, who grow up together and are initiated at the same time, represent these polarities.

Still another manifestation of the principle of opposition is apparent in Salt's mentor, the Holy One, a wise old man who speaks in riddles, or "backward talk—a trick of saying the opposite that he means," in order to make the villagers think he is crazy when he is actually sane and very wise. No one in the village knows how old he is, but sometimes he hops around like a child or even crawls on his hands and knees. At times he seems not to know where he is in the world. The people call him the Holy One "because it was thought that he had been touched by the spirits of the other world."[15] Yet the Holy One is not ignorant of happenings in the village below. Quite the contrary; he already knows of Salt's loss of status and of troubles brewing in the village.

The reciprocity of opposites appears yet again in the relationship between the Holy One and Eldest Woman, his clan sister and the senior female member of the Turquoise Clan.[16] The people sometimes call her "the mother of mothers." She, too, is ancient, but unlike the Holy One she has remained active in village affairs and is the final arbiter in clan matters. While Eldest Woman protects Salt by reversing his initiation and removing his turquoise amulet, thus returning him to childhood, the Holy One protects him by giving him his own amulet and by offering the means of restoration. These two protectors, one male, supposedly withdrawn and seemingly senile, the other female, still involved in village affairs, respected and revered by the people, together provide still another set of opposing elements within the story.

As familiar to McNickle as these various elements of Navajo mythology were, however, they did not of themselves constitute a plot. As he contemplated the material at his disposal, McNickle cast about for a story line that would permit him to utilize these motifs in a mythical form that would appeal to young readers. While Navajo mythology suggested a hero's quest, Joseph Campbell's *The Hero With a Thousand Faces* may well have suggested the specifics of the story that emerged.[17]

Campbell's well-known work was the result of an intensive study of the mythologies of prescientific peoples around the world. His interpretation of the universal hero derives from both Jungian and Freudian understanding of human experience.[18] He clearly shares Carl Jung's belief that myth originates in and gives expression to the universal fears and aspirations that Jung considered part of the "collective unconscious." Campbell sees these universals expressed in similar archtypal images in myths throughout the world. He also borrows from Freud, to translate the mythic components into the framework of modern psychology. The literature of modern psychoanalysis, he tells us, contains abundant examples of the struggle to outgrow an infantile ego. "One is bound in by the walls of childhood," he maintains, "and fails to make the passage through the door and come to birth in the world without."[19] Later he explains that "the hero-deed to be wrought is . . . that of making it possible for men and women to come to full human maturity through the conditions of contemporary life."[20] In other words, individuals must conquer their childish self-centered impulses and fears before they can achieve their full potential as mature adults. This conquest, he believes, is the essence of the heroic experience.

Campbell also believes in transcendant spiritual realities, or Powers, as he calls them, that are available to aid in this conquest. The transcendant is not easily reduced to words, however, and world myths have evolved to provide the means to communicate the universal experience of that spiritual reality. He believed that, despite a tremendous variety of specific detail, the hero myths possess an underlying thematic integrity that reveals their origin in the broadest human experience and in the collective unconscious. In the mythic mode, they describe how men and women heroically have acquired the spiritual power to achieve self-realization.

Campbell describes this universal experience through the archetype, or "monomyth," of the saving hero who rescues a people from destructive forces attacking it from within or without. He defines the nuclear unit of the monomyth this way: "A hero ventures forth from the world of common day into a region of supernatural wonder: fabulous forces are there encountered and a decisive victory is won: the hero comes back from this mysterious adventure with the power to bestow boons on his fellow man."[21] The development of the monomyth, Campbell tells us, follows a specific sequence of separation, initiation, and the final return of the hero to his people, to ordinary reality.

The first stage, that of "separation," usually begins with a chance event, sometimes even a blunder, that becomes a prelude to the hero's "call to adventure." Such an accidental event, Campbell believes, "reveals an unsuspected world, and the individual is drawn into a relationship with forces that are not rightly understood." These are the creative, generative, spiritual forces of the universe, or Powers, that will be released as the hero moves toward fulfillment and destiny. In order to accomplish this task, however, the hero must overcome the (Freudian) "infantile ego," which shrinks from personal danger and refuses to accept the possibility of death. By the completion of the hero's adventure, the egocentric impulses are conquered and regeneration, transformation, or even resurrection effected. "The call [to adventure]," Campbell maintains, "rings up the curtain, always, on a mystery of transfiguration."[22]

In *Runner in the Sun*, McNickle broadly follows Campbell's outline of the heroic monomyth. The tale begins with Salt's "call to adventure" and concludes with his return and transformation. Flute Man, an unscrupulous follower of the evil Dark Dealer, precipitates the crisis when he tells the clan leaders of Salt's disregard for tradition in planting his corn.[23] Flute Man thus becomes what Campbell calls the "herald." He acts as the forerunner of the forces that are about to break into the world to activate Salt's "call to adventure." When the clan leaders take away Salt's status, McNickle again follows the pattern of the monomyth. Campbell describes the hero's lowered status as a precursor for the transformation that will follow. A reduction in status is necessary, he maintains, so that the hero may begin his task from a marginal position relative to others. He is not fully accepted as one of them. He may be an adopted child, or handicapped, or an outcast, but for whatever reason, he is or becomes an outsider, often facing a long period of obscurity, before he finally reappears to respond to destiny's call.[24] Spencer, too, points out that the hero of Navajo myths is frequently separated from family, sometimes by personal choice, sometimes by overt and deliberate rejection, but eventually triumphs. (She describes the circumstance of a young boy, for instance, as a "male Cinderella.")[25]

According to Campbell, the hero's acceptance of destiny, the "call to adventure" or summons from that initial obscurity, is clearly dangerous. Psychological risks will be encountered as the hero moves toward psychic reintegration. But rejecting the call, refusing to give up one's own self-interest, is likewise dangerous. "Refusal of the summons," Campbell tells us, "converts the adventure into its negative. . . . All he [who refuses] can do is create new problems for himself and await the gradual approach of his disintegration."[26] Such, he says, is the fate of those who turn their backs on their destiny.

Once again, McNickle adheres to the pattern of the monomyth. The Holy One makes it clear to Salt that danger awaits him should he accept the call to adventure. Dark Dealer has already committed murder. He is rumored even to possess the power of witchcraft. Salt will have to venture dangerously if he would acquire the power to defeat such evil, but there are also risks in refusal. Should Salt reject the charge that he has been given, the Holy One must put his own knife to the boy's throat. Salt now knows too much about the forces arrayed against the village to be allowed to live, should he turn away from the work he is being called upon to perform.[27]

So it happens that Salt, who has sought out the Holy One only to ask how he might regain his lost status, is called instead to the great adventure. In appealing to the old man for help, he has put himself under the tutelage of the next significant element in Campbell's heroic myth, which he calls "the protective figure." Such a figure is not always human; it might be a totemic animal, a fairy godmother, or some other personage whose appearance represents "the benign, protecting power of destiny." This protective figure makes itself known to the hero only after the hero has responded affirmatively to the initial call. The hero "has only to know and to trust and the ageless guardians will appear," Campbell assures us. "Having responded to his own call, and continuing to follow courageously as the consequences unfold, the hero finds all the forces of the unconscious at his side."[28]

The role of the "protective figure" in McNickle's novel, however, does not belong exclusively to the Holy One. Eldest Woman, his sister, is also a protector. The Holy One tells Salt, "Eldest Woman acted in her right and in her power in returning you to your childhood. She is your godmother . . . she is responsible for you and she did this to protect you."[29] Campbell suggests that the protective figure is often mythically both ageless and androgynous, and by joining Eldest Woman and the Holy One together as Salt's protectors, McNickle has followed Campbell's delineation of this character.[30]

The transformation of Campbell's hero, and of McNickle's, begins at this point. According to Campbell, the hero's initial childish desires are increasingly called into question and the entire orientation of the hero to the world begins to change. Confronted by the call to adventure, "that which has to be faced . . . makes itself known, and what formerly was meaningful may become strangely emptied of value." As the call becomes more emphatic, "a series of signs of increasing force" bear upon the hero until "the summons can no longer be denied."[31] So it is with Salt. In the beginning he mourns the loss of his turquoise amulet and his status in the clan, but his self-centered concern is soon replaced by a larger one. The Holy One points to the danger Dark Dealer represents, and Salt responds to the challenge. He feels "as if the image in which he had been born had been broken, and he had been born a new person."[32] Now, with this larger sense of his mission, he is prepared to venture beyond the boundaries of his world into the dangerous unknown. As Campbell has anticipated, "the imperative of the call to adventure" has replaced all his other concerns. Armed with the protective Power of the guardian spirit mediated through the turquoise amulet given him by the Holy One, Salt prepares for the second phase of the adventure, his initiation.

In Campbell's view, the hero's initiation is a process, rather than an event, that signifies an approach to the source of ultimate Power. In describing this initiation, Campbell repeatedly returns to the Freudian concept that the death of the infantile ego is necessary for regeneration. For even as the hero accepts the call, other Powers, psychic or supernatural, stand guard at the boundaries of the hero's familiar world to prevent venturing beyond. These other Powers protect against the chaotic and the unknown, and they attempt to dissuade the hero's affirmative response. Through the instrumentalities of family and society, those Powers have always instructed the infant ego to ensure that the child internalizes societal boundaries. Fear of the unknown and a reluctance to venture therein, the result of this early training, is part of the child's universe and is supported by popular belief, by rulers who have a stake in the status quo, and by cultural tradition. The creative, regenerative Powers issuing the "call to adventure," however, are "beyond the sphere of the measured and the named," beyond the security of the familiar. While they may pose a fundamental threat to life, the hero must be willing, under their protection, to move and act beyond the limitations of the known. Subsequent events will recreate a new self "so that he comes back as one reborn, made great and filled with creative power."[33]

Campbell notes that most people of any age are generally unaware of the variety of possibilities available to them in alternate ways of living out their lives. Rather than explore other possibilities, they prefer the safety of the known and familiar, and they refuse to recognize the intrinsic value of cultures other than their own. Yet, Campbell maintains, "It is only by advancing beyond those [traditional] bounds. . .that the individual passes, either alive or in death, into a new zone of experience."[34] So it is that Salt, himself, prepares to face the natural and supernatural phenomena that challenge his intent and purpose, while Star Climber, who represents the Powers that oppose Salt's call to adventure, retreats into his fears. He clings to the tradition-bound elements that stand in the way of meaningful change for himself and for his people.

As Campbell points out, the trials that comprise the hero's initiation are immensely varied and often quite incredible. McNickle, however, purposefully avoids monsters and other fantastic hazards that would move the action of his story into the realm of make-believe. As he points out in the book's Foreword, his story is about real people who actually lived in communities such as Salt's village, and throughout the novel he provides alternatives for the supernatural or magical. Even the Holy One, who appears to represent the

Sun Old Man, is authentically human. In McNickle's myth the hero's journey must be realistic, and the obstacles overcome must be within the realm of possibility.

Unfortunately, in his attempt to avoid the fanciful in Salt's journey, McNickle fails to maintain the elements of danger and suspense he created earlier. He describes with some sensitivity the land Salt passes through and the various people he meets along the way, but the events themselves do not seem to be genuinely life threatening. As John Purdy notes in his analysis of *Runner in the Sun*, "McNickle's most obvious deviation from oral narrative traditions is the brevity with which he handles the journey itself."[35] As Salt moves south, he rests briefly along the way a mythical four times, first among the Tohono O'odham (Pima/Papago) Indians, second in Culiacan, third in a village on Lake Patzcuaro, and finally in the city of Culhuacan, or Mexico City. In Culhuacan, his daring and potentially life-threatening rescue of Quail, who is a slave girl in the household of his host, becomes his ultimate adventure and the climax of his initiation. Risking his life to save her, he proves himself worthy of her, of adulthood, and of his destiny. His initiation is thus complete, although it is curiously unsatisfying for the reader.

In representing the culmination of Salt's adventure, the young woman in McNickle's story is as significant in Campbell's monomyth as she is in Native American mythologies generally. Campbell maintains that "the ultimate adventure, when all the barriers and ogres have been overcome, is commonly represented as a mystical marriage of the triumphant hero-soul with the Queen Goddess of the World."[36] In McNickle's novel, the girl Quail represents that figure. Not only is she the Indians' Red Corn Woman, but she is Campbell's Universal Mother, the Earth Mother, who is the generator of renewed life. The Universal Mother nourishes and protects, and she embodies all the sustaining Powers of renewal. By returning with Quail, Salt ensures the survival of the clan, as together they represent the continuing capacity for the ever renewing cycle of life. Her rescue thus fulfills Salt's call to adventure.

The third stage of Campbell's heroic monomyth is the transformed hero's return, bringing the Power acquired through the successful completion of tasks. Sometimes, according to Campbell, the hero is reluctant to return from the Fabled Land. Why go back? Having achieved the final bliss of union, what more could be desired? On the other hand, Campbell maintains, "if the hero in his triumph wins the blessing of the goddess or god and is then expressly commissioned to return to the world with some elixir for the restoration of society, the final stage of his adventure is supported by all the powers of his supernatural patron." The hero's gift of life will then "rebound to the renewing of the community, the nation, the planet, or the ten thousand worlds."[37] Whatever form the gift may take, as a symbol of life energy it will be perfectly adapted to the needs of the hero's own people.

So it is with Salt. By the time he and Quail reach the Village of the White Rocks, he has begun to understand the nature of the divine gift. Renewal resides not only in the new strains of corn brought by Quail but in new blood from the Earth Mother herself. The old village will not die; instead, the people will survive and prosper.

The conclusive evidence of Salt's transformation is revealed in the final scene of the novel. Both Salt and Dark Dealer have returned to the village. Acknowledging Dark Dealer's submission, the Holy One points to Salt as the one who will determine whether to accept him back into the village. "This night, and our future, belongs to our grandson," he tells the people. "Let him say what we are to do." Salt then reveals divine mercy rather than human justice. He tells the villagers, "If Dark Dealer finds in his heart that he has not done well, and asks us to take him back, we cannot refuse.

We cannot deny him his chance to make the gift which will fulfill his life. I say, bring them all back [the Spider Clan people], and make our people whole again." The Holy One agrees. "Power is here," he declares, "the power to restore peace in a bad heart. The very power needed by our people."[38] By responding without fear to his "call to adventure," Salt has, indeed, achieved his destiny.

Throughout this narrative, McNickle has followed the outline of Campbell's monomyth. The various motifs he employs from Navajo mythology are not new; they have been described previously by a number of ethnographers. The heroic quest was an essential aspect of Navajo chantways for as long as the myths had been told. It was the timing of the two works, Campbell's in 1949 and McNickle's in 1954, that suggests McNickle's reordering of the familiar elements to conform to Campbell's interpretation of the hero myth.

Given that assumption, whether or not one agrees with Campbell that elemental myths convey a human response to deep psychic needs, it is interesting to then ask whether McNickle himself was also responding to those needs. Campbell recognized that today's rational cultures no longer accept as a reality the transcendant Powers tapped by the hero of the monomyth, and that young people today might ask what meaning, if any, the hero's "call to adventure" has for them. Most of us no longer live in small communities such as the Village of the White Rocks, and we are reluctant to believe that an entire people can be saved by one person's response to the "call to adventure." Science, not the individual's grappling with supernatural Powers, has for several centuries provided the rationale and the impetus for social change, and it is science, most of us believe, that will create a better world.

It was just this loss of a spiritual dimension in modern life, however, that led Campbell to conjoin the psychoanalytic insights of Freud and Jung into his interpretation of the heroic myth. While our rationalized culture has deprived us of the spiritual element we need in our growth toward true psychological maturity, he believed that modern psychology provides insight into that struggle through the implications of the monomyth. "The hero-deed to be wrought is not today what it was in the century of Galileo," he explains. "Where then there was darkness, now there is light; but also, where light was, there now is darkness. The modern hero-deed must be that of questing to bring to light again the lost Atlantis of the co-ordinated soul." The functioning world of today, he believes, needs "a transmutation of the whole social order, . . . so that through every detail and act of secular life the vitalizing image of the universal god-man who is actually immanent and effective in all of us may be somehow made known to consciousness." Through the conquest of the infantile ego of each individual, the hero's intensely personal quest for spiritual health and psychic regeneration will ultimately accrue to the benefit of all.[39]

It is difficult to tell, from McNickle's story of Salt, whether he also shared Campbell's psychological interpretation of the heroic monomyth. He obviously felt, however, that mythic stories do indeed convey vital aspects of communal life, of the collective unconscious, that are true to broad human experience. Those tribal myths whose motifs he borrowed had been told to uncounted generations of Native children, and each time they were told, they recreated the mythical events in the present moment. Thus they carried forward cultural values crucial to the survival of the community. McNickle was well aware of this contemporary aspect of myth and believed in its validity. *Runner in the Sun* begins and ends as stories do that are told in the traditional manner, with formulae that create a context for the storytelling event,[40] and while it is obviously rooted in the history McNickle knew so well, by relating it as myth he provided it with new dimensions of time and space.

If McNickle purposefully created a myth, however, and if myths endure because they embody timeless truths about the world we live in, then even if we disagree with Campbell's interpretation, we may look for a deeper meaning in *Runner* than the idealized characterization of its hero. As noted earlier, McNickle claimed that the story was about the innate peace keeping habits of the first Americans, whose gift of peace was rejected by the Europeans who arrived later.[41] But another theme is present as well, a theme to which McNickle repeatedly returned in his writing, and that is the persistence and continuity of the Native American tribal experience. The single idea he expressed most consistently throughout his life was the ability of Native people to incorporate into their lives those elements of the dominant culture that enhanced their traditional lifeways, while rejecting those that threatened their identity as Native Americans. These adaptations even suggested the title of one of his later historical narratives, *Native American Tribalism: Indian Survivals and Renewals* (1973). McNickle believed that Indian people, given the freedom to change at their own pace, would continue to make constructive adaptations to the modern world. As Alfonso Ortiz has pointed out in his Afterword to the recently reprinted edition of the novel, *Runner in the Sun* is a statement in mythical form that reasserts McNickle's faith in Native ethnic and cultural survival, despite the fact that survival was being deeply threatened in the 1950s by the possibility of tribal termination.[42]

Above and beyond all the analyses, however, recall that McNickle's story was written for the young reader, and McNickle's hero is a worthy role model. Salt is brave in the face of danger, trustworthy and compassionate, respectful of his elders, and sensitive to the ways of others whose lifestyle differs from his own. Above all, he has his priorities in order—as he matures, he forgoes his own desires for the welfare of his people. While he knows that tradition is important, he discovers that it is sometimes necessary to disregard tradition and venture into the unknown if an individual, or a people, is to endure in a changing world.

McNickle spent his life working for the continuing survival of Indian people, raising money, teaching, writing, and inspiring young Native Americans with his faith in the Indian tribal experience. He was one of the founders of the National Congress of American Indians in 1944 and one of the organizers at the American Indian Chicago Conference in 1961. Sadly, his third and final novel suggests that at the end of his life he was beginning to doubt. *Wind from an Enemy Sky* is an elegy for a way of life drowned in the flood of modern civilization. The whites' new dam finally "killed the water," and the old tribal ways are doomed. In *Runner in the Sun*, though, Salt and Red Corn Woman bring hope and the promise of renewed life to the people who live in the Village of the White Rocks.

Chapter Eight

Cultural Survival in
Runner in the Sun

Lori Burlingame

In *Runner in the Sun: A Story of Indian Maize* (1954), McNickle gives his readers a historical and mythic vision of Native American life before the tensions and conflicts that erupted with the coming of the Europeans to this continent. As in his other two novels, McNickle deals with the issues of cultural survival and individual development, but in this novel, he affirms the title-theme of his nonfiction historical text, *They Came Here First* (1949).[1] His aims are to present an insider perspective on Native cultures, to debunk the notion that the history of "America" began with Columbus's "discovery" of it,[2] and to counter the stereotypes that have plagued Native Americans since the coming of the whites. In his foreword to *Runner in the Sun*, McNickle writes: "Most of us grow up believing that the history of America begins with the men who came across from Europe and settled in New World wilderness. The real story of our country is much older, much richer, than this usual history book account."[3]

Runner in the Sun was published in the terrible early years of the "termination era," during which the United States government set out to destroy the remnants of traditional

Native American tribal structures and loyalties by terminating the tribal status of and ceasing to provide federal funding and support for numerous Indian tribes. Implicit in *Runner in the Sun* is a belief that Native cultures will endure despite white efforts either to assimilate or eradicate them. As Franco Meli notes, McNickle is concerned with "the issue of tribalism, that is the multiplicity of distinctive traditional cultures, which gives the lie to all stereotypes and resists the forces of assimilation."[4] McNickle's depictions of distinctly different Native cultures and customs thwart Anglo-European stereotypes about the sameness of Native peoples and the uniformity of Indian life.

Runner in the Sun is significant because it provides a general yet historically-based account of Native American life in the Southwest in the Mesa Verde period (A.D. 550–1300). McNickle's vision does not idealize or romanticize Indian life; he strives to recreate a realistic or true-to-life depiction of Indian life in the precontact era. The tribal society that he describes is not without conflict, and the struggle for survival, both culturally and personally, is ever present. The difference is that these conflicts and tensions are resolved by the people themselves, whom McNickle characterizes as essentially peace loving.

McNickle's depictions of a Native American society in the midst of conflict and potentially ruinous upheaval break the stereotype that all Native cultures are static and unchanging. They also confound the idea that conflict only came to Native peoples with the arrival of the whites; *Runner in the Sun* overturns white notions of precontact perfection. McNickle does not give us the stereotypical romantic vision of a "noble savage" society; rather, he presents us with a highly organized and civilized, realistic society that, like all societies, experiences internal discord. The notion that Native American cultures are set in their ways and opposed to change is also countered; as a result of internal conflict and the lessening supply of water from the village stream, the Indians of *Runner in the Sun* must adapt their ways of life and even move from their cliff dwellings.

When the Europeans came to this continent, they seemed to think that Native American peoples should completely change their ways of living and adapt to European ways, and when they failed to do so, Anglo-European cultures tended to regard them as rigid and primitive. McNickle undercuts this ethnocentric stereotype by depicting change from within in a precontact culture; his dynamic delineations[5] of Native peoples and cultures subvert the fixed, two-dimensional representations that are found in James Fenimore Cooper's novels and in Hollywood films. McNickle shows his readers that change and adaptation were and are essential to the survival and maintenance of traditional Native lifeways, values, and conceptions of personal and tribal identity; he says:

> "Those who insist that Indians must change their way of life if they are to survive are really insisting that the change must be made at once. They ignore or minimize the fact that Indians have been changing their habits, their material culture, and their outlook since the coming of the first white man. . . . If the Indian accepted some objects and customs from the white world, why did he not accept them all?" Most whites have failed to understand that the Indian used whatever he adopted "as a more effective tool for carrying on the kind of life he knew." (quoted in Ortiz, "Afterword" 244)

Runner in the Sun was written primarily for an adolescent audience, as part of "the Land of the Free series of juvenile historical fiction."[6] Through this novel, McNickle seeks to educate American youths, both Native and non-Native, about Native American cultures and their place in the history of the Americas. Like most myths and stories in Native traditions, this story serves primarily to educate, but it also serves to entertain; however, to dismiss this novel as less than serious or as escapist literature either because of its intended audience or its fable-like quality is to miss the very relevant historical, political, and cultural perspectives and implications of the novel.[7]

Unlike *The Surrounded*, which was written largely for the dominant white literary audience of the time, *Runner in the Sun* speaks more specifically to a Native audience. Bruce Grant, a reviewer for the *Chicago Sunday Tribune* writes, "This book is all Indian—the artist [Allan C. Houser] is a full blooded Apache."[8] In the sense that this novel, unlike McNickle's other two, deals solely with Native American cultures, Grant is correct, but this is not to say that McNickle did not intend to address, inform, and educate his non-Native audience as well; throughout his career as a writer and as an advocate in government and Indian affairs that was his intent. While *Runner in the Sun* offers encouragement to and kindles pride in a Native audience, it also asks non-Native readers to "re-read" "American" cultural myths and history. Through identification with McNickle's protagonist Salt, any reader, juvenile or adult, Native American or European-American, can come to a deeper understanding of and gain greater respect for the traditions and values of Native cultures.

McNickle employs oral narrative structures and tropes in *Runner in the Sun*; Alfonso Ortiz observes that the novel "resembles a story that is told more than one that is written. Sentences are brief, coordination prevails over subordination, and nouns are repeated rather than represented by pronouns, to make the listener's task easier. The narrator is obviously omniscient as well, as in traditional tale-telling" (Afterword 248). Although McNickle's story is a product of the oral tradition, it is told in written form, and is, hence, an adaptation of traditional storytelling methods. Like Salt, who encourages his people to adapt their ways of life in order to ensure their continued survival, McNickle adapts the oral narrative ways of storytelling to novel form, and in so doing, he makes his story accessible to a larger audience and bridges the gap between Native American and white cultures.[9]

As is the case in Silko's *Ceremony*, the idea of the story is central in *Runner in the Sun*. Salt's journey/quest culminates in a new story that validates Native American history and traditions and a new ceremony, called the Red Corn Dance, that revitalizes and strengthens his community.[10] Just as the new strains of corn and the new blood of Red Corn Woman bring about new ceremonies and enduring hope, so too, does McNickle's story about Salt create a new myth meant to provide hope for contemporary Native peoples. In so doing, it perpetuates the creative flow of stories that is the hallmark of the oral tradition.

Like his other novels, the early drafts of *Runner in the Sun* had different titles, among them were "The Boy Who Stole the Sun" and "Journey into the Sky."[11] Yet, even in his drafts, the impetus for McNickle's novel appears to have been a desire "to explore the origins of contemporary peoples, as well as their literatures."[12] Hence, although McNickle has written it with the inescapable hindsight of a postcontact writer, the novel itself is set in the precontact era before relations with the whites irrevocably influenced and altered Native American lifeways, beliefs, stories, and storytelling methods.[13]

There are varying hypotheses about the approximate time frame in which *Runner in the Sun* is set. John Purdy suggests that the novel takes place approximately 4,000 to 4,500 years ago in the Southwest; in *Indians and Other Americans*, McNickle mentions that it was at about this time that the use of maize began in the area that he writes about in *Runner in the Sun* (Purdy 86). *Runner*, however, is about the search for a new and hardier strain of corn rather than about the advent of maize farming in the Southwest. Based on this and some historical connections between Salt's people and the Anasazi

Indians, one could argue that the novel is likely set much later, at about A.D. 1300.

Several theories address when and from where maize farming developed and spread into the Southwest.[14] Alvin Josephy Jr. says that maize farming appears to have spread from Mexico into the southernmost part of the Southwest (151).[15] Salt's journey to the Land of Fable (in *Runner*) takes him to the place we now call Mexico City, and the people whom he meets there are most likely the Aztec Indians. As Purdy observes, Salt's journey backtracks along the course of "Mother Corn" as she originally came to Salt's people (99–100).

Although McNickle never provides a definitive time frame, tribal or historical background, or geographical setting for the novel, there is evidence to support the idea that he is talking about the Anasazi Indians.[16] Josephy notes that the Anasazis were the "ancestors of the present-day Pueblos" (160). In his preface McNickle says of Salt's people, "They were real people, as were all the people Salt encountered on his journey south into the country we call Mexico" (viii), perhaps by way of emphasizing the historical reality and existence of the Native cultures he depicts.

Josephy traces the development of the Anasazi and Pueblo cultures. He notes that during the Developmental Pueblo stage (ca. A.D. 700–1100), the Anasazis, like Salt's people, began to use a large ceremonial chamber called the "Great Kiva." The height of Pueblo culture was reached during the Great Pueblo period (ca. A.D. 1100–1300) when different clan units lived together in individual settlements, as do the seven clans in *Runner in the Sun*. These Anasazi settlements were often located in the recesses of cliff walls or on top of mesas in Mesa Verde, Colorado; Chaco Canyon, Arizona, and the Colorado River Basin in southeastern Utah. The Anasazi Indians were noted for their turquoise jewelry. During the Great Pueblo period, which was characterized by complex social and religious organization, the Anasazis ceased to use the Great Kiva. Small kivas were still employed, and new architectural types and structures, which may have originated in Mexico, emerged.[17]

Like the Anasazis, Salt's people, who are called the Turquoise people, live in cliff dwellings, and they wear turquoise jewelry; in fact, Salt's turquoise necklace signifies his initiation into adulthood. The kiva is the center of the community, and it is used for meetings and ceremonies; the opening chapter of *Runner in the Sun* is titled, "Call to the Kiva," and like the Anasazi Indians, each of the seven clans in Runner appears to have its own kiva.

Like Salt's people, the Anasazis left their cliff dwellings and moved away. From the end of the Great Pueblo period to the beginning of the sixteenth century, the Anasazis withdrew very suddenly from their homelands (Josephy 159–60). For reasons that are still unclear, they vacated the Mesa Verde site around A.D. 1300, and their cliff dwellings remained abandoned and undisturbed until the late-nineteenth century.[18] A number of theories explore the reasons the Anasazis left, among them, an epidemic, fluctuations in rainfall patterns, pressure from antagonistic nomadic invaders, factionalism among Pueblo clans, and exhaustion of the wood supply (Josephy 159). Salt's people leave their cliff dwellings because of drought and the exhaustion of the soil: "The years had been growing drier in Salt's lifetime, and there came a succession of seasons when no rain fell, the spring ceased to flow at summer's peak, and they almost lost even the precious new seed" (McNickle 233).

From approximately 1300 until the appearance of the Spaniards in 1540 (sometimes called the Regressive Pueblo period), the Pueblos experienced a "golden age" in their new locations (Josephy 160).[19] The ending of *Runner in the Sun* is consonant with the "golden age" of the Pueblos.[20] Like the Anasazi Indians, Salt's people moved to greener lands, "and the new corn, when planted and watered abundantly, produced such harvests as had never been known" (McNickle 233).

While it is not possible to ascertain definitively why McNickle based *Runner in the Sun* on the history of the Anasazi Indians, it is probable that he did it to give added strength to the idea that Native American cultures have survived and adapted in the face of adverse circumstances and will continue to do so. The futures of the Anasazis and of their fictional counterparts, the Turquoise Indians, seem bright, even though they have had to leave their lands and adapt to life elsewhere. During the termination era, Native Americans were denied their very identities: their status as tribes and any federal support or protection that went with it, and they were encouraged to leave their reservations and relocate in large cities. In *Runner in the Sun*, McNickle presents us with an historically-based account of adaptation and change in the face of calamity. His message is that Native American cultures can overcome and be strengthened by even the worst threats to their identities, if they are courageous and adaptable.

Runner in the Sun is also the story of the adolescent Salt's initiation or coming-of-age; in this respect, it is a Bildungs-roman, and it follows a long tradition of such stories and novels, in both American and British literature, by writers (with whom McNickle was undoubtedly familiar) like Charlotte Brönte, Charles Dickens, Ernest Hemingway, John Steinbeck, James Joyce, and Jack London. McNickle's novel, however, is different from the works of these writers in that his emphasis is on the growth of the individual in relationship to society, whereas in, for example, Joyce's *Portrait of the Artist as a Young Man*, Stephen Dedalus's development leads to individualistic detachment from his origins; Dedalus must transcend the boundaries of religion, nationality, and culture in order to be a great artist. Salt leaves his people so that he may return and help them, Stephen leaves his family and country so that he may have greater personal and artistic freedom.

The individual's development, usually in opposition to culture or environment, is frequently the focus of the "American" novel. Huck Finn is the archetype of the American individualist—in an attempt to escape from society's "civilizing" influence, he lights out. In contrast, McNickle's Salt goes from being an isolated individual to a representative of his community, and as a result he is able to lead his people out of their unhealthy and stagnant isolation to a new place of green valleys where they will better be able to survive. Salt becomes an heroic leader of his people because he is both respectful of tradition and willing to initiate change when it is in the best interest of his people. Unlike Dark Dealer, who places his own ambitions above the welfare of tribe when he tries to take control by instilling fear in the people, Salt puts the good of his community above his personal safety.

Salt's development from an individual to a "mythic hero" (Purdy 88) proceeds according to traditional Native American patterns found in the oral narrative tradition. When Salt goes to visit the Holy One, he is receiving counsel and assistance from his elder. The Holy One acts as a mentor to Salt. Although he admires Salt's creativity and resourcefulness, the Holy One upbraids Salt for acting without considering his people's traditions when he planted his corn by the stream. He also gives Salt a chance to prove himself and displays his confidence in Salt when he gives him the task of finding the secret path from the village to the upper fields[21]: "To find the way, Salt must look, literally, below surface appearances, as the readers must if they are to understand that Native peoples and their traditions are not relics of the past but lively forces in the present, which have faced millennia of threats and catastrophes and have survived" (Purdy 99).

The Holy One shares with Salt a recurring dream. In many Native American cultures, dreams and wishes are socially significant, powerful, and often prophetic. Like stories and myths, they call things into being and create reality. The Holy One feels that Salt may be implicated in his dream about a journey; he tells him: " 'Three different times I have had a certain dream. Each time a sacred person talks about our village and tells me that our trouble will not be solved by ourselves alone, that we must go outside of ourselves to find help. . . . Someone may have to make a journey . . . it will have to fall on a young man; one who thinks of his people, not of himself; one who will give his life, if necessary, in order to save his people' " (McNickle 54). The Holy One's dream foretells the journey and metaphorical vision quest that Salt makes to the Land of Fable. Salt's traditional vision quest, which reflects an important phase of his development into a leader of his people and a hero, involves three things: "the desire for knowledge of how to help, the aid of a helper (Sun), and the removal, for a time, from his people" (Purdy 98). As Franco Meli observes, the vision quest typifies the central characteristics of tribalism; it is cyclic in nature, and it requires the visionary to leave the tribe and to make the quest alone (363). This solitude, however, is only temporary; the visionary leaves the community "only in order to return with powers to share, to be validated by the tribe, that is interpreted and applied in a social context" (363).

Thus, while Salt's vision quest involves a demanding and solitary journey, its main purpose is so that Salt's growth and discoveries may benefit his tribe. The Holy One tells Salt that he must go for the sake of his people, and he advises Salt:

> We will survive what Dark Dealer has done, but our life here is broken and will never be put together again in the way it was before. We must find a new way, and I have no knowledge of what that will be. . . . I cannot tell you what to look for, or what to bring back. That is the terrible thing about this journey of yours. I can only tell you that somewhere in the south lies a land our fathers called the Land of Fable. . . . Is it a new race of corn

that is needed, then? Maybe what is needed is that our people should change. . . . I think that what you must look for will be something that comes from our Father the Sun. (McNickle 164–66).

Before Salt leaves for his journey, the Holy One takes his own turquoise necklace off and puts it around Salt's neck. For Salt, it is a "shattering experience" (166). He "felt as if the image in which he had been born had been broken, and he had been born a new person" (166). In the act of giving Salt his Turquoise necklace, the Holy One makes him into a representative of his people and indicates that Salt may take his place as a leader of his tribe. Salt is no longer solely an individual. He has taken on a new identity, and his future and ability to survive are now synonymous with those of his people; his quest is for that which will save them.

According to Purdy, McNickle deviates from traditional oral narrative stories in that he does not devote a great deal of the novel to Salt's journey; however, the events leading up to the journey are more crucial because they depict Salt's growth and his loyalty to his community, and they identify him as an innovative and worthy leader of his people. As Purdy notes, however, McNickle's narrative of Salt's journey follows the traditional pattern. There are four (four is a Pueblo sacred number) main events in his journey or vision quest.[22] First he visits his kin to the southwest, next Yucca Flower Woman in Culiacan, then Ocelot near Lake Patzcuaro, and finally Tula in Culhuacan; each step of his journey takes him farther from his home and his traditional values and reflects a new stage of his development into a hero of his people (Purdy 99–100).

As Purdy notes, Salt is increasingly attracted to the sun as he journeys south, but the societies that he encounters become more and more materialistic and less humanistic. Culhuacan, the final stopping place in his journey, appears on the surface to be a great city, but below the surface are emptiness and disrespect for human life and tradition. Even though Ocelot and Tula are good men, they are powerless to turn back the tide of destructive behavior that seems to have overwhelmed their societies.

Tula tells Salt that Quetzalcoatl,[23] an Aztec "deity and legendary human hero,"[24] who was once revered as the god of his city is no longer respected. According to Tula, Quetzalcoatl was responsible for bringing many good things, most especially corn, to his people.[25]

Cinteotl was a male deity who oversaw food plants in Aztec culture, and Chicomecoatl was the corresponding female goddess.[26] According to Paul Weatherwax, Chicomecoatl was said to have been pleased with sacrifices of flowers, agricultural products, birds, and small animals, but it was said that she found human sacrifice repugnant. In the Aztec fourth month, which started on our fifth of April, a great festival was held for Chicomecoatl (229). The beginning of the celebration was marked by a " 'great watch' " (229), during which the people fasted; following this, rushes and reeds sprinkled with sacrificial blood (drawn from the bodies of festival participants) were set at the doors of houses (229). Xilomen was the goddess of new or green corn, and the Aztecs honored her with a festival from June 25 through July 14 (Weatherwax 233). Unlike Chicomecoatl, however, Xilomen required human sacrifice; some accounts indicate that the girl to be sacrificed was, like Quail, a slave, who was not native to the Aztec culture and who did not know about the ceremony or her intended part as an offering in it (233).[27]

It is difficult to say with certainty whether McNickle is drawing on these Aztec corn myths and ceremonies in *Runner in the Sun*, but internal evidence suggests that he is. Tula tells Salt about a change in the customs of his people, and this change typifies the difference between the ceremonies honoring Chicomecoatl and Xilomen: " 'In the former days it was our custom to draw blood from our bodies as a token in payment for the gift of life. Now come these men without reason and shame, these believers in numbers and size, and they turn the simple ceremonies of our fathers into spectacles of horror. Our temples are washed in blood. . . . We are soon to celebrate the Feast of the Eighth Month . . . in which the maturing of the new corn is honored by cutting off the head of a young girl' " (McNickle 205). This change in customs is regarded as negative by Salt, Tula, and Ocelot, with whom the readers' sympathies lie. The change is also forced on Tula and his people; if Tula refuses to comply, his family may be harmed, and he is afraid to stand up to those who demand this sacrifice.

McNickle uses a change in ceremonies in the novel as a metaphor for the changes in values that later came about with the entrance of the whites into the Americas. Although McNickle demonstrates, via his fiction, the central roles that change and adaptation play in cultural survival, he also clearly indicates that not all change is positive. The need for human sacrifice and the change in sacrificial customs in the novel may metaphorically represent (or stand for) the introduction of Native peoples to Christianity, the new religion, which emphasizes the life-giving power of Christ's death and sacrifice. Seen from this perspective, McNickle's depictions of the changing ceremonies suggests that the acceptance of Anglo-European religious systems and values have had detrimental effects on Native cultures and peoples.

These outside influences may also intensify negative trends already present in a culture. According to Purdy, Culhuacan in particular embodies many of the characteristics of progressive European and "American" cultures:

> [McNickle presents] either directly or obliquely—the cultures in which European explorers recognized qualities somewhat akin to their own. Ironically, their recognition of shared motivations led them to believe that they had found the pinnacles of Native "civilizations": the Mayan, Aztec, and Toltec. By the time Salt

reaches the home of Tula, however, it has become obvious that each culture is increasingly class-structured, increasingly oriented by individuality, and therefore, in Native terms, inflexible and doomed to destruction. (Purdy 100)

Individual ambition, selfishness, the desire for personal power, and materialism, which are qualities often encouraged and rewarded by Anglo-European cultures, are depicted as destructive because they disregard the sanctity of human life and instead pay homage to property and power. In most Anglo-European cultures, the word "successful" is applied to those with wealth and the power that accompanies it; it usually has very little to do with moral character. As Jean Giraudoux wryly observes in his play *The Madwoman of Chaillott*, "to have money is to be virtuous, honest, beautiful, and witty. And to be without is to be ugly and boring and stupid and useless" (59).

While McNickle has given us a straightforward depiction of pre-Columbian Native American life, his story operates on a number of prophetic levels. On one level, the story functions as a form of "retroactive prophecy," which is defined by Jarold Ramsey as: "one of a numerous set of native texts, some mythological and others historical or personal, in which an event or deed in precontact times is dramatized as being prophetic of some consequence of the coming of the whites."[28] McNickle's depiction of Aztec society, as seen through the disenchanted eyes of Tula who mourns the loss of traditional ways and values, closely resembles Euro-American society. The disrespect for and destruction of tradition and life implicit in the practice of human sacrifice is suggestive of the disruption and havoc wrought on the Indians by the coming of the whites to the Americas. In this sense, *Runner in the Sun* can be seen as a form of "retroactive prophecy."[29]

The novel can also function as a prophecy about the future set in past times. The individualistic values that Salt observes already exist in his own culture in the character of Dark

Dealer.[30] In *Runner in the Sun*, however, tradition and community triumph over the values, individuality, selfishness, and personal power that Dark Dealer embodies. While McNickle celebrates and affirms this triumph, he also issues a warning to contemporary Native American and European-American cultures alike. The message for Native Americans is that buying into Anglo-European systems of value can bring about destruction. Like Tula, who is afraid to stand up to those who demand human sacrifices, Native American cultures will be doomed to despair and emptiness, if they do not resist that which goes against their values. The message for the whites is that, like the ancient Aztec society whose greed and disrespect for human life brought about its death, the majority culture will be overtaken by that fate unless society's ways are altered and people learn to respect each other and the Earth.

There is hope, however, in the positive ending of the novel and in the fact that even someone like Dark Dealer may change. Because of his concern for the hungry women and children of his clan, Dark Dealer humbles himself and asks for the forgiveness of the Turquoise Clan and its new leader, Salt. Dark Dealer has learned to value his people's welfare above his own pride.

Salt develops into a mythic hero and a great leader of his people because he is not taken in by materialism and the lust for personal power; as he grows into a man, he learns to place his people's welfare above his own, and he becomes their representative. Salt looks beneath the surface of things. He sees the necessity of change while at the same time respecting tradition. He and Red Corn Woman are able to lead his people into a new place and a new way of life that will ensure their continuance. "There they lived in peace and supported one another" (McNickle 234).

In *Runner in the Sun*, McNickle affirms the enduring power of traditional Native American values and lifeways, subverts stereotypes about Native Americans, and asserts the necessity of change and adaptation in Native American cultures. McNickle's vision is one of hope and understanding, and he offers it to those who hear and heed the messages in his story.

Chapter Nine

A Legend of Culture:
D'Arcy McNickle's
Runner in the Sun

Jay Hansford C. Vest

As a novelist, D'Arcy McNickle is best known for vividly portraying the conflict between Native and white cultures. When interpreting his other novels, *The Surrounded* and *Wind from an Enemy Sky,* critics have primarily focused their attention upon a vision of despair and an inevitable sense of tragedy. These powerful novels of cultural conflict are said to convey wholesale rejection and renunciation of the white world.[1] Softening this reading, one scholar, James Ruppert, has cited McNickle's interest in exploring the societal implications of cultural confrontation. Ruppert further acknowledges McNickle's attention to realism rather than romanticism; emphasizing the tradition of American naturalism, he proposes a regionalist framework for judging McNickle's works.[2]

McNickle's experiences—as Native traditionalist, bureaucrat, anthropologist, and novelist—and his innate genius nurtured the development of the modern Native American novel. Although two of his novels originate in the thirties, his writings are characteristic of what Kenneth Lincoln has termed a renaissance of American literature. Creatively drawing upon his ethnohistorical scholarship, McNickle's novels generate significant insights into Native cultures, as well as supply essential knowledge fostering traditional cultural continuation through time. Accordingly, many scholars characterize him as the grandfather of both contemporary Native American literature and modern Indian ethnohistory.[3]

Set in the pre-Columbian Southwest, *Runner*[4] is McNickle's creative interpretation of traditional Pueblo civilization prior to conquest and the taint of acculturation. On the surface, the novel is an account of a youth's initiation into adulthood. The protagonist, a boy called Salt, is given the challenge of leadership; to be successful, he must discover a carefully guarded secret while surviving intrigue and mortal danger. Following this trial, he must undertake the fabled quest—a journey into an unknown land, for an unknown thing that, when discovered and returned, will save his people. He returns with a young woman bearing a slave mark upon her forehead that the people honor as the sign of the sun; he also bears with him the wisdom of peace.

Focusing upon the novel's youthful hero, critics tend to view *Runner* as juvenile fiction aimed at the education of American youth to Native values.[5] Alfonso Ortiz has rightly responded that it "is not simply an innocent book for juveniles, although juveniles can read it for profit and pleasure." Concluding that *Runner* is McNickle's "response to the tragic policy of termination," Ortiz champions the novel as a literary ethnohistory "claiming for Indian people a reality apart from that granted to them by white people, and . . . a reality whites cannot erase nor, eventually, fail to face."[6]

Ortiz's last point is sustained in McNickle's preface to *Runner*; moreover, McNickle explicitly confronts the ethnocentric accounts of American history that have ignored America's pre-Columbian civilizations. Declaring the people of Salt and their village of the White Rocks to be real "hundreds of years before Columbus and his three little ships set sail from Isabella's Spain," McNickle presents a list of the many domesticated plants and food crops contributed to the world by Native America (vii–viii).

When opening one of his scholarly articles, McNickle commented: "The Americans called Indians wrote no histories, and their past was only dimly told in oral tradition and legend. When strangers came to write about the land that had been theirs, the Indians somehow turned into flora and fauna and where hardly visible as men. Their global experience had been reduced to scattered footnotes in world history."[7] McNickle's remarks indicate his concern over the manifold misconceptions directed at Native Americans; and as Ortiz suggests, *Runner* is "a frontal assault on the many negative stereotypes long prevalent in American culture, stereotypes which had as their common purpose to alienate Indians from their land."[8]

McNickle's ethnohistorical writings reveal his familiarity with the foundations of these negative stereotypes; moreover, as an anthropologist, he addresses both the savagism dogma and the illusion that is primitive society theory.[9] Expression of these highly destructive dogmas appears in the following tenets: first, Indians, as non-Christians, were deemed unenlightened and therefore noncivilized. Second, Indians were determined not to utilize properly the natural environment; and under this ruling, their rights were declared ephemeral. These tenets were based upon erroneous assumptions: that all Indians were hunters, that said hunters required too much land for their stalking, and that such activities are bloodthirsty and characteristic to the "Natural Man" as opposed to a "Civilized Man." From this premise, a third tenet was devised that held Native peoples as a lower grade of humanity. Since Natives, under these misconceptions, did not properly use nature, Christian princes and their vassals, the presumed farmers and "husbandmen" of Europe, were declared to have right of acquisition of the newly "discovered" lands. In a fourth tenet, the Europeans had already begun to establish literacy as the "true" mark of civilized humanity; lacking a written language, Natives were, therefore, viewed as childlike and often rated as little better than the beasts of the forests.[10] Writing for young people, McNickle sought to dispel these erroneous notions via his creative pre-Columbian novel, *Runner.*

Interrupting his work on *Wind from an Enemy Sky*, begun in the 1930s, McNickle published *Runner* in 1954 at the midpoint of his literary career, that is, halfway between his powerful novels, *The Surrounded* (1936) and *Wind* (1978). In part his reason for writing *Runner* is revealed in his passionate but controlled response to the termination policies of the 1950s. *Runner* is also clearly a response to the savagism dogma and primitive society theory; moreover, he hoped to replace the stereotypical perceptions of Natives as wild warriors, hunters, and savages, with a more accurate view of Native agriculturalists. *Runner* is a gentle but firm rebuke of savagism. This rebuttal is highly developed in his ethno-history, *They Came Here First* (1949).[11] The effectiveness of his argument is, however, no less significant in the fictive genre. The novel's creation must also be understood in the larger context of McNickle's emergent sense of place in the Southwest.

In the summer and fall of 1952, McNickle initiated a health care and education project at Crownpoint on the Navajo Reservation. Buying a home in Albuquerque, he was capti-vated with the Southwest landscape and its Native peoples.[12] During his visits to the Crownpoint area, he encountered archeological evidence of the Anasazi people; in so doing, "he sensed a direct contact with people who had lived in the area before the Navajos arrived, people untouched by [W]estern civilization, whose way of life seemed totally adapted to their environment. Their artifacts were all around him at Crownpoint, drawing him almost irresistibly."[13]

He was further compelled in his writing by an earlier visit to the area with John Collier. During that visit, a Hopi elder raised the questions concerning the whites' claim to the land and authority over Native governments. These questions of sovereignty and moral accountability disturbed McNickle and he felt that the man deserved an answer. Recalling this incident, he wrote: "I was present at that conversation on the mesa. I tried to frame answers to the questions. As it turned out, there were hundreds of questions; one led into another and gave the mind no rest."[14] Consequently, McNickle constructed an ethnohistory—*They Came Here First*—designed to confront the Western antecedents to these questions and the concomitant illusions—savagism and primitive society theory—that accompany them.

Declaring McNickle's message in *They Came Here First* to be a "moral imperative," Parker notes: "All Americans, he believed, should address themselves to the questions the Hopi man had raised. Europeans had come as uninvited intruders, and the Indians, though hospitable at first, did not ask the strangers to stay. But they did stay, and because of their superior technology they were able to impose their will on those who were there first. Despite that imposition the Indians had survived and now they were asking troubling questions that ought to be addressed."[15] In the preface to *Runner*, McNickle affirms the novel's design to challenge the ethnocentricism characteristic to American ideology; writing for a youthful audience, he declares:

> Most of us grow up believing that the history of America begins with the men who came across from Europe and settled in New World wilderness. The real story of our country is much older, much richer, than this usual history book account.
>
> Thousands of years before Europeans, by accident, stumbled upon the American continents, men were living here, scattered between the two polar oceans. They lived under a variety of conditions, and they developed tools, clothing, shelter, food habits, customs, and beliefs to fit their conditions. In some areas, they felled trees in the forest and built houses out of planks split from the trees. Elsewhere, they erected great mounds of earth

and stone and placed their houses and temples on the summits. In still other places, they quarried rock and built houses of stone. (vi)[16]

During his efforts with the ethnohistory, McNickle learned from archeological sources that no evidence of warfare had been found among the Anasazi people and their neighbors to the south for over six hundred years. Deeply moved by this example of peace, he decided to develop a fictional account of the Pueblo people's peaceful lives.[17]

In staging this pre-Columbian narrative, McNickle created a legend of culture. Legends attend to an oral tradition's conceptualization of the past and sense of history, whereas myth addresses the eternal verities or mysterious powers of the world in an atemporal, metaphorical logic. Legend and myth are both modes of storytelling used traditionally to address cultural concerns in a sacred manner. Opening with "This is the story of a town that refused to die. It is the story of the angry men who tried to destroy, and of the Indian boy Salt, in the language of his people, who stood against them" (1), McNickle implies a legendary rendering of events.[18]

Purdy acknowledges this identification of a legend narration motif in the novel declaring that "in *Runner*, McNickle is a storyteller speaking to children." Accordingly, the goal of *Runner* is the education of American youth to proto-Pueblo culture and Native American civilizations.[19] Something of this narrative education approach is present when Salt and his younger sister "lay [awake] and told stories about the beasts of earth and sky—idle caricatures of the stories their elders told in high seriousness" (25). This method of utilizing traditional Native legends juxtaposed against the implicit Western stereotypes of American Indian cultures manifests the Native American intellectual tradition of Trickster-Transformation characteristic to Native oral narratives. As a literary device, trickster-transformation alters the listener's or reader's perception of the status quo via intentional deception and concomitive transformation of the *prima facie* wisdom. The device exposes a powerful irony in the author's intention of transforming the novel's readers—presumably Anglo-American youth whose forebears had applied these negative stereotypes for the conquest of the Americas—into an appreciation of pre-Columbian civilizations and support for contemporary Native American societies.

Engaging a teenage boy as hero, McNickle affirms his understanding of the responsibilities traditionally entrusted to Native youth. This claim is manifest in his scholarly work where he cites Dorthy Lee's remarks concerning Sioux boyhood; Lee had written: "A boy had a duty to develop himself, to increase in hardihood, in physical prowess, in skill, in bravery, because through enhancing himself he enhanced his society."[20] With his protagonist's long arduous journey to the valley of Mexico and his traditional running, McNickle successfully conveys these attributes of physical prowess, skill, and bravery; furthermore, his youthful readers are subtly prepared to enhance American society with a more accurate and faithful understanding of pre-Columbian Native American civilizations.

The novel manifests clear connections to the traditional indigenous cultures of the Southwest; particularly evident is an historical base centered upon the predecessors of the modern-day Hopi. Affirming this perspective, McNickle's field notes reveal an entry that provides a synopsis of Hopi history including their traditional emergence narrative and conflicts with white invaders. Purdy notes that "the entry on the Hopi contains an interesting, yet brief notation":

1—Source of Power
2—Written vs. Tradition
3—Policy vs. Tradition.[21]

These apparently obscure entries imply McNickle's understanding of a Hopi world view. In this sense, his reference to a "Source of Power" suggests the Native American metaphysic of nature and mythological epistemology. In citing "Written vs. Tradition," he is specifically acknowledging the oral character or legend motif characteristic to these societies. This action affirms the pattern of indigenous wisdom and its transmission. Further, the notation of "Policy vs. Tradition" conveys his attention to explicating Native governments and their cultural based laws. Consequently, this citation provides a clear intent to articulate a traditional world view and civilization grounded in a Native philosophical tradition. It further suggests an alternate context for reading this novel; specifically implying a narrative style characteristic to Native American methodologies. In *Runner*, McNickle describes an enchanted landscape:

> The country which held this town was so broad and flat that the horizon seemed to lie at the end of the world. The soil underfoot was light gray in color, but so thickly was the land covered with pinion and juniper and dwarf oak that the distances looked black. It was high country, a land of little rain, where rocks turned black under the sun's intensity. At day's end, after heat had poured for long hours upon the parched earth, waves of blue haze rose against the horizon until earth and sky blurred and the tops of distant turreted rocks seemed to float on empty space. The people living there sometimes called it the Enchanted Land. (2)

This description, while accurate, has a mythical quality—a place were earth and sky blur—and the reader is filled with a sense of power derived from an aesthetic experience of the infinite in McNickle's imagery.

His village of the White Rocks conveys an imaginative blending of historic Chaco Canyon and Canyon de Chelly: "At last the town would emerge out of shadow. It was not at the bottom of the chasm, but in the wall of gray rock standing opposite. Streaks of brown weathering extended downward from the top of the canyon, then disappeared where the rock bulged inward to form the roof of a cave. The houses inside the cave were perfectly sheltered. They were built of stone and stood in some places four stories high" (2–3). The metaphor of a town emerging from the shadows invokes McNickle's intent to convey an enlightened understanding of a pre-Columbian civilization. In painting this picture of Pueblo Indian culture, McNickle's *Runner* supplies a foundation for dispelling the savagism stereotypes in the ethos of American youth. His village manifests a 4,000- to 4,500-year history of maize-growing agriculturalists which is characteristic of the proto-Pueblo—including the Hopi— Anasazi cultures.[22]

The degree to which the novel can captivate and stimulate youthful understanding is evident in an anecdote that Ortiz cites in the 1987 afterward concerning a Cree student who traveled to the Southwest to retrace Salt's journey (235–36). As a Native of an extremely different cultural perspective, McNickle's Cree student was captivated by the story and its explication of pre-Columbian civilizations. Clearly this student was inspired and prepared to champion the Native American cultural heritage and civilization in the face of the stereotypes characteristic to Western ideologies. In this manner the novel speaks philosophically, preparing the literary foundations for a Native American paradigm as legitimate and substantial as either Western or Eastern world views. Moreover, McNickle's notations of Hopi world view implicitly affirm a philosophical paradigm identifying metaphysics, epistemology, and axiology; surely these perspectives may be distinguished from both Western and Eastern philosophical traditions and they are in no way inferior. *Runner*, thus, champions the study of Native American cultures within the reader's discursive heart.

Purdy has declared *Runner* as "a fictional equivalent to *They Came Here First*";[23] in affirming this claim, we may observe a correspondence of the themes of civilization between the ethnohistory and the novel. These themes are: one, the material complexity and multiplicity of Native American cultures; two, their many languages; three, a trade economy and maize agriculture; four, a system of law and peace; and five, their art and religion.

In developing the material culture for *Runner*, McNickle clearly references Chaco Canyon and Mesa Verde; he also discusses the Hohokam cultural sequence.[24] Mirroring these proto-Pueblos and their material culture in the novel, he writes of Eldest Woman's entrance into the village storeroom:

> She moved across the enclosure and squeezed herself through an entrance as narrow as the one from her sleeping room. House doors were built with a high sill that helped to check cold air from creeping in at the floor level, and their narrowness also made it easier to keep out an unwelcome intruder. In really cold weather a hanging of thick cotton cloth or a fur robe was placed over the opening.
>
> "Now, my daughters, bring your jars, or whatever you have. Here is corn, dried squash, beans, and dried meat for your babes and your ailing ones. Bring a jar here, where my hand is reaching. Our storeroom may not be bottomless, but for our mothers who are without men and our children who are without elders, we always have enough. You belong to the House of Turquoise, and there is abundance among us."
>
> Eldest Woman continued to chatter as she filled jars and baskets. Each woman, upon receiving a brimming measure in her receptacle, murmured a blessing and hurried away. In the darkness of the early dawn, none might see who came to the storehouse to receive a gift of food. No one ever spoke of such things. The names of the women, or the children, who appeared at the storehouse were never uttered in the hearing of others. (84–85)

The reader expecting savagery is transformed by passages such as this one that convey a complex material culture and a social welfare system that is free of stigmatizing poverty.

A rich multiplicity of cultures is revealed in Salt's journey to the south. With his entrance into a broad valley with many homes, a picture of a complex civilization is generated.

It was more the countryside that had altered. Looking down in astonishment upon the flood-plain, he saw a community of houses exceeding in number anything he had ever imagined. In the broad valley it seemed as if dwellings extended all the way to the horizon; not scattered aimlessly across the valley, but divided into planned sections, with roads between. The houses were of mud, fashioned in square blocks like the stones of which his own village was built, the roofs a thick covering of long bleached grass. Here and there among the houses, on low man-built earth hills, large buildings had been erected. Salt recognized these as holy places. (176–77)

Not only do these Indians plan and erect vast cities, they also have buildings for worship.

During his journey, Salt encounters a multiplicity of languages and is surprised to find some people who understand his own tongue. Despite the difficulty of communication, he follows a code of honor that is respected and he is allowed to pass undetained (127). Here, McNickle has taken the reader past the implied stereotype that all Indians speak "Indin." He further constructs the text to reveal the richness of specific languages in their shaping of inward habits of thought; this theme is manifest in *They Came Here First* where he discusses the Hopi use of tensors when qualifying meaning.[25]

The story of maize or Indian corn is a central topic of discussion in *They Came Here First*; McNickle explains its arrival among the Pueblos over 2,500 years ago. In *Runner*, the story of maize is a central vehicle of the plot and McNickle supplies vivid descriptions of this rich and complex indigenous agriculture.

Up here in the flat country were the planted fields from which the village of the White Rocks drew life and the songs that fill a life. These fields stretched from almost the rim of the canyon to the very point at which the sky came down to the land. Along this entire reach, the earth was quite level, except that it had been the bowl of an old lake. The field that belonged to Salt's family was about midway along and toward the low center. Each of the Seven Clans making up the village had its own land, and these lands, too, were marked off and a boundary post gave the sign for the clan. (75)

Later Salt is astonished by the irrigated fields and canals that he finds on his journey, which carried water to the fields (172). The widespread fields and irrigation demonstrate a rich agricultural economy, which arrests the idea that all Indians are hunters.

Perhaps his richest depiction of Southwestern Indian civilizations occurred with his attention to Native law, government and peaceful relations. As noted earlier, McNickle was impressed by the Pueblo history and centuries of peace among them. In *They Came Here First*, he describes tribal law and the young men's responsibility to keep the peace; he is particularly attentive to the Hopi system.[26] In *Runner*, he shows how this Native law is grounded in respect for elders (29) and other traditions, for example:

> It was not a lonely land. The farther south he traveled, the more thickly populated he found it. Even when he encountered no man or woman, he knew that people were nearby. Everywhere along the trail, he found wayside shrines. These might appear to be no more than a heap of rocks piled at the trailside, with bright-colored feathers attached to protruding sticks. But he never failed to take up a rock from the roadside, breathe upon it, and, as taught him in childhood, lay it atop the pile. This courtesy to the Cloud People. . . . Trailing him silently . . . they saw him perform his act of grace; thereafter he went on unmolested.
> It was not a lonely land. (174–75)

This acknowledgment of other cultures and their traditions stands in stark contrast with the savagery of the invading Europeans, and particularly in view of the Hopi elder's question to McNickle and Collier that was the impetus for the novel and therefore sets Salt on his journey. Laws, governments and systems of justice abound throughout the novel. Perhaps the most important theme McNickle conveys is the role of religion in securing respect for all. Contrast the White Rocks pueblo kiva pipe ceremony (15) with one in the valley of Mexico (190); both manifest a respect for the ultimate mysteries of life and encourage a way of life that embraces moral reciprocity. Far more faithful to Native traditions than a work by Fennimore Cooper or even La Farge, *Runner* offers a rich and complex view of Native American cultures that transforms readers' perceptions.

The savagism dogma that was used to rationalize the European and Anglo-American genocidal conquest of Native American civilizations does not withstand scrutiny. Exposing this erroneous doctrine in his ethnohistorical account, *They Came Here First*, McNickle's highly engaging pre-Columbian novel transforms the youthful reader's imagination and creates a faithful metaphorical representation of Native American cultural sophistication. In *Runner*, readers are taken beyond the idea of "discovered lands" and engage a pre-Columbian civilized society where law, peace, art, and religion occupy center stage. McNickle's emphasis upon Native laws, governments, and peaceful coexistence is quite remarkable given the political climate of 1954—the publication of *Runner* paralleled the Korean and Cold Wars.

Runner is distinguished from *They Came Here First* by several features. Through a youthful protagonist *Runner* presents a complex picture of Native civilizations that transcends juvenile fiction. McNickle's use of simile in describing the many cultures that Salt must contact throughout his journey allegorically challenges the negative stereotypes that have affected the American public's perception of Native Americans. Consequently, the novel works to arrest fantasy illusions while, at the same time, conveying historical accuracy. Nevertheless, a deeper reading derived from mythological study is possible that places *Runner* on a level with McNickle's other powerful novels.[27] McNickle, in his preface to *Runner*, declares: "Corn was, indeed, a great gift to the world; but a greater gift was one that the world let lie and never gathered up for its own. That was the gift of peace on earth" (x). With a novel born of his meditations upon an Hopi elder's difficult questions, McNickle created an allegory of that tradition's greatest promise.

Chapter Ten

Wards of the Government:
Federal Indian Policy
in "How Anger Died"

Birgit Hans

Throughout his writing career, D'Arcy McNickle was concerned
with federal Indian policy and its impact on Native American
peoples. While his nonfiction works offer historical frameworks, his novels and their manuscript versions offer a more
personal view of the policies' impacts, but none in more
detail than the manuscript version of *Wind from an Enemy
Sky*, which is titled, "How Anger Died," and deals with the
Indian Reorganization Act of 1934. The published version,
Wind from an Enemy Sky (1978), deals primarily with the
destructive power of the Allotment Act of 1887, as does *The
Surrounded* (1936).[1]

McNickle's preoccupation with changing Indian policies
in his fictions is not surprising during the early part of his
writing career, however. He had spent formative years on
the Flathead Reservation in Montana and in the Chemawa
boarding school in Oregon, exposed to the federal government's policy of assimilation and eradication of all Native
cultures. From these experiences he took away the conviction
that tribal cultures were doomed to disappear and that, in
order to achieve any measure of success, the individual Native

American had to become a part of white mainstream culture, a conviction that must have been reinforced by his European experiences. During his residence abroad (Oxford University in 1925 to 1926 and the University of Grenoble in the summer of 1931) he must have encountered either a romanticized view of the Noble Savage or, more likely, was exposed to Hitler's fascist ideas of race, i.e., the supremacy of the white Aryan. In fact, one of his short stories, "Six Beautiful in Paris," explores the idea of racial mixtures; here it is an American member of Paris's intelligentsia who raises the question of racial purity, questioning his American nephew's attachment to a Jewish girl.

On his return to the United States McNickle seems to have felt comfortable in the anonymity of the city. His diaries, though full of the financial worries and horrors of the Great Depression that was gathering momentum, do not indicate that he experienced problems because of his ethnic background. However, McNickle, who was interested in history as well as literature, observed racial biases, more or less veiled, and ethnocentrisms in contemporary works on American history. All in all though, life in the city proved interesting and stimulating for McNickle, and as late as 1932 he wrote in his diary: "I knew that I wanted to write and that I did not want to return to the scenes from which I had fled" (McNickle Collection, Newberry Library). Considering his personal experiences, the uncritical reflection of federal Indian policies in the manuscript versions of both published novels does not surprise the reader.

The year 1932, however, proved a turning point, and McNickle admitted to his growing disillusionment with American democracy, and the bitter financial pressures of the Depression forced him to reexamine the feasibility of a writing career. The birth of his first daughter in 1933 forced McNickle to make another important decision. Was he to make his stepfather's name, "Dahlberg," which he had used since his return from Chemawa after his parents' acrimonious divorce, his legal surname, or was he to return to "McNickle" and, thereby, reclaim his ethnic heritage? He not only returned to "McNickle," but he renewed contact with his mixed-blood mother. At the same time, he was drastically revising the manuscript version of *The Surrounded* into a novel that did not advocate acculturation as did the contemporary work of other Native American writers.[2]

McNickle, with his interest in politics and his daily study of newspapers, was definitely aware of the changing political climate toward Native Americans in Washington. In 1934 he expressed his changed view in a letter to Professor Gates: "my interest is that of one of the original Americans hounded into the earth who sees, at last, the beginning of a wholly devoted and wholly sincere effort to recreate the glory that was in these Americas before Christian barbarians came to impose a 'higher' civilization upon the innocents" (McNickle Collection). It is not surprising then that "How Anger Died," the extant manuscript version of his third novel, *Wind from an Enemy Sky*, which—as his diaries indicate—he had started even before *The Surrounded* was finally accepted for publication in 1935, reflects merely the possibilities inherent in the Indian Reorganization Act of 1934.[3]

While working on the earliest version of *Wind from an Enemy Sky*, McNickle was waiting to be appointed to a position in the Bureau of Indian Affairs, a step that he could not have contemplated before John Collier's reform administration. The Indian Reorganization Act, part of the New Deal for the American people, was to reverse the tragic failure of the Allotment Act and, for the first time, the federal government passed legislation that acknowledged Chief Justice John Marshall's supreme court decisions of the 1830s that Native Americans were "domestic dependent nations" with aboriginal title to their lands and a right to their own government and culture. It was a hopeful time for those tribes that adopted the

Indian Reorganization Act. Interestingly, however, McNickle, as becomes evident in "How Anger Died," did not subscribe to the general enthusiasm accorded the Indian Reorganization Act. Even during these hopeful, early years the manuscript version explored the potential of its merely being another piece of legislation that would continue to administer the "wards" of the government rather than treat Native Americans as responsible beings who should be given a voice in their own affairs.

One of the most controversial issues under the Indian Reorganization Act proved to be spirituality. In "How Anger Died" McNickle chose to use Native spirituality, in this case the recovery of the sacred Feather Boy medicine bundle that had been removed by a missionary, as a test case for the Indian Reorganization Act. Superintendent Rafferty learns about the story of the sacred bundle from one of the Little Elk tribe's old people, Two Sleeps. "Long ago," the old man begins, "when animals talked like men, the Thunderbird was flying up this way" (90). Thunderbird, whose intentions are to observe the people and help them if he can, transforms himself into a feather, something "small and soft" like the people, and impregnates a girl after he has floated down to the camp. Her son, Feather Boy, reveals himself to his mother who asks him for a reliable food source for her people. The Thunderbird, after bringing corn, beans, and squash from the south, teaches his mother how to grow these plants. Her people, who fear that he has brought evil to them, are pacified by the harvest. Ultimately, Thunderbird leaves his mother's people but a medicine bundle remains with them: "this thing from my body will protect your lives and you will never want for food" (93). At the same time, Feather Boy, the Thunderbird, issues a warning: "Be careful of it [the bundle], because if your enemies should win it from you, then all these good things will fall to them and you will starve" (93).

In the case of the Little Elk people in "How Anger Died," the government program to "civilize the Indians," i.e., to make them into farmers and Christians, has destroyed an already existing, viable horticulture established, according to legend, in mythical times. The white's idea of farming denies another tenet of Little Elk culture. "Corn, beans, and squash" were given the tribe by the Thunderbird and, therefore, they are sacred crops and their cultivation precludes their being farmed for profit. The Little Elk, as do other Native peoples, believe that everything in nature is embued with a spirit and that they should only take what is necessary for survival. In a reciprocal relationship, "corn, beans, and squash" give themselves to the Little Elk people to ensure their well-being, and the Little Elk people take care of the Feather Boy medicine bundle, the spiritual representative of agriculture. Because of inner strife the Feather Boy medicine bundle was removed by the Christian missionaries (keepers of a different spirituality), and consequently, its power was turned against the Little Elk people, upsetting the delicate balance between all elements of creation. As Feather Boy had warned them in mythical times, "all . . . good things will fall to them [your enemies] and you will starve" (93). The loss of horticulture removes the tribe's subsistence, as even Bull finally recognizes, as well as their spiritual center. Fear and lethargy set in and are quickly condemned by the whites, because they defeat their attempts to turn the Little Elk people into farmers, ranchers, and Christians. Their failure to reintroduce what they did not know they had taken away from the tribe reinforces centuries-old preconceptions: Indians refuse to be productive members of white society, that is, Indians cannot assume responsibility for themselves and will become—if they are not already—mere relics.

McNickle also addresses the basic irony in the relationship of the federal government and Native American tribes. The government bases its Indian policy on stereotypes and misconceptions as old as the Euroamerican settlement of the continent itself. All Native American tribes, federal authorities firmly believe, chase the buffalo and refuse to farm the land, that is, to make effective use of the land by Euroamerican standards. The advent of a superior race, the white race, dooms the Native cultures. McNickle's description of the Commissioner of Indian Affairs' office in "How Anger Died" shows that the myth of the "Vanishing Indian" is still very much alive: "On the wall behind him was a massive show-case filled with the relics of a life that was rapidly falling into dust—Sioux war bonnets, an infant's cradle board, ponder-ously decorated pipe stems, painted rawhide shields, a buckskin dress heavy with beadwork mossaic, weapons and tools of a lost economy. On the wall behind Rafferty a pen-dulum clock beat the grave seconds away" (154–55). McNickle refers to the objects displayed on the wall as "relics," obsolete reminders of a life that has already disappeared, according to the adminstration that chooses not to distinguish between the physical and spiritual life of the various tribes.

Interestingly, the objects are either decaying or full of dust, but they cover all aspects of stereotyped "Indian" life: war, child rearing, and dress. These objects, once part of the every-day life of the Plains Indians, are reduced to mere decorations, and indifferent decorations at that, since they are permitted to decay in the office of the man appointed to preserve them. That their fading is linked with the Indians' vanishing culture is emphasized by the clock whose audible beat removes these "relics" further and further from contemporary life. The Commissioner of Indian Affairs, barricaded behind his desk like an executive administering objects instead of people, chooses to maintain the fiction of the disappearing and decaying Indian culture.

The Commissioner's encounters with Bull, the traditional leader of the Little Elk people, and Mrs. Johnny Two-and-a-Half illustrate that attitude. Bull's promise to cooperate with the Bureau of Indian Affairs' policies and programs provokes only an inane response: "I am glad to know you feel that way about your superintendent. I'm sure he is also gratified" (160). Eaton's inability to talk to and understand the people in his charge becomes even more obvious in his encounter with Mrs. Johnny Two and-a-Half during his official visit to the Little Elk Reservation:

> He [Commissioner Eaton] did not want to talk, since anything he said would only encourage her to begin a general conversation or possibly even to ask for some favor. It was always that way with Indians—if you said "Good day" to one of them, he immediately expected his share of the money paid for Manhattan Island. . . .
> He yielded and greeted her with "How!" He repressed an impulse to raise an open palm.
> "How are you?" the woman asked.
> At that, he stopped with one foot on the lower step and looked intently in her face. She seemed to lean toward him, returning his gaze.
> "I am fine, thank you. You speak English?"
> "Not too good. They understand me here O.K. except when I ask for more lease money for my land. Then they act dumb, these Agency people." (248–49)

Clearly, Commissioner Eaton has had very little exposure to Indian cultures, and he does not wish for any physical contact with the Indian people he administers. After all, he already knows what to expect and, as an administrator, he is interested in objects, not humans. The government's inability to look beyond the stereotypes and preconceptions about Native peoples denies the richness, variety and endurance of contemporary Native American cultures.

In the manuscript, "How Anger Died," the Indian Reorganization Act is ineffective in changing existing attitudes, since federal Indian policy is made by government officials in Washington. It better suits their purpose to consider Natives faceless "wards of the government." The figurehead administrator of the Bureau of Indian Affairs gets positive character references from various political and religious groups, but he is the subject of severe political pressure and without any real power. He will only support Rafferty's plans to restore the tribe's land base, if the Superintendent does not get "too radical," in other words if he does not contest the Bureau's long-term leases of tribal lands to white ranchers. The Indian Reorganization Act may acknowledge the Native Americans' right to their land, but white ranchers and farmers currently utilizing the tribe's land ultimately have the stronger Washington lobby. He states his position clearly in a talk with Rafferty:

> "I want to tell you something, Mr. Rafferty. Before I accepted this job, I was convinced, as I take it you are, that the Indians should use what they have, timber, land, everything. I was in Congress before I moved in here. I'd been watching this Indian business. When I went up to meet the President and he asked me what I meant to do for the redmen, that was the one thing I had in mind and I expressed myself in plain language. How do you think he reacted? He smiled. 'Go to it,' he said. But he smiled. Now I know why."
>
> "I don't follow you. What did he mean?"
>
> "He didn't think it would work, and he was right. Sometimes it's the Indians. We turn land over to them, with wagons, plows, harness, seeds, a farmer to show them how to put the things together—and then nothing happens. And then again, a man like Senator Newmark gets so purturbed [sic] and raises such cain that we don't even get started. The President knew his Indian business a little bit better than I did when he asked me the question." (153)

The Commissioner's words are frightening in their matter-of-factness; his idealism has evaporated along with the will to fight for what he believed in. Indian policy is regarded as mere "business" and, consequently, depends on the business interests of other groups. The Commissioner finds it easier to manage the situation if he maintains his distance from the people it will affect. In keeping with this attitude, he refuses to listen to Bull, who tries to explain to him the importance of Feather Boy: "Feather Boy is our power. If we have him, we will use the land just like you say. We will get along fine" (159). Ultimately, Feather Boy becomes the symbol of defeat for the Commissioner.

In "How Anger Died" political pressure is brought to bear primarily through the state senator who represents the ranchers. Their attitude toward the Native Americans from whom they lease the land has certainly not been altered by the change in Indian policy, which has officially shifted from assimilation to limited self-determination. Arguing with Superintendent Rafferty, one of the ranchers says: "We figure they're part of our country and we see to it they get something to eat. It's worth remembering" (47). Their using *our* during an interview with the white superintendent deliberately excludes the Little Elk people. Since they do not make proper use of the land by the ranchers' and farmers' standards, they have no right to it. Long-term leases, in leaseholders' minds, have transferred the ownership of the land to them. Senator Newmark, trying to intimidate Superintendent Rafferty, expresses this idea without hesitation:

> "Some of the men who run cattle on the Little Elk range have been talking to me—in a friendly, over-the back-fence sort of way, understand. Nothing official. Some of those men have been using that range for ten, fifteen years. It's good range, as you know. Lots of water and the grass always reliable. Those fellows can't afford to move, even if there was some place for them to move to. Which there isn't. . . .
> "The Indians get along. They always do. I know the Indians and they always get special consideration from me. But you know their needs are simple, not like the rest of us. Give an Indian a pair of pants and a little meat—Besides, you know as well as I do, they don't want to use that land. You throw good stockmen out of business, and what do you get? Something that you wouldn't want to gamble on." (150–51)

The choice of whom to support, the ranchers or Rafferty and the Little Elk people, is not really a choice for Senator Newmark who represents both groups in the capital. He knows "the Indians," but his "special consideration[s]" are limited to physical things, clothes and food. His statement is reminiscent of the earlier treaty negotiations of the United States with Native peoples all over the North American continent; there, too, similar goods were "magnanimously" given in compensation for the cession of huge tracts of land and used to discipline the Native peoples. The Senator looks back on a long, well-established tradition that legitimizes his political pressure on the Commissioner of Indian Affairs and that frees him essentially from all moral restraints.

Land, to the Senator as well as the ranchers, simply means profit; there is no spirituality involved, no reciprocal relationship with the land. Capitalism, therefore, is a revered element of democracy and even replaces legal rights if it must. The Little Elk people are not even protected by American law that, ironically, was forced on them by the federal government, first, with the establishment of the reservations and, later, by the Allotment Act and citizenship. In contrast to the nebulous "[t]he Indians" who are not even dignified by their tribal name, the ranchers are friends, neighbors and—most importantly—voters. If Senator Newmark wishes to remain in Washington, he cannot afford to let go of his ethnocentrism. Federal policy toward Native Americans may have changed, but the Senator is dependent on his constituents, and their attitude toward Native Americans is not dictated by legislation but by more practical, economical considerations. He simply refuses to listen to the politically weaker part of his constituency and, thereby, denies it the basic rights of American people.

Another powerful political group is the Missionary Board as represented by Reverend Welles. Being Christian—a vital element of being civilized—means, to Reverend Welles, blind obedience to the dictates of the church and simply abandoning all prior beliefs. There is no attempt even to find out what is being replaced: "The Indian people start from origins about which we speculate but know next to nothing" (61). The Little Elk people's origin story of agriculture is dismissed, and their reluctance to relinquish their hold on a "heathenish" past makes the Little Elk people into an even more inferior species that will never attain the same level—intellectually and morally—as Euroamericans:

> "We do know that the effect of that original beginning has been to produce a people who are quite unlike us—in attitude—in outlook—and in destination, unless we forcefully change the destination. . . .
> "The Indian, sir, is anti-civilization. I would call him anti-humanity. Because of the place he started from, and the road he has traveled, he is not where we are now and is not even going our way. When we talk across the distance to him, he dissolves and we never touch him. If there were two humanities, I would say he was with the other body. Since there is but one human family, and the Indian is within it, I can only describe his relationship to the rest of the family by saying that he is both opposed to it and escaping from it." (61)

Indians in Welles's view are something apart, only grudgingly considered human. They will never hold a place among the civilized peoples of the world. His prediction is that the Native peoples will become extinct, which is, in his own mind, a reasonable solution of the Indian-white conflict. The disposal of the Feather Boy bundle requires no justification in Welles's eyes, since this symbol of a barely human superstition was replaced by enlightened Christianity.

Thus, McNickle exposes a rather common and pernicious attitude towards Native American spiritual beliefs. As recently as May 1992, Andy Rooney expressed similar ideas in the *Chicago Tribune*:

> They [Native peoples] hang onto remnants of their religion and superstitions that may have been useful to savages 500 years ago but which are meaningless in 1992. No one would force another

religion on them but what if an Indian belief, involving ritualistic dances with strong sexual overtones, is demeaning to Indian women and degrading to Indian women and degrading to Indian children? Should they, on Indian land within the United States, be encouraged, with government money, to continue that? Should Indians be preserved on reservations like the redwoods and the American eagle, or should they join the mainstream?

Welles also reflects, of course, a more fully developed version of the young priest in the earlier novel, *The Surrounded*. Interestingly, it is the old missionary in that earlier novel, Father Grepilloux, who symbolizes the religious tolerance his successors should be required to have under the Indian Reorganization Act. Locked into their struggle to save souls (even if it killed the person as Richard Henry Pratt, the pioneer of government boarding schools put it) and supported by a powerful lobby in Washington, the missionaries simply continue their practice in the way most of them have always done.

McNickle, while writing the manuscript version of *Wind from an Enemy Sky*, had also reached a point in his personal development that permitted him to reevaluate his view of the early missionaries. Father Grepilloux in *The Surrounded* is a larger-than-life reminder of what could have been if the white ranchers in the Flathead Valley had included the Flathead in their dream of an agrarian paradise. The ranchers' greed and federal Indian policy were responsible for the failure of that dream and, therefore, Father Grepilloux fails as a cultural mediator. Even in *The Surrounded* Father Grepilloux is seen as an exceptional individual rather than the representative of the Church. The deception of the altar, which turns out to be nothing but a beautiful facade to conceal a shabby space, is closely aligned with the description of the young priest whose concern is merely the *form* of worship.

McNickle's diaries indicate that he was working on "How Anger Died" in the 1940s, after he joined the Bureau of Indian Affairs. The knowledge of the inner workings of the

Bureau displayed in "How Anger Died" lend verisimilitude to his discussion of federal policies and the political pressures brought to bear on the Bureau by special interest groups such as, for instance, the Missionary Board. These experiences led McNickle to a very different evaluation of missionary work from that in *The Surrounded*. No longer can an individual representative of the Church represent its ideals. Mr. Welles is given no redeeming qualities, none of the affection and understanding for the Native peoples in his charge that are associated with Father Grepilloux. Instead, Mr. Welles sees the "savage butchering committed by the Indians" (60) in terms of gain for the missionaries: "A man who has dedicated his life to God and loses it in the battle of faith, derives a fulfilling glory which his co-workers must ever keep bright" (60). The possibility of martyrdom is even more attractive than conversion, especially if the Native peoples are regarded as a part of humanity that is different and inferior. One belief system must replace the other wholesale and, according to the Church in "How Anger Died," the Little Elk people can have no say in their spiritual destination. The Churches, no matter whether Catholic or Protestant, remain fossilized, unreceptive to new ideas, and intolerant.

It is most disturbing that, with the exception of Adam Pell whose museum houses the Feather Boy medicine bundle, none of the administrators in Washington or "Friends of the Indians" asks what the Little Elk people want. McNickle makes this point even more forcefully in *Wind from an Enemy Sky*. In the novel's published version Pell is as willing to return Feather Boy as he is in "How Anger Died." He is aware of the medicine bundle's cultural and spiritual significance. Feather Boy, however, has been destroyed by rats in his museum basement and Pell offers a golden statue as replacement. The underlying assumption is that each "primitive" faith is the same and the fetish of one primitive culture can be replaced with that of another. Furthermore, the monetary value of the gold statue far outweighs that of the bundle, as he is careful to point out. Bull shoots him. At the end of *Wind from an Enemy Sky* no hope remains for the Little Elk people; the spiritual destruction of the Native peoples will lead inevitably to their physical destruction. While McNickle expresses his doubts about the Indian Reorganization Act in the manuscript version, "How Anger Died," he does not consider the situation desperate, merely unchanged on the federal level. Ultimately, though, his long personal involvement in federal Indian policy bore out his initial scepticism and, perhaps, cautious optimism but at the end of his life, he was pessimistic about the relationship of the federal government and Native peoples.

"How Anger Died" ends with Adam Pell returning the Feather Boy medicine bundle to its rightful owners, unharmed and even refurbished. The return of the bundle by plane parallels the mythical arrival of Feather Boy among the people. At the conclusion of the spectacular and melodramatic scene, heavy rain clouds build up. As Bull opens the bundle, a thunderstorm erupts over the parched land to ensure, once more, the food supply of the Little Elk people, as it had done in the centuries before its disappearance. For the Little Elk people who know the legend, Feather Boy is a bringer of change. In the legend he brought the people seeds and taught them horticulture. The bundle's return encourages the Little Elk people to learn about cattle raising from their superintendent. The spiritual power that the medicine bundle has, despite its decades in Pell's Institute of the Americas, will help the people accommodate to a changed world without losing their spirituality. The Commissioner of Indian Affairs, forced against his will to accept the return of Feather Boy and reinstate the reservation's superintendent whom he has fired, is pressured by Adam Pell's political clout and the news media to act on the spirit of the Indian Reorganization Act rather than doing so by conviction. As Bull points out just before Feather Boy's return and after Rafferty's dismissal: "My superintendent had me believing that maybe they had made a new law in Congress and that Indians would be treated like white people because of it. Now I see there is no such law and Indians are the same as always—not like dogs, because they have only two legs, and not like horses, because they cannot feed their bellies on grass. Just Indians" (269). It is the individual Rafferty and his willingness to face repercussions that make a difference on the Little Elk Reservation and not the official change in Indian policy.[4]

Help, according to "How Anger Died" and some of Mc-Nickle's short fiction as well, can only be expected on a local, tribal, and personal level after mutual respect has been established. People like Pell are to be considered exceptions that confirm the rule. Even that basic human understanding cannot be expected of the majority of agency employees who rarely manage to look beyond established stereotypes and prejudices, despite their daily encounters with Native American people. "There were lady clerks here," Rafferty's secretary tells him, "who barred their doors every night and tied their scalps on with lacey caps" (35). Another agency employee responds to Rafferty's reform idea:

"You talked like an injun lover." . . .

"Been in the Service twenty years now. Apache, Blackfeet, Pine Ridge, Kiowa. Indians is all alike. Haven't seen 'em change a hair in twenty years. Government goes on a spending money and doing things. Indians just sit there looking on." . . .

"You can't shoot 'em, you can't move 'em out, you can't let 'em alone. All you can do is spend money on 'em." (193–94)

Rafferty describes the school on the reservation as following the dictates of the assimilation era, which was so much a part of the Allotment Act nearly fifty years earlier: "It [the school] followed a curriculum of sheer nonsense puffed into imbecility by a handful of nasal-toned, shirtwaisted old girls" (37).

It is the school curriculum, however, that Rafferty manages to infuse with the spirit of the Indian Reorganization Act. Ignoring the rigidity of the teachers and the incompetence of the principal, he manages to introduce a viable, cultural education for the Little Elk people. The curriculum will reflect their needs as residents of the Little Elk Reservation rather than the white bureaucracy's idea of required information for members of mainstream society. The entire agency personnel, with the exception of Rafferty's secretary and the doctor, take their cues from the Commissioner as the representative of the federal government in Washington, and like him, find it easier to "administrate" than to rethink their ethnocentric views and the prejudices that are reaffirmed on a weekly basis by Mr. Welles's sermons. Consequently, they turn against Rafferty and provide the reasons for Rafferty's dismissal on the Commissioner's arrival on the reservation.

McNickle portrays Superintendent Rafferty as a rare being whose courage in opposing the Commissioner and the federal government as well as the ranchers and the church is exceptional. Bull says of him: "I will say he is the first superintendent who hasn't tried to steal from us. The first who has never lied to us. . . . For the first time our people are not afraid of the Government man, and that's a good thing" (158). Ironically, the support of the Little Elk people, those "wards" whose guardian he is, does not count with the federal government. Even if disagreements with the federal government do not lead to the loss of their jobs, superintendents with Rafferty's commitment ultimately pay a high, mental price. McNickle describes this additional burden in his short story "Snowfall," which developed from "How Anger Died": " 'We don't just grow old,' Ephraim Morse would tell his wife, explaining himself and his brothers in service. 'We pass through ten lifetimes. We become a walking tomb of people who died waiting for a short word from us, when we had to wait on somebody else. We bury them, then carry them with us' " (76).

In "How Anger Died" federal legislation has very little impact on the spiritual universe of most of the Little Elk people, but it has caused a deep chasm between their spiritual universe and their physical existence. Unfortunately, Bull is the only, somewhat developed Native American character in "How Anger Died"; however, throughout the manuscript the reader gets glimpses of an older, perhaps mythical relationship between all beings, a spiritual realm whose very existence holds out hope for bridging the chasm. The medicine bundle is responsible for healing the breach between Bull and his uncle Henry Jim that was caused by Bull's killing an agency employee and the subsequent loss of Feather Boy. Animals might not talk like men anymore, as they did in mythical times when the Thunderbird came, but there is a spiritual bond between them and Native peoples that Christianity has not yet managed to destroy. One example is Henry Jim's horse that commits suicide after his death. To prove that the bond still exists, the Feather Boy/Thunderbird medicine bundle, the physical representation of the union between the powerful mythical spirit and a woman, retains its power, despite its thirty-year captivity. As Bull says to the Commissioner of Indian Affairs: "Feather Boy is our power. If we have him, we will use the land just like you say" (159). They will return to the life and horticulture they had before government interference; however, the return of their medicine bundle also reminds them of the inevitability of change. Decades of senseless, extreme poverty were caused by the Euroamericans' unwillingness to listen.

It is obvious from the manuscript, that in the 1930s and 1940s McNickle believed that the Indian Reorganization Act had very little impact, since the change in federal Indian policy was as usual implemented by those geographically removed from the daily reality of Native American life by those caught up in their stereotypes, prejudices, and ethnocentric views, and by those involved in political power games.

The federal government's inability, even disinterest, to look beyond established biases inherited from colonial governments dooms the Indian Reorganization Act, which would affirm aboriginal rights of Native American tribes.

Federal legislation, McNickle asserts, can only be effective if the government ceases to administer the "wards," those faceless Indians, and learns to recognize tribal cultures and their varying and viable traditions. In the manuscript version this discernment is only possible for the individual government official, the superintendent of the Little Elk people. In the published version, however, thirty years later, McNickle has lost even that hope; in *Wind from an Enemy Sky* the superintendent also becomes the victim of cultural and administrative insensitivity. According to the later novel, the federal government will never be able to put aside the burden of history and will continue to do its "duty to its wards."

McNickle's novels, *The Surrounded* and *Wind from an Enemy Sky*, both deal with the Allotment Act whose enduring, destructive power remains a reality for tribes even today. That piece of legislation certainly had profound impact on McNickle's own life growing up in rural Montana. The difficulties of dealing with his mixed blood heritage, his time at the Chemawa boarding school at a time when unconditional assimilation was official governmental policy, and the sale of his allotment on the Flathead Reservation to finance his education at Oxford University had certainly weakened McNickle's ties to his heritage. His complete rejection of all things Indian as a city dweller was followed by a slow rediscovery of his "Indianness," but, McNickle never reestablished his ties to the Flathead Reservation. He talks about the problems of urbanization in "John Collier's Vision":

> Urbanization had uprooted populations, destroyed neighborhoods, impoverished the relationship between generations, expanded enormously such escape devices as commercialized recreation, and favored the lowest common denominator in

entertainment and mass communication. In all this urbanized man stood bewildered, confronting ultimate destruction. (718) It may yet happen that fragmented, depersonalized urban man will give thanks that the Indians were not totally destroyed. (719)

Of course, urbanization here refers to the relocation policy of the government in the 1950s, another attempt to force assimilation. McNickle had "relocated" earlier, in the late 1920s; nevertheless, the impact had been the same. He, too, had become one of the "uprooted populations." The loss of his specific tribal heritage may explain why McNickle turned to writing nonfiction after the publication of *The Surrounded* and why *Wind from an Enemy Sky* and its manuscript version use a fictional tribe and are highly didactic in nature.

The Indian Reorganization Act roughly marked the beginning of another important stage of McNickle's life, his reclaiming of his Native heritage. The intent of this piece of legislation made it morally acceptable for McNickle to work for the federal government, but its official rejection also marked his resignation from the Bureau of Indian Affairs in 1952. It is not surprising then that the federal legislation that had had such an impact on his own life would play such a prominent role in his published fiction.

Chapter Eleven

Two Humanities:
Mediational Discourse in
Wind from an Enemy Sky

James Ruppert

D'Arcy McNickle spent years revising his novel, *Wind from an Enemy Sky*, in order to reflect his experience in white/ Native affairs. Some of that experience was gained under the auspices of the Bureau of Indian Affairs (BIA), some with pan-tribal organizations like the American Indian Development fund and the National Congress of American Indians, and in a personal capacity as critic, editor, and teacher. He wrote in 1976, "The present draft of the novel is the last of many versions of the story I attempted over a twenty year period. I experienced many interruptions in the writing, and each interruption seemed to result in a new approach to the material. . . . About two years ago I returned to the manuscript and rewrote the entire script in about six months" (Purdy 106).

John Purdy perceptively discusses some of the revisions in the novel's development, and in considering these revisions, one thing is clear: McNickle tried with each draft to refocus his message while he reconstituted the text. The interruptions from novel writing gave McNickle new insights into how best to construct a text to move his readers. Certainly how his audience reacted to the text was of utmost importance to McNickle. His purpose was also mediative: McNickle aimed to reeducate both Native and non-Native readers so they could better understand each other's cultural codes. *Wind from an Enemy Sky* was his last and best attempt to illuminate the cognitive structures in this cross-cultural dynamic, reflecting years of personal experience and his refined literary talent.

Part of the novel's success derives from the agile manner in which McNickle satisfies the expectations of a Native and non-Native audience. The role of each implied reader can be deduced by following the shifts in textual perspectives and by identifying the cultural discourse fields surrounding each reader's role. The text attempts to reinforce enough of each reader's precognitive epistemology in order not to alienate, yet it strives to restructure insights to allow each reader to perceive textual meaning with new appreciation, and also to move that insight into socio-political actions. This process is called mediation.[1]

Starting from the supposition that McNickle addressed both a non-Native and a Native reader, it is fruitful to explore the nature of those readers as implied in the roles assigned each by McNickle. Wolfgang Iser's construction of the implied reader is useful as a model, but with modifications. Iser, for example, does not take into theoretical consideration the existence of two separate implied readers, one with a Western values system and another capable of applying both Native and Western values to events in the text. By defining the cognitive position of his readers in relation to their appropriate discourse fields, McNickle establishes a starting point for them. He then positions each to move through the shifting textual perspectives on events in the novel. As implied readers move through the text, they develop a new perception of the meaning of the text and a new way of thinking about the world around them.

As a mediative enterprise then, *Wind from an Enemy Sky* must engage not only the reader's present perception but respond to the discourse field upon which the text builds because the field is the source of those perceptions. Reading the novel then could become a crosscultural event. As both implied readers become aware of the discourse field of the other, they begin Mikhail Bakhtin's ideological translation and come to an appreciation of the goals of such discourse. The readers also begin to perceive the intersubjectivity or intertextuality of the novel's discourse. A useful way of discussing this dimension is to apply in a cultural context Donald Bialostosky's formulation of the "dialogic conversation" in order to understand the nature of the discourse field that each new text advances.[2]

Wind From an Enemy Sky has at least two cultural conversations and a dual set of textual and cultural goals. While we may assume that readers can easily reconstruct how McNickle appreciated the cultural conversation of the dominant culture in the early 1970s, we may have more trouble identifying the outlines of the cultural conversation addressed to the implied Native reader.

The trend of much of the research on contemporary Native American written literature has been to seek out the cultural referents from specific tribal traditions in order to understand the cultural conversation in the narrative. Indeed some critics suggest that we should examine writers primarily in the context of their tribal traditions. According to this perspective, Leslie Silko's is seen as contributing only to Laguna literature and Simon Ortiz's work only to Acoma literature. While there is some value to this approach, the methodology does not really delineate the ways in which the discourse of a text may be addressed to a non-Laguna or non-Acoma Native audience as well. For *Wind from an Enemy Sky* such a cultural approach would yield only limited insights, for though McNickle drew on his tribal experience for some background, the book addressed a pan-tribal audience in ways that none of his other novels did. In other words, McNickle used his appreciation of Native thought and values to create a pan-tribal cognitive system for the novel rather than promote Cree, Salish, or any other specifically tribal outlook. It is in this broader context that the Native cultural conversation is framed.

This position also gives him a flexible standpoint from which to address his non-Native implied reader. McNickle viewed his mainstream American implied reader as someone who knew little of actual Native American life and thought, but who had some interest in the Indian. McNickle obviously knew he needed to break the stereotype of the stoic Native traditionalist obstructing the benefits of progress for no good reason. For years the author had aimed to negate stereotypes in his ethnohistorical writing and in his previous novels. His approach in *Wind* was to define "the map of the mind" (125) of his Native American characters, or as John Purdy puts it, "to attract his readers into his primary lesson: an understanding of how and why, the Indians react as they do" (128). To show why Indians reacted as they did, McNickle condensed various elements of Native American cultures and sought to establish this map for a non-Native implied reader; moreover, he included in *Wind* some overtly political discourse directing it toward the non-Native reader who lived during the social upheaval of the 1960s.

During those years, the counterculture resurrected many romantic images of the Indian. Frederick Turner gives perhaps the best outline of white romantic thinking about Native Americans in his Introduction to *The Portable North American Indian Reader*. Turner identified six essential 1960s beliefs: the Indian was (1) the original ecologist, (2) the original communist with a small "c", (3) not an aggressive fighter, (4) a natural democrat, (5) noncompetitive, and (6) wise because the Native was prescientific (10).

By 1974, the image of the peace loving, communal, spiritual Indian was tarnished by the violence of AIM and Wounded Knee. Many liberal readers were taken aback. In the early seventies *Black Elk Speaks* had reached innumerable readers and brought awareness of injustice while reinforcing a sense of Indian nobility. As McNickle finished the last draft of *Wind*, interest in and confusion about Indians was at a high point. His narrative, set in a past era, was meant to explain something of the cultural differences that kept the dominant culture from understanding Native Americans. This temporal distancing allowed him to avoid a defense of AIM-type violence; he argued though that suppression of Native rights would inevitably lead to violence.

In 1973 McNickle published a revised version of *The Indian Tribes of the United States*. He used its introduction to address the 1972 takeover of the BIA and the events at Wounded Knee in the spring of 1973. Like a good historian, McNickle advised his readers of the persistent pattern of federal usurpation of Native American rights and the specifically odious Eisenhower years of termination and relocation: he then linked the present violence and the divisiveness created in Native American communities with the detrimental effect of outside interference in the internal social dynamic of change, even if that interference was with the best of good will. He concluded:

> Older Indians had tried to live with that reality, seeing no way around it, hence their unwillingness to challenge the forces around them. If they waited and talked quietly among themselves, perhaps the forces would wither away and they would not have to surrender what was left.
>
> So the anger of the young was in part directed at the old men of the tribe, but that was anger within the family. The real targets were the men in far places, of good faith or bad, who still thought themselves as the only proper source of Indian well being.
>
> It now seems likely after Washington and Wounded Knee, that anger will hang in the air, like a combustible vapor, for some

time to come. Indian Americans need assurance that riots are not essential preliminaries for purposeful talk. (xiii)

McNickle's literary texts are suffused with social insights. It is not a large step to see how this political discourse becomes dramatized in Bull's initial unwillingness to challenge the forces around him and his hope that they will wither away, or in Jim's anger with the old men of the tribe who were holding the people back. McNickle's viewpoint is apparent in many passages such as when Iron Child concludes that Henry Jim was not to blame for the quarrel that has split the tribe, but rather that the white intrusion is to blame and that the tribe reacted as it did because it was "losing out" (84) to the whites. Pell's actions in constructing the dam and in offering the gold statue not only characterize him as the type of reformer with which McNickle must have dealt, but also reveal him to be one of those "in far places" who think they know what is best for the Indian. While in the previously cited passage McNickle was speaking of anger in the air following Wounded Knee, *Wind from an Enemy Sky* also expresses anger: white anger over the killing and perceived backwardness of the Natives, and Indian anger over continued white domination and oppression. In the tragedy at the end, Indian anger finally explodes. McNickle hopes that riots are not essential, yet *Wind* can be read as implying that they might prepare the ground for purposeful political talk, if only to discuss the causes of violence. This foregrounding of overtly political Native perceptions introduces the non-Native implied reader to the causes of Indian anger and frustration. Moreover, the sense of the inadequacy of non-Native understanding of Indian thought (best exemplified by Pell) keeps the implied non-Native reader from rushing into a specific solution. Implied non-Native readers are led to see that the "real targets" are those like themselves who come with solutions to Indian problems.

McNickle's writings and correspondence contain a number of explicitly political passages since his insights and attitudes were honed over decades of work at the cross-cultural barricades. It is also important for an understanding of McNickle's text to focus on the ways the novel engages non-Native discourse of the 1970s on a cultural as well as political basis.

Throughout the novel there is a conscious effort to contrast a number of important cultural concepts: sources of knowledge, senses of the past, ideas of justice, the roles of leaders, modes of education, and appropriate use of land to name only a few. This mediating exploration of epistemology and cultural values is embedded to evoke a greater sense of tolerance and understanding in the non-Native reader, while validating the Native world view for the implied Native reader. There are many sections in which McNickle directly addresses his readers, adopting a position similar to oral storytellers who will insert direct interpretation into their tellings. These intrusions serve to prevent the non-Native reader from making quick conclusions about the meaning of events. For example, he reminds us how difficult it is "to translate one man's life to another's" (26), or he comments that "ends are never seen in beginnings" (238). Rafferty's realization that he must judge others by their fitness to their world, and that the Little Elk have a different map of mind (125), makes him more willing to listen before he acts. Pell's insight that Native ideas are rational, though they work from "different data and a different order of reality" (210) is similarly enlightening for him. However, Pell's assumptions are fundamentally wrong and when translated into action, they precipitate tragedy. Pell's and Rafferty's revelations negate stereotypes without acknowledging that Native American world view is something that can be learned by non-Natives.

These authorial intrusions and moments of illumination by key non-Native characters open up some elbow room for Native culture and thought. They reveal acceptable attitudes for implied non-Native readers to identify with, but the cautionary quality of these attitudes, and the fact that they are foregrounded in the text, encourage the non-Native reader to delay the construction of the meaning from that which has passed over the event horizon of the text.

The use of contrasting sections acknowledges a history of non-Native discourse about Natives that has not included Native voices. McNickle reinstates the Native voice by adopting the storyteller's stance and allowing the character Henry Jim to do so too. Jim cannot shape an action in the present without telling a story from the past, a story "carried back to the beginnings." He explains, "today talks in yesterday's voice, the old people said. The white man must hear yesterday's voice" (28). To shape the actions of today, McNickle's novel tells a story of the past, of an imaginary Indian tribe at the time of a reform administration and its great dam building projects similar to the ones in the United States in the 1930s. As he does so, he reestablishes the non-Native discourse field about Indians, especially through characters like Marshal Sid Grant, Adam Pell, and Reverend Stephen Welles. Reverend Welles voices the bitter conviction of the failed missionary: "The Indian people start from origins about which we speculate but know next to nothing. . . . The Indian is anticivilization! . . . If there were two humanities, I'd say he is with the other party. . . . They will not abandon the old and the familiar, if left to themselves. They can only choose what they have always known, and that choice means extinction for them" (51–52). These convictions express the old belief that whites must "kill the Indian to save the man," for the only means of survival is to wrench the Indian from traditional culture and force the adoption of mainstream American culture.

In contrast to this late-nineteenth century and early-twentieth century rhetoric is the discourse of reformers such as Adam Pell. Pell, the romanticist, who has made a hobby of Indians, has modern progressive plans. He believes that the Indians are capable of being empowered. He says of the Peruvian Indians, "When opportunity came to them they were quite capable of adopting new ideas" (145). The opportunity, however, is created by one rich non-Native who has a vision of how to better the lives of the oppressed Natives. He initiates a plan of social reform devised by himself. Through the concerted actions of one individual, Carlos, "an extraordinary human community" develops where "people were discovering what it meant to be human" (148). Pell wants his actions to live up to this dream. He sees something better than wardship for the Indians and acknowledges the failure of previous interfering plans, but still must try to meddle to "restore something of what they lost through my carelessness" (234). He acts under the reformist belief that his values can be transferred to another group of people.

These threads of discourse form the contemporary historical and cultural conversation about Indians and their relationship to European America. McNickle lets the character Rafferty learn and grow through his responses to the frontier, missionary, and reformist discourse about Indians. As he does so, he assumes the role implied for the non-Native reader. Rafferty's introduction to Native life is gradual. He adopts a reasonable attitude, which serves as a model for the implied non-Native reader. As his awareness of the externally created problems of the Little Elk Indians grows, his sincere desire to help establishes a paradigm for the non-Native readers looking for a way to respond to the problems presented in the text. Yet even Rafferty does not embody the restrained role that McNickle wished contemporary America would adopt. As Rafferty dies, so also does the in-text substitute reader—the non-Native reader who started the book. The specific constellation of attitudes of that self must die as well so that the cultural conversation can evolve past even reformist thinking. McNickle wants the non-Native implied reader to hear the voice of yesterday before advocating the actions of today.

As the non-Native discourse field about Natives is explored, countered, and expanded, one of the primary formal elements of this mediational goal takes shape. What starts out as a murder mystery quickly changes into the type of mystery known as a procedural, since we know who is the killer and only the questions of whether they will find him, and why he did it remain. Yet after awhile it is hard for most readers to sustain a strong desire to take Pock-Face to trial and hang him. It seems ever so much more reasonable that the Indian system of justice should prevail and the two families should get together and settle the problem. Sid Grant proves to be an arrogant, intrusive detective. Because of his smug and superior frontier manner and his automatic assumption of Indian culpability, non-Native implied readers start to lose not only identification with him, but with the system of justice he represents. The scene in Rafferty's office, which brings all the principals together, is a perfect parody of the murder mystery convention where the detective assembles the suspects to reveal the murderer. In *Wind*, however, the murderer unexpectedly confesses, and nobody knows exactly what to do about it. The Indians expect that they must immediately respond in order to compensate the family. The whites want Pock-Face to remain quiet. They are uncomfortable, expecting impersonal legal proceedings that will, as Bull says, make everyone angry. The two perceptions of justice are juxtaposed in a convention of non-Native discourse concerning the murder mystery. The non-Native belief that revealing the murderer will lead to justice is thwarted. In the conventions of the murder mystery, the revelation of the murderer brings closure and a sense of understanding, but here only more questions are created. When faced with people holding different cultural attitudes about the individual's responsibility toward society and the spiritual world, the Native concept of justice highlights the inadequacy of the Western concept of justice. More importantly, that implied reader is pushed to reexamine how to make sense of the death and the events leading up to it. The non-Native reader is encouraged to reconsider the circumstances in text that have slipped over the event horizon in order to understand how meaning has developed.

The Native implied reader might feel that a Native world view is validated, but the murder is sufficiently random that it does not fit comfortably into a Native sense of personal justice. The question to be examined is how does this Native sense of justice fit into a new, modern world. The mystery for this reader involves the question of whether Feather Boy will be returned. Epistemologically, the issue is the significance of a medicine bundle: Why is it so important and how can it influence the life of a people? On a more practical social level, the question becomes: what will the Little Elk people do if it is not returned? By the end of the novel, the cultural conversation about Native Americans is engaged and redirected, first into a contemporary discussion about violence and then into a validation of a different world view. With this textual shift in perspective, the conventions of discourse about Natives and the Western system of justice are appropriated for decidedly Native goals.

Of course key determinants in all readers' responses are the questions asked of Antoine in the beginning that resurface in the middle and at the end of the novel: What did you see? What did you learn? What will you remember? (8, 116, 238). Both Native and non-Native implied readers must answer those questions for themselves. The final meanings of the text then are not in the novel but in the readers' appreciation as they take this voice of the past into present action and insight. The non-Native readers are encouraged to conclude that their actions can hurt both non-Natives and Natives, that cultural misunderstanding too easily leads to tragedy, and that they need to respect Native conclusions and be slow to interfere even when they think they see the right answer. The questions are foregrounded in much the same way as Iser describes the wandering perspective. While initially they are associated with the narrator, they quickly become internalized as questions in Antoine's mind. With the death of Rafferty, the non-Native reader is guided to shift perspective to that of McNickle, the storyteller, and ask what Antoine has learned. As these questions are directed to the implied readers, however, their answers are the raison d'être for the text. The attempt to shift the reader's perception to a more Native perspective is made more explicit in McNickle's nonfiction prose where he often argues for an "enduring policy of self-determined cultural pluralism" toward Indians (Native 169).

Through the authorial intrusions, the contrasting chapters, the death of the non-Native implied reader in the text (via Rafferty), the parody of the mystery form, and the use of questions, McNickle embeds a high degree of self-reflexiveness, guiding the non-Native implied reader to view the novel as a narrative whose meaning must be discovered. The authorial comments and questions also create a tone that is personal in a way reminiscent of oral storytelling. In a sense, McNickle is adopting a mediational strategy common in traditional Native oral narratives, perhaps even encouraging non-Native implied readers to acknowledge an unexpected form of knowledge derived from storytelling. They are directed to adopt a world view where dreams reveal truth and a song can keep a person alive, where stories from the past provide the meaning for events of the present. They must live in that world view, if only for a moment. Consequently, new elements have entered the cultural conversation in the process of redirecting the discourse about Natives.

McNickle's storytelling also creates a mediative frame with which Native readers might be familiar. The power of songs, visions, and traditional stories reinforces certain cultural precognitive positions since the voice of the past speaks to today's world. Moreover, the questions asked of Antoine obviously serve to focus the perspective for the implied Native reader. They require not only a reaffirmation of tribal values and an appreciation of injustice (already present in most Native readers), but they also present historical, political, and scientific analyses, that go beyond an emotional and cultural response. At first the Little Elk people think that the whites are awkward and unable to survive (135), but eventually they realize that though they are "a people without respect . . . they managed to get what they wanted" (131). While Jim moves to adopt white ways, Bull withdraws to "a time when people waited and did nothing" (133). Native implied readers are encouraged to analyze change, identity, and community, not just respond. The death of Bull, a viewpoint character for a Native implied reader with activist tendencies, pushes that Native reader to calculate the dynamics of isolation and violence. Bull's move from his confined world where he saw that "death always waited beyond the camp circle" (93) to his violent response at the end of the novel reminds the Native reader that cultural continuity is not synonymous with isolation and that reaction is a victim's strategy.

The parameters of the cultural conversation to which McNickle saw this book responding are delineated in his other writing from the 1970s. McNickle's revision of *Indians and Other Americans* in 1970 offers an insight into his implied Native reader. The 1959 edition of *Indians and Other Americans* ended with an appeal for a four point plan similar to the one Congress approved for Iran. The 1970 edition concluded with the promotion of an identity that would be pan-Indian as opposed to tribal specific, pointing to the political influence that the Red Power movement brought to national Indian policy and the awareness of Native American concerns. Also the revised edition emphasized the importance of independent community-based projects. While the first edition was clearly aimed at a non-Native reader, the second attempted to reach both audiences, and especially a young, politically active, pan-tribal audience. It offered young Native American readers a political and historical understanding of the present struggle and proposed the community as the locus of political activity.

In 1962, McNickle concluded his *Indian Tribes of the United States* with a quotation from the "Declaration of Indian Purpose," which was composed during the 1961 University of Chicago conference where Native American representatives from ninety tribes gathered. For McNickle, this event marked the advent of an era of pan-tribalism even more than did the creation of the National Congress of American Indians in 1944. The manifesto, aimed at non-Native America, pleads for material assistance but also asks for ample time to adjust to the pressures of the dominant culture without interference. In 1973, McNickle revised *Indian Tribes of the United States*, changing the title to *Native American Tribalism: Indian Survivals and Renewals*. In this new edition, McNickle added an epilogue that concerned the Alaska Native Claims Settlement Act; in it he expressed the opinion that the act was a victory for Indians because the government had been forced to accept a proposal that would assure some measure of Native self-determination (167). The new conclusion emphasized the oscillation of federal Indian policy, its periodic acceptance and then denial of Native rights. The section ended by expressing cautious hope that a policy of self-determination was about to be universally accepted. McNickle cited the government's return of the Taos Pueblo sacred lake whose significance was religious rather than economic, as an example of greater tolerance by contemporary America, and he insisted that the efforts of the new Native American writers were vital to the growing sense of pan-tribalism (168).

McNickle believed that though the elders might not be comfortable with the terms pan-tribalism and Indian nationalism, they were sure of their common identity. The angry young people would have to find common ground in their different senses of tribal identity, and they would also need to understand the political necessity of pantribal unity. McNickle concluded: "Finally, it can be noted in closing that the spokesmen of earlier years who tried to accept what an alien world offered their people, seeing no other choice open, are now silent. If the Indian race is to be destroyed, the new voices avow, the destroying agent will have to contend with an integrating people, not with isolated individuals lost in anonymity" (170). Thus, in this concluding chapter when discussing the relations between elders and politically active youth, McNickle clearly emphasizes the role of pan-tribal rather than tribal-specific identity. When he reminded the youth of the vacillation of white attitudes toward Natives, he also advised them to use those attitudes, when encountered, to further the cause of Native rights, but not to be lulled into a false sense of security. *Wind from an Enemy Sky* reinforces and dramatizes this advice.

In his introduction to *Native American Tribalism*, McNickle included a section pointedly aimed at militant youth. He criticized AIM's attempt to use the Bureau of Indian Affairs to dissolve the Sioux Indian Reorganization Act's constitution, claiming that if this were to have happened, "the last vestige of a tribe's sovereign right to govern itself in internal matters would have vanished" (xi). These questions of identity, relations to elders, political strategy, and the dynamics of American perception of Native Americans map the field of Indian political discourse to which McNickle saw himself responding. His experience of working with Native youth, university students, and scholarship committees, and as a lecturer, and reviewer kept him abreast of current Indian affairs and mindful that there was a young Native audience out there for him.

Wind from an Enemy Sky addresses this pan-tribal and political young audience in some very specific ways and for some very well-defined goals. One way it does this is through reference to specific events that McNickle actually experienced. The BIA reform administration, which in the novel places the educated social worker in the Little Elk agency, is obviously modeled after the Collier administration. The dam on the Little Elk land in the novel was probably not modeled after Kerr Dam. The Flathead tribe was relatively receptive to that dam (Dunsmore 40). More likely the dam in *Wind* was inspired by Garrison Dam near Fort Berthold and the controversy surrounding the construction of this dam because it flooded sacred burial sites. The South American dam of the novel paralleled a real South American dam project with which he was familiar. Likewise, much of the action in *Wind* centers on the Indians' attempt to have the Feather Boy sacred bundle returned. McNickle worked on the successful negotiations to return the Mandan sacred bundle,[3] but the most recent event in his mind might have been the successful return of the sacred lake to Taos Pueblo. In both cases, the tribes were successful in having sacred objects returned.

Clearly the landscape in the novel resembles the geography of the Salish reservation where McNickle grew up. Similarly, some of the characters in the novel resemble real life figures. McNickle's diaries for 1957 discussed the quarrel between two brothers in Crownpoint, New Mexico. The quarrel was very political and involved issues concerning leadership of some local organizations. The tensions were high because one brother was considered educated and one not. Significantly, the uneducated brother was named Sam Jim.

It would appear that McNickle adapted some historical and political events for his literary goals. This kind of adaptation, which Iser refers to as depragmatization, is the source of much of McNickle's creative structuring in *Wind*. Iser explains the general process:

A further complication consists in the fact that literary texts do not serve merely to denote empirically existing objects. Even though they may select objects from the empirical world . . . they depragmatize them, for these objects are not to be denoted. The literary text, however, takes its selected objects out of their pragmatic context and so shatters their original frame of reference; the result is to reveal aspects (e.g., of social norms) which had remained hidden as long as the frame of reference remained intact. (109)

The incorporation of known political events required for McNickle a depragmatization unlike that in James Welch's *Winter in the Blood* or in Louise Erdrich's *Love Medicine*. The events in these two novels are not of such a political nature that their denotations must be completely depragmatized. In *Wind*, the denotations of events are not only depragmatized but transformed because the frame of reference is so strongly fixed in the perspective of both audiences. In pushing for a pan-tribal frame of reference, McNickle engaged a highly political discourse about progress and violence in Native communities. The discourse was drawn from the political conversations of educated Indian youth conducted in publications like *Akwesasne Notes* in the mid-seventies.[4] He depragmatized the dam project, the successfully returned bundle, and the victory of the Taos Pueblo in order to "heighten the contradictions" (as activists from the seventies phrased it) inherent in Native/non-Native relations.

He went on to identify in the conclusion to *Native American Tribalism* the vital role Native American artists and intellectuals played in expressing tribal views, in voicing common goals, and identifying similar problems. He saw their contribution as essential in establishing a basis for the pan-Indian perspective. Soon after writing this conclusion, he moved on to completing his final revision of *Wind*. In writing his text, he attempted to play the same role he assigned to other Native writers: that of fostering a pan-tribal perspective in his Native readers.

In *Wind*, McNickle's implied Native reader is expected to recognize that cultural unity is more important than any issue facing an Indian group. Henry Jim's lesson is that only if the people are united will significant change come about and that change can only proceed at the pace set by the people themselves. The struggle between Henry Jim and Bull forces the implied Native reader to adopt an opinion on the traditionalist/progressive debate that is the subtext of the novel. The necessity of cultural unity on the textual level is mirrored by the necessity of unity on the national political level. The activist cannot separate from the people and set up individually as a model on the communal or national arena. The alien concept of individual responsibility would not only deconstruct that person's Indian identity, but it would impede the social dynamic necessary for change. Only if the forces of a unified Native American society confronted the forces of the mainstream could positive change come about. In a letter to Sol Tax, McNickle explained:

> I think you are quite right, i.e., perceptive, in your observation that what most disrupts tribal capacity to act, (to carry on), is the divisiveness that results from imposing an alien concept of individual responsibility in the group. The pulling and hauling between (traditionalist) and (progressive) parties which characterizes so many Indian communities flows immediately from this outside imposition. Every Indian generation has to be made over in the quest for harmony. Fortunately, it always seems to work out and the community in the end remains intact; but at great cost. And to add to the travail, the Indians are blamed for their factional splits, as if they were in charge and able to prevent self-injury. The answer, as you rightly assume, is to restore the autonomy they once enjoyed, which made possible useful and meaningful adaptations.[5]

The ultimate effects of federal policy or tribal decisions on tribal communities may not be clearly visible. Indeed controlling the outcome of such restructuring may be out of the hands of tribal communities, but the internal social dynamic and especially the creation of identity *are* open to structuring. McNickle believed that each Indian generation remade itself: personally, culturally, and, in the contemporary world, politically. *Wind from an Enemy Sky* emerged out of a field of tumultuous discourse on identity, community, and political action.

What did you see? What did you learn? These two questions condense the responses of both sets of implied readers as the text becomes a self-conscious attempt to engage both recent and long-standing cultural conversations, to respond to positions, ideas, actions, fears, and events: to define identity by speaking.

Chapter Twelve

"What Did You See?
What Did You Learn?
What Will You Remember?":
Wind from an Enemy Sky

Alanna Kathleen Brown

D'Arcy McNickle set himself a very demanding task in the writing of *Wind from an Enemy Sky*. His intent was to explore the mind sets of two different peoples, and through both Native and white characters, to expose the great difficulties in achieving bicultural understanding. Through numerous characters he explores the shifts of heart and mind that illustrate how personally challenging such movements are, how courageous, how tenuous, and how breakable. His technique is not merely to illustrate through character. From page one, D'Arcy McNickle actively provokes his readers toward an inner dialogue in which they must find their way on uncertain ground. A chapter by chapter textual reading reveals both his artistry and his achievement.

The novel begins with two cataclysmic events, one technological and the other personal. A holy place, a place of power for the Little Elk people, has been turned into a reservoir for a dam, and Bull, their leader, discovers his foolishness in denying that water could be controlled in such a manner. He shames himself in front of his grandson, Antoine, when he loses himself to his rage and his powerlessness. The essence of the chapter, however, has a different focus. That focus is actually on the relationship between grandfather and grandchild: the significance of their bonding to the boy, Antoine; how the grandfather, Bull, teaches and how Antoine learns; and the difficulty of bespeaking a people in a language that is not their own. By page two, McNickle is already engaging the reader in a more plotted intellectual inquiry: "He was named Bull—that was the English form of it. But the words men speak never pass from one language to another without some loss of flavor and ultimate meaning." This problem is further illustrated when Antoine is described as "a coming-man" (3), clearly a transliteration of an Indian concept, and the disciplinarian at the government school is described as "man with one long arm,—that is, man with a whip in his hand" (9).

Three other critical observations also are introduced. When Antoine is speaking of what he has read about the construction of the dam, Bull responds, "Am I talking to you or to a piece of paper?" (1). For Bull, corporal experience is essential to knowledge. Literacy is not a source of knowing. It is as unreal to him as the white world of the valley below, a "world he sometimes passed through, but never visited" (2). Further, Bull can only put the dam in the context known to him, the genesis stories of his people. When he asks who the creature is who made the dam and wonders if it is "a monster first-man, who decides things in his own way?" (7), Bull is asking a critical ethical question which, when understood, pits Western individualism against the balances essential to social and natural order. As his tribe would understand, before humans could come to inhabit this world, monsters had to be defeated through cunning to create the balances essential for human survival. Yet, as Bull recognizes, his question will not be respected because Indians have been denied a full cultural humanity by those in power: "The white man makes us forget our holy places. He makes us small" (9). The first nine pages of the text have already engaged the reader in very complex issues involving the problems of translation, literacy, religious world view, and the denial of social equality.

The second chapter in which Henry Jim comes to Bull's camp fleshes out both Indian social and etiquette systems and the Indian spiritual world view. Much like Ella Cara Deloria chose to do through *Waterlily*,[1] McNickle uses *Wind from an Enemy Sky* to guide his readers toward an anthropological appreciation of culture. He is encouraging the stance of nonjudgmental observation. The chapter begins with a reference to Bull's two wives, the family organization of Bull's camp, and the generational organization of relationship terms such as grandfather. This chapter also begins to outline the sharp contrasts in freedom of movement before and after settlement for Native peoples. Where white readers will again face complex challenges to their own cultural assumptions is in the significance of dreams as a source of spiritual interpretive guidance, and in a world view that does not presume the preeminence of human beings. "Were the animals and the trees asked to give their consent" (24) to their deaths when the dam was built? The reader has entered a world where the shaman, Two Sleeps, will assert that sources of knowledge are due to "listening to my grandfather, the badger. And to my aunt, the bluebird" (20).

Chapter two and chapter three also introduce readers to the dual tugs that still divide opinion within Indian families and within Indian communities, the choice of how much to assimilate and/or to maintain traditional ways. Furthermore, in these chapters the dilemma surrounding the sacred Feather Boy bundle is introduced. As McNickle forces the reader to consider: "How to translate from one man's life to another's— that is difficult. It is more difficult than translating a man's name into another man's language" (26). That is why McNickle does not give a simple, analytic discussion of the bundle to white readers who undoubtedly fail to grasp its significance. Meaning must unfold within a context. Henry Jim takes a long look backward at the lives of his people in order to bring up the subject of the bundle and its return with the new superintendent of the Little Elk Agency. The meaning of the bundle will take the entire novel to unfold. An anthropological stance can go only so far. Definitions do not encompass meaning, observations cannot encompass the whole. McNickle's challenge to the reader is a penetrating one. Crucial to understanding those different from ourselves is honoring what they hold sacred. Not being able to do that unravels all the rest, as we come to understand through the tragic ending of the novel.

That tragic ending is but one of the probable outcomes of the story. First we must enter within the frames of dialogue that McNickle establishes, and the next three chapters clearly outline McNickle's approach. He introduces us to three characters: Pock Face, an Indian youth who wishes to demonstrate his warrior prowess to his people by killing the man who built the dam; Stephen Welles, the Protestant missionary who thirty years ago furtively sent the bundle on to the Americana Museum in hopes of redirecting the Little Elk people to Christianity and civilization; and Toby Rafferty, the new superintendent of the Little Elk Agency, who is willing to take on the role of cultural intermediary. What gives this structure coherence is that the first two characters clearly grow out of the historic pasts appropriate to their cultural heritages. What makes Rafferty's position particularly poignant and vulnerable is that he, at first, perhaps like the reader, is only a man of good intentions. He has no knowledge that will make smooth the path he is following. Then in chapter four, actual history intertwines with the text, for in 1934 John Collier was appointed by Franklin Delano Roosevelt to direct the Bureau of Indian Affairs, and as the fictional character, Rafferty, recognizes, that appointment and the hiring of a number of people like him were meant to be "a repudiation of the military-political-missionary tradition that had prevailed in the past" (33). Nonetheless, those new hires, committed to something called "cultural relativity," were surrounded by veteran Bureau employees who distrusted the new direction and its implied judgment of past actions. The new agents also had to work with Indians who assumed exploitation and expected corrupt and arrogant patronage from federal officials. While men like Rafferty thought they knew what needed to be changed, there were no road maps for the direction they wished to take. The changes in attitude and action would have to evolve community by community.

Chapter six expands on Rafferty's situation. It begins with his recognition that he is "an outsider, trying to find his way inside" (46) to the Little Elk people, and ends, after his discussion with Stephen Welles, at Rafferty's realization that he is an outsider to the belief in Indian savagery and the passion for conversion that drives the white minister. It is to McNickle's credit that although he has difficulty developing psychologically complex portraits, he does create (male) characters whose positions are consonant with real life, and who cannot be easily dismissed. The actions and beliefs that determine their actions are wholly recognizable, as is the position of go-between.

Chapters six through ten set up a crucial contrast for the reader. Through the thoughts of Reverend Welles the notions of Indian as enemy come into sharp focus. Welles asserts quite simply: "The Indian is anti-civilization!" (52). His explanation of this is telling: "The Indian people start from origins about which we speculate but know next to nothing. We do know they are a people who are unlike us—in attitude, in outlook, and in destination, unless we change that destination" (51). Welles finds difference to be fearful and objectionable. He also assumes the right to redirect a people and a culture, that is, an authority granted by Manifest

Destiny. Part of McNickle's technique is to have such assumptions stated clearly so that readers must confront the more visceral emotions galvanizing such beliefs. He then immediately brings the reader's attention to some of the differences whites find so befuddling or fearful.

In chapter seven, Henry Jim is traveling to the various encampments to inform all the Little Elk people that the quarrel dividing them is over and that he is taking steps to redress his part in the stealing away of the Feather Boy bundle. In the midst of that process he has a dream about his imminent death (55) and immediately begins to sing to stave off that death. His tribesmen join him, and through the ensuing chapters until Henry Jim dies, his tribesmen sing for him, speak for him, keep him alive long enough that his vision of a unified tribe may come into being. What is striking about their actions is the formalism that also empowers them. The men surrounding Henry Jim ride in formation, take responsibility for giving rest to one another in the singing of Henry Jim's song, but also come to full chorus to acknowledge their unified commitment to the man and to his vision. When the tribesmen come to speak for Henry Jim with Rafferty, the very closing and opening of the gate into the compound bespeak their sense of somberness and importance in the delivery of the message. Moreover, each man repeats the message as a sign of its significance and power.

The responses of the white characters indicate either their inability to comprehend the actions of the Indians, or their total misjudgment of the situation. Sid Grant, the U.S. Marshall who has just taken Bull and his men into custody, can only comprehend the singing as threat: "And stop singing those damned war songs!" (57). Even Rafferty, watching the men leave after their formal request for help, finds himself questioning out loud: "Do they really think they can keep him alive by singing—?" (85). Their unification, which provokes fear in the one and amazement in the other, is further compounded by the difficulty the Indians have in explaining how an object of historical curiosity to one culture could be a venerated object of spiritual power to another. As Iron Child instructs Son Child: "Just tell him we lost our Indian flag, our Indian Lord Jesus, maybe he'll understand it better" (84). Having heard the harsh but commonly held judgments of Welles, the chapters immediately following Welles's assertions pull the readers into comprehensible, if different, behaviors and beliefs, which enable readers to both identify with and critique the responses of the whites.

The next chapter, eleven, asserts that strong notions of justice can work themselves out differently in different cultures, while at the same time illustrating that those, Native or white, who reach out to be cultural intermediaries are distrusted for actions that appear to be accommodation and betrayal by both groups. In this pivotal chapter, Bull describes how, among the Little Elk people, a man would be held accountable for injuring a family, and that if he chose not to compensate the family, he would be banished from the tribe. Bull cannot comprehend any justice in holding himself and all the men of his band hostage for the death of a single man, but he knows that white justice does not work in the same way, that it requires a death for a death. He urges his tribesmen to remain calm and silent about Pock Face's action, for the loss of even one man lessens them, whereas the loss of one white man means nothing in the face of so much conquest and settlement (92). Since the whites' law allow no way to redress a wrong to the injured family, and as Indian numbers have already been so seriously eroded, the only action for them is to maintain unity. Individual actions must be understood in the light of tribal survival. All their past has taught them that, "Death always waited beyond the camp circle"(93).

Yet beyond the camp circle is exactly where Boy, a severe and undercutting translation of the name Son Child, has chosen to go. It is in this and the previous chapter that we learn how Son Child's interest in language led him to act as translator on behalf of Native speakers (80–81), and ultimately, through a series of jobs at the agency, to an appointment as chief of the tribal police force. Yet, his speaking on behalf of others has ironically isolated him. In chapter eleven, Son Child makes a moving plea to be understood in his choices, for were a compassionate Indian concerned about the well-being of his people not the tribal policeman, Native peoples would be treated with far more harshness and insensitivity (91). He asks Bull's people not to misjudge him. He is not an extension of white authority over them, a betrayer of his own kind. He understands clearly that he provides a buffer to the abuses of power and authority a figure like Sid Grant represents in the novel, and whose rough justice Bull and his men are experiencing. The contrast also is clear to McNickle's readers. McNickle wants the readers to grasp the day-to-day choices, the emotional complexities of being one who bridges the chasms dividing cultures. There are personal costs as well as satisfactions in making such choices, and people need support who accept such demanding paths of responsibility.

After such an evocative chapter, the next two, twelve and thirteen, provide some comic relief and move the plot forward. Having guided his readers to a more receptive place of engagement, however, with the lives of his Indian characters, at chapter fourteen through sexteen, McNickle then examines settlement/assimilation from the Indian perspective, and it is a very painful look. Through Antoine, McNickle exposes the mission-BIA schooling Native children were coerced into undergoing, and through Henry Jim, he exposes the abuse of the "token" assimilating Indian. What Reverend Welles had implied was ultimately a benefit to Native peoples, the massive effort to eradicate "whitemanize" indigenous peoples,[2] in reality isolated, shamed, and splintered them.

The offensive nature of the education system is made clear in Antoine's memory of the Long-Armed-Man's warning: "You students, now, you listen to me. I want you to appreciate what we're doing for you. We're taking you out of that filth and ignorance, lice in your heads, all that, the way you lived before you came here, and we're going to fix you up clean and polite so no man will be ashamed to have you in his home. Forget where you came from, what you were before; let all of that go out of your minds and listen only to what your teachers tell you" (106). Four years of marching, cleaning, learning English and European table manners, and experiencing the threats of humiliating public punishments or closet isolation have left Antoine scarred with fears and nightmares and the belief that whites are a powerful enemy to be avoided (3, 106, 112). The immediacy of Antoine's memories is made more poignant when one realizes that in 1915, McNickle, himself, at eleven, was sent off to the Chemawa Indian School in Oregon when his parents went through a rending divorce.[3] McNickle's knowledge of the situation he is describing is intimate. Because of his later BIA work, so is his knowledge of how federal agencies rewarded and used "token" Indians.

It is a very moving approach to a problematic subject to have Henry Jim follow-up Antoine's revelations in chapter fourteen with a reflection in chapter fifteen on his choices to assimilate. Henry Jim recounts his muddled sense of what white people did for him and his non-comprehension about why, and he remembers the costs in terms of isolation and loss of community. He rejects that assimilation when he acts on behalf of his tribe at the end of his life and returns to the tepee and to his Native language. Henry Jim's story, combined with Antoine's, shows readers that the whites' promise of a better life for Native Americans was a lie. Instead, those who believed themselves to be culturally superior are exposed as arrogant, abusive of power, and self-knowingly manipulative.

In contrast, when Antoine and Henry Jim "return to the blanket," they are enfolded in family and community, given leadership roles, and a language and a music that have profound meaning for them. This is most eloquently stated when Antoine is on his way to the agency to check up on his grandfather:

> It was a time of pleasure, to be riding in the early morning air, to feel the drumming earth come upward through the pony's legs and enter his own flesh. Yes, the earth power coming into him as he moved over it. And a thing of the air, like a bird. He breathed deeply of the bird-air, and that was power too. He held his head high, a being in flight. And he sang, as his people sang, of the gray rising sun and the shadows that were only emerging from the night.
>
> To be one among his people, to grow up in their respect, to be his grandfather's kinsman—this was a power in itself, the power that flows between people and makes them one. He could feel it now, a healing warmth that flowed into his center from many-reaching body parts. (106)

Why would Antoine's joy in feeling connected to his own people, or Henry Jim's success in reunifying the tribe, be threatening? It is Toby Rafferty who helps McNickle's readers step beyond the parameters of the thought patterns of dominant power. Rafferty does not require submission to feel safe in the world, nor does he view the strengths in others with hostility. When Doc Edwards and he have come to check on Henry Jim's condition, he observes Son Child's tending of the tepee fire and he is struck by Son Child's competence, grace, and social ease. He thinks to himself: "What a man learned, and it was all he learned in a lifetime, was a degree of fitness for the things he had to do" (125). As his meditation continues, he considers how snug the tepee is and he can understand its appeal to others, matching anything he knew of "a house of stone and mortar" (125). He then considers the problem of how to communicate mutual respect, especially when a past strewn with disrespect has already determined the direction of a conversation. Moreover, as he recognizes, language itself, and culture, already embed differences in meaning that make the best of conversations complex. This thought process leads Rafferty to a decided and important conclusion: "I am glad I left this man [Son Child] free to make his own decision, this deft man at the fire. He will know how to decide. Not only for me and my way, but for all these people" (125). Rafferty chooses to trust and to respect rather than to command. His choice shows in his compassion towards Bull and his faith that Bull will come in to see him about the death of Jimmy Cooke after Bull has fulfilled his family obligations to his brother. His kindness does not go unnoticed. As Bull replies: "Maybe this one is different, as you said. He doesn't push" (128). The interaction is short in duration, but the ground has shifted.

One chapter is left before McNickle switches to the white story. Chapter seventeen focuses on Bull, and it is here that white readers will finally hear the voice of Indian anger and despair. It is the next morning and Bull is riding to the agency, Antoine at his side, but as McNickle points out, Bull is also "traveling through time and over mountains and prairies of thought and feeling" (129). His first memories are of shame, how he held his heart hard against his brother for those thirty years and played his own part in maintaining the quarrel that divided the people when there were forms of tribal etiquette that could have been followed to heal the breach. Then he recalls the past, what really was at the base of his anger at his brother:

> It was not his elder brother on whom at first he had cast his anger—that came later. That was when the anger settled and turned to rock. It had come first when these men from across the world, from he knew not where, had told him that he could not have his own country, that he no longer belonged in it. They would make it into a better country and let him have just a small piece of it. He wouldn't need a big piece because it would be

easier to live in the new country. These mountains, trees, streams, the earth and the grass, from which his people learned the language of respect—all of it would pass into the hands of strangers, who would dig into it, chop it down, burn it up. They came with great beards on their faces, smelling of sweat, but smiling all the time and talking without pausing. They left big scars in the mountains where they went digging for gold. They cut down the biggest trees and hauled them away to make houses—or sometimes they just let them rot in the forest. They scared away the game with their heavy tramping feet. They plowed up the prairie grass and spoke out in anger when stones broke their plows. They were a people without respect, but they managed to get what they wanted. (130–31)

Bull wonders how he can explain to Antoine that the Little Elk people never foresaw the danger until it was too late. He recalls one story after another of how foolish and vulnerable the first whites seemed, the laughter they generated, but their numbers, not their skills, ultimately overwhelmed the tribe. In his despair, it is as if he twists the racist saying, "The only good Indian is a dead Indian" into "The only happy Indians are dead Indians because they don't have to care" (136). He cannot see that his anger is eroding his spirit.

It is at this point, midway through the novel, that Adam Pell, the industrialist, steps into the text. While there were earlier references to him, it is significant that events have unfolded as much as they have before he enters the scene, and that the readers have come to know all the other characters who will be the significant players at the ending of the novel.

The reasons for a dominant critical approach to *Wind from an Enemy Sky* are evident as well at this juncture. In the afterward to the University of New Mexico Press edition, Louis Owens asserts that while Adam Pell "may talk to Indians he has never learned to listen to them. Adam makes the fatal mistake of generalizing about Indians, perhaps the most common error in the history of Indian-white relations" (236).

He expands the theme of misunderstanding to include "the barrier of silence between Indian brothers . . . the miscommunication between Indian and white, and . . . the seeming impossibility of dialogue between all men" (259). Considering *Wind* to be an extension of the fatalism McNickle developed in *The Surrounded*, Louis Owens asserts that this later novel "gives us a dark picture of mistrust, misunderstanding, and death" (259). Though not as pessimistic as Owens's interpretation, James Ruppert does believe that McNickle implies, "after his years of working between two cultures, that it is close to impossible for those cultures to truly understand and respect each other's worldviews."[4] Certainly the issues both critics address are aspects of the novel readers must take into account, but is the story ultimately such a statement of hopelessness? McNickle is in a discourse with his readers to engage them in a process that encompasses much more than the tragic ending of the novel. He is saying to them, just as Bull asked of Antoine: "What did you see? What did you learn? What will you remember?" (116) The implication of such a series of questions inevitably leads to: "And how will you act?"

In chapter eighteen we learn what Adam Pell saw, learned, and remembered to better understand the choices he will make. The story of Adam Pell's friendship with Carlos Mendoza is a story of crucial importance to him. That friendship brought Pell beyond being a select collector of Indian antiquities into being an active participant in social change. The dam that he helped finance and build in Peru is less significant than the fact that his story demonstrates how people move beyond the assigned roles of conquest to create a new community of shared economic prosperity and political-social participation. Both humbling and touching to Pell is the city's response to him. He is embraced as an honorary citizen. As he explains to his sister, Geneva, and his brother-in-law, Thomas Cooke, that experience changed him. "Until I went to Cuno and lived with its problems for a while, I had never given much thought to the living Indians—our own, or those in South America" (149). Suddenly he realized that the artisans of the past who had "created those wonders were still with us" (150). His aesthetic sensibility, curiosity, and skills as an engineer and financier have come together in a beneficial way not only for others, but for himself.

Pell is a man of progress. He believes in the efficacy of technology and universal suffrage and education. He believes that tomorrow can be better for everyone, and as we will learn in chapter twenty-three, is thus horrified to discover that the dam built on the Little Elk Reservation not only does not improve the lot of the Little Elk people, it has been built without their consent on land that belongs to them. That revelation, however, is yet to come in the novel. What does concern Pell when he arrives in Elk City, besides the death of his nephew, is that no miscarriage of justice happen to an Indian because of that death. Pell does not want racial prejudice engendered by the cause of the family's personal sorrow. Such a character will generate respect among a number of readers.

Having now sympathetically introduced all the main characters as well as guiding readers toward a more comprehensible understanding of both the Little Elk people and the whites who have authority on the reservation, the dam and Feather Boy medicine bundle plots converge. In chapters nineteen and twenty, Adam Pell, Toby Rafferty, Sid Grant, Boy (Sun Child), Bull, Antoine, and Pock Face come together in the Superintendent's office. The meeting has not been planned nor are the events that unfold expected. In some cases the individuals have not even met each other before. In the newness and awkwardness of the situation, people try to size each other up. Rafferty tries to fathom Pell's motives in dropping by to visit and is cautious of a man he views as "domineering" (153). Bull, on the other hand, is attracted to Pell's self-command: "One would have to watch him, listen carefully to what he said, and try to decide what manner of man he was. This one had sharp, clear eyes, the eyes of a man who could find his way" (160).

Sid Grant, in his eagerness to capture the Indian murderer, is the proverbial bull in a china shop. He does not have Bull's grace of manner, his self-possession, nor the ability to speak to Geneva's grief as Bull does (160), but he has found the gun that shot the bullet that killed Jimmy Cooke. Sid Grant is crudely working toward an inquiry that will entrap Bull and force out the information he needs, though Bull would have to injure his own to reveal it. Into this situation comes Pock Face with his second confession of the shooting. His motive for confessing unites the two plots: he is afraid that Rafferty will not help the tribe get the Feather Boy bundle back if he believes that Bull is the killer. To help the tribe continue its healing and to restore the sacred bundle, he will submit himself to the whites' law. It is his explanation, however, of why he shot Jimmy Cooke that shocks Pell into new awareness: "That bullet was meant for me" (171), and which brings Bull consciously, for the first time, face-to-face with the "monster first-man" (7) of chapter one. Antoine immediately recognizes the danger in such revelations and fears the explosive anger they will trigger in his grandfather (169). Yet Bull's commitment to his brother to regain the Feather Boy bundle matches Pock Face's commitment, and Bull keeps his anger in check. As he recedes back into his chair, Bull feels "that a great danger [has] passed" (169). The component here that keeps the violence from occurring is hope. Communication is not the determining issue. The importance of hope is reiterated by Pell almost immediately. When Pell learns that the Feather Boy medicine bundle has been sent to his Americana Institute, he instantly assumes personal responsibility: "Am I culpable here also?" (173). That expression of guilt, however, is followed by an immediate hope of expiation: "If I find this medicine bundle, I'd like to bring it back myself. Maybe I'll be forgiven then, for killing the water" (173). While the latter notion is extraordinary to him, he nonetheless accepts that such a belief explains and justifies to the Little Elk people the killing of his nephew.

What do these men do when the ground of their understanding shifts right under them? Their interactive responses become the focus of the following three chapters, twenty-one through twenty-three. Readers see both what is released and what is held back. On the positive side, Henry Two-Bits comes to Rafferty to initiate farming on his land for he has seen through Henry Jim that Indians can assimilate to a certain degree without turning their backs on their own people. Moreover, farming will solve an intergenerational conflict, for Two Bit's sons will now come home if they can make a living on the reservation. As significant on the interpersonal plane is the growing friendship between Bull and Son Child. When Bull chooses to accept Son Child as a son both for who he is and for his skills in mastering the languages of the two cultures, a very positive tone is set for bridging the divisions between Indians and whites and Indian and Indian. This possibility, this hope, is at the heart of efforts many like McNickle dedicated their adult energies to create.

Nevertheless, the very shifts toward positive change evoke their own doubts. While Bull can warm to Son Child, at the same time he can harbor doubts about Rafferty: "What does he want for his help?" (180), and distrust the movement towards assimilation: How many of those taking up farming "will turn back once they go away?" (186). He simply cannot see the choice to farm as an Indian choice. Moreover, deep in his soul, Bull distrusts Pell. He has someone on whom to focus his animosity for the grave betrayals of settlement. He has needed to frame that overwhelming historical event within a human context: "Why should he do this to me? I have not offended him. How could I, when I don't know his name?" (7). Now Bull has a name and a person: "That man from the East took the water from the mountains and spread it over the land, and some of our people will say it was a good thing. Maybe he is a good man—I watched him, and that is what I think—and yet he will destroy us" (187). Bull's distrust is also echoed by Rafferty who continues to see Pell as an obtuse and arrogant man (175).

Yet it is through Adam Pell's personal angst that McNickle will guide the reader to understand how the government has colluded with settlers to deprive Indians of even the minimal reservation lands set aside for them. In chapter twenty-three, Pell describes himself as "feeling exposed and naked, and considerably embarrassed" (190) as well as outraged at the degree of injustice perpetrated on Indians both through the legal system and in spite of it. His is a journey of uncovering how the allotment system really worked to coerce indigenous peoples into a cash nexus as well as to open up reservation lands to white settlement. He is shocked beyond belief to learn that the minimal amount of money paid to Indians for the "selling" of their land has been used almost entirely for surveys, irrigation projects, and so forth, that benefit white homesteaders. Moreover, water rights and land resources still legally in the hands of Indians have been taken over without recompense. Pell's assertion, "I'm not talking against progress. That's how I make my living, . . . [but] these people should also share in that progress" (191), is more moving to McNickle's white readers because Pell's sense of justice is one in which most of them share. His idealism, rather than political cynicism, actually reinforces the notions of foul play and betrayal of fundamental democratic principles.

It is Pell's response to all his discoveries that could bridge the two cultures with an even stronger tie. Rather than accept that he can do nothing about the injustices he has come to understand, he does choose to take responsibility for his part in disrupting the world of the Little Elk people. That notion of directly taking responsibility for injury caused to others is exactly what Bull had outlined in chapter eleven. Pell wants to "show good faith" (194, 210) like Carlos Mendoza, and he has come to understand through the examination of the record of his own people that: "The Indians say we killed the water, and damned if they aren't right!" (193). His movements are not those of a shallow or self-serving and self-deluded man. Nonetheless, both Pell and Bull have personal shortcomings alluded to throughout the text that have the potential to lead to tragedy. Bull can be a poor listener, and he is a brooding man with a quick-fire temper who can slip into despair. Pell is a man of decisive action who rarely shares thought processes. Decision making is not a collective process for him. Pell is a man who acts in moral isolation. The loss of the Feather Boy medicine bundle will sorely test them both.

Not until four-fifths of the novel has unfolded does McNickle allow Bull to tell the Thunderbird story. Only now are readers sufficiently engaged with people and events to listen and comprehend its meaning. That sacred story tells of a time long, long ago when the people were starving because they did not know how to survive. Thunderbird came to them out of pity and brought them tobacco and gave them the Feather Boy bundle with this injunction: "All the good things of life are inside. Never let it get away from your people. So long as you have this holy bundle, your people will be strong and brave and life will be good to them. My own body is in this forever" (208). The meaning of the bundle for the Little Elk people is self-evident. Yet because of the events of the previous chapter and Two Sleeps' unwillingness to share what he foresaw of the future, readers are not surprised to learn, following the telling of the tale, that the bundle is gone. It has been carelessly lost. Tossed into a lumber room, mice have eaten away through the buckskin covering, and all that remains are a few pebbles, shafts of feathers, tattered hide, and binding thongs (209–10). While McNickle interrupts the narrative to engage readers with the problem of sacred power pieces out of context in museum settings, the profound problem that must be faced is how to handle the revelation of the bundle's loss.

Two Sleeps has chosen to remain silent about what he has learned, for "men together, each acting for each other and as one—even a strong wind from an enemy sky had to respect their power" (197). He cannot be the bearer of such grief to those who have taken him in. For Bull, who does not yet know of the loss but who senses an on-coming tragedy, the thought of revealing to Antoine that they are a people who can "no longer protect themselves or their own children" (203) is devastating. "A boy should not grow up feeling that his life would be worthless" (203), so he tells the Thunderbird story, not realizing how that telling heightens its loss for Antoine and readers alike. Pell must struggle with a guilty conscience about all that he has learned about the building of the dam, and for the carelessness of a museum staff that cannot be defended. He decides to make recompense by giving the Little Elk people what is most precious to him, the Virgin of the Andes, a small gold Peruvian statue. It is, at once, a very personal and very valuable gift, but no one knows of Pell's process of thought, and the Little Elk people will not be given the time to experience their loss and to grieve before a gift is offered.

From this point on, the denouement of the book moves quickly, although what is described are periods of waiting and reflection. Those final talks from chapters twenty-seven to twenty-nine flesh out old stories and introduce new ones. There is no lack of communication as the novel draws to its conclusion. In the camp where Bull's men locate those who have been rounding up horses it is remarked that they would have been divided by the quarrel between Henry Jim and Bull in the past, but now, "they could sit at the same fire," talk together, "and everything seemed natural" (223). Even Toby Rafferty and Adam Pell discover that they like one another as they agree on their perceptions about the exploitation of the Indians on the Little Elk reservation (228–29), but they are all vulnerable to a past that will reassert itself. In chapter twenty-eight readers will learn about the rape and murder of Louis's daughter. The dreams of her cries push Louis to insist on bringing his gun to the gathering at the agency. He will protect his only other child, Pock Face, at any cost. It is also Louis who gives words to the band's feeling of entrapment: "The outside is closing in on us and I am growing small. They took our land. Next it was our water. Now they want to take my boy. When will they take our women, this grandchild?" (220–21). The car trip that Boy, Pell, Rafferty, and Doc Edwards take leads them to a vista overlooking the valley and reinforces the Indians' sense of encirclement. All the fenced-in land of settlement, the grid squares of ownership bespeak a travesty to land and to an Indian way of life that cannot be reversed. The loss of the Feather Boy bundle in the face of so much dissolution is unthinkable. Yet that is what has happened.

The final movement of the novel juxtaposes great hope and inordinate despair. On the one hand, Two Sleeps weeps at the personal knowledge that "Feather Boy is dead" (246), yet can only say to his camp, "I wanted to know everything, to be inside of everything—I thought. But my brothers, that is a terrible thing to want. My heart is already dead" (220). On the other hand, there is Iron Child who has a sudden premonition that the man from the East has brought them back their medicine bundle: "[N]ow we will have our life again, the way it was" (226). Pock Face and Antoine echo his expectancy. Rafferty, himself, has hoped for such a positive conclusion, knowing what it would mean for his work.

Even Bull has been "lifted out of fear" (239) for though his people will never be as strong as they once were, with the return of Feather Boy they can "be proud again" (239). All that hope and good feeling is blasted away by Adam Pell's revelation, and the novel ends with three good men dead: Pell, Rafferty, and Bull. What does McNickle want his readers to understand? What does he want them to grapple with?

Is it to acquiesce in Bull's despair or to presume that meaningful efforts at bicultural understanding are essentially doomed? Just as Henry Jim took a long time to tell the story to explain his request for aid in getting back the Feather Boy medicine bundle, so we as readers have been asked to think about a long story to help us understand what happened at the agency on that terrible day "the world fell apart" (256). We have been asked to consider character as it impacts events: Bull's brooding anger, Pell's need for control and understanding, Two Sleeps's pain in foreknowledge. We have been asked to consider context: how settlement was experienced by Native peoples, how notions of justice, even responses to something as technical as a dam, reflect cultural assumptions and beliefs. We have been encouraged throughout the text to listen attentively to words and characters speak to or with one another, and consider how translations can make a mockery of life (Mr. Two Bits, Mr. Bull, Boy). We have especially been asked to reflect on the positive, yet tenuous, movements that can grow out of trusting enemies and seeking healing change. We have to appreciate the courage that it takes to step out into the middle, to mediate like Rafferty or Son Child or Henry Jim, and to see that such actions can make a difference. We have also been shown how easily past hurts and pain can haunt the present and disrupt movements toward trust. We have been taught to think about the sacred, what it means to us and what it means to others, and perhaps above all, brought to understand how essential hope is to human survival and dignity.

No one is evil in *Wind from an Enemy Sky*. Human beings can be thoughtless, can be careless, but cruelty plays no part in the tragic ending of the novel. What we may be confronted with is our own need to blame, to find the reason why events happened as they did, to name the guilty party or to focus on the problem that, if understood, would make the ending comprehensible and thus within human control. If only Adam Pell had not been so proud and obtuse, if only Boy had not pulled the trigger and betrayed his people, if only Two Sleeps had spoken up sooner, if only the museum personnel had taken better care of the Feather Boy medicine bundle, or if only these men knew how to talk to one another. The novel evades all such "answers." The readers, like Antoine, face overwhelming experiences, which they must incorporate into personal understanding and go on in the world. That process is complex and takes time. What did we see? What did we learn? What will we remember? How will we act? D'Arcy McNickle has written a profoundly engaging and open-ended novel.

Notes

Chapter One

1. Larson, *American Indian Fiction* chapter 4; Priscilla Oaks, "The First Generation," 57–65; Louis Owens, 'Map of the Mind': 275–83.

2. Verne Dusenberry, "Waiting for a Day That Never Comes," *Montana Magazine of Western History* (April 1958): 26–39.

3. House Committee on Indian Affairs, *Wheeler-Howard Act, Exempt Certain Indians, Hearings on S. Rept. 2130*, 76th Congress, 3rd session.

4. Nancy Oestreich Lurie, "The Voice of the American Indian," *Current Anthropology* 2 (December 1961): 478–500.

5. Stuart Levine and Nancy O. Lurie, eds., *The American Indian Today* (Baltimore: Penguin Books, 1968), 295–328.

6. Lawrence Kelly, "Anthropology and Anthropologists in the Indian New Deal," *Journal of the History of the Behavioral Sciences* 16 (1980): 6–24; and Lawrence Kelly, "Anthropologists in the Soil Conservation Service," *Agricultural History* 59 (April 1985): 136–47.

Chapter Two

1. Richard Hofstadter discusses Theodore Roosevelt's racial theories in *The American Political Thought* (1948), theories that

he considers grounded in Roosevelt's childhood struggle to overcome his own physical weakness and to attain physical perfection. Roosevelt also held, according to Hofstadter, that, in the encounter between two races, the superior race has the right to replace the inferior one. Needless to say, Hofstadter distances himself from Roosevelt's comments. Hofstadter's *The American Political Tradition* was published at least a decade too late to openly express the sentiments of the histories discussed in this paper.

Chapter Three

1. I take expression in this instance to mean the manner in which thought is formed into language. In Saussurean terms, it is the *parole* extracted from *langue*. Every language has a set of possibilities for expression (determined by many variables, one of which is the medium of expression). Each speech event is the realization of one (or more) of those possibilities.

2. Foucault's use of the term "fundamental will" indicates that in the Western metaphysical tradition the concept of will is not always and wholly individual.

3. As always, any discussion of purity leads one close to an abyss. Jacques Derrida argues in several places that form and content are correlative terms. Cf. particularly *Writing and Difference*, 12 ff. (Chicago: University of Chicago Press, 1978). Any entity that is so organized that we may recognize its form necessarily has attached to it a content (semantic value). My point here is that it is possible to privilege either form or content, to lean over the abyss of one or the other, as it were. The expression to which Momaday refers in the following statement is primarily emotive and only secondarily cognitive, and is a comment upon the psycho-physicality inherent in an oral tradition. This emotive aspect of individual expression differs from that in which the reciprocity of speaker and tradition is bound up with exercising and restoring memory.

4. Throughout his work, however, Foley emphasizes the vitality of oral tradition.

5. In a similar argument, Ong notes that Milman Parry's most fruitful discovery was that "virtually every distinctive feature of Homeric poetry is due to the economy enforced on it by oral methods of composition" (21). This necessity for

economy of expression derives from the limitations of human memory. Parry's field studies were of Serbo-Croatian oral epic.

6. Literacy also avoids transmogrifications (to a certain extent) because literate traditions are transmitted in documents. Cf. Havelock, 70 ff.

7. Part of the function of such vocables is to establish or maintain rhythmic patterns. Cf. Bierhorst, 269.

8. The systematic aspects of ceremony are also evident in the Navaho *Nightway, Blessingway,* and so forth. Native American healing ceremonies in general address the various levels of relationship among individual and community. Cf. Donald Sandner, *Navaho Symbols of Healing,* for a discussion of the medicinal aspects of ceremony. Sandner notes that healing is not directed at symptoms, but at the entire social and natural complex of forces (3).

9. Momaday's comment is in regard to the story of the arrowmaker, which he includes in *The Way to Rainy Mountain.*

10. Ong makes a distinction between "primary" and "secondary" orality. The latter, such as the orality of electronic broadcast media, is based upon literacy. Limón is discussing primary orality here.

11. Limón speaks of the "Chicano literary renaissance," which has continued to gain strength since the 1960s: "The literary flowering occurred in the context of a militant redefinition of the political and cultural relations between the dominant society and a still subordinated Mexican American community" (125). I am grateful to Ken Roemer for his discussions of the concept of audience in oral narratives.

12. It should be noted that trickster narratives express social resistance. Historical narratives do include episodes of political resistance, but almost always to outside groups.

13. The framework "fits" *The Surrounded,* in a modified form, and is one of the work's Modernist characteristics. This framework, interestingly, could be derived from oral stories, "Vision Quest," for example.

14. Notable exceptions might be the Native American empires of Central and South America.

15. The power of a uniform cultural field is that allusions work. The danger of such uniformity is that hegemonies (of all types) become imbedded in cultural ideologies. The best of both worlds would be a "reverberant" field that adjusted itself rather

than its adherents, something that oral traditions do much more readily than do literate ones. Stability within a literate tradition resides in the document. Stability within an oral tradition is much less time- and space-specific. When the echoed voices of allusion speak loudly, as they do in a cohesive cultural context, all the connotative harmonies that are generated by allusion reaffirm, and simultaneously recreate, the culture's fundamental tone. This, I think, is the distinction between harmony and uniformity.

16. It should be noted that although oral traditional cultures are "unified," they are not isolated monocultures. There is, for example, significant borrowing of tribal stories, as the stories within *The Surrounded* illustrate. Cf. McNickle's note following the dedication.

17. The irony of miscommunication is revealed by McNickle's manipulation of point of view, another modern literary technique. Throughout the work at various times we enter the consciousness of Archilde, Catharine, Max, George Moser, Father Grepilloux, and Agent Parker.

18. This is not to infer that McNickle's style is Faulknerian, which it certainly is not, particularly if style exists only at the level of sentence construction. I would argue that style includes other, larger, semantic units and that McNickle's use of these units can be characterized as modern. At the level of the sentence McNickle's style is, among the "mainstream" moderns, most like that of Hemingway. I am grateful to Philip Cohen for helping me to place *The Surrounded* in a historical context.

Chapter Four

1. This essay grows out of an earlier one written for a special pedagogical issue of *Studies in American Indian Literatures*.

2. For his use of the term, "utterances," see Bakhtin's essay, "Discourse in the Novel" (264, 272, 276 ff.)

3. I thank Professor Tedlock for showing me the term, "included narrative." I also thank him for help in researching Salish material and for editorial comments. Thanks, also to Professor Bruce Jackson for his editorial help.

4. I owe much to Purdy's study of McNickle. His use of material from the Newberry Library has proved especially helpful. Much of this essay is an attempt to build on his foundation.

5. The introduction to Tedlock's *Finding the Center* provides clear examples of verse-tendencies, while Phinney gives representative examples of interlinear translation, along with free translations of the same texts.

6. For a representation of pauses, see "Guide to Reading Aloud" in *Finding the Center*.

7. I use the relatively formal, mechanical appellation *transmitted* to reflect the channels through which Sanders received the story. In her preface, she gratefully acknowledges "Mr. Edward Morgan, the faithful and just agent at the Flathead Reservation, [who] has given me priceless information which I could never have obtained save through his kindly interest. He secured [*sic*] for me the legend of the Flint, the last tale told by Charlot and rendered into English by Michel Rivais, the blind interpreter who has served in that capacity for thirty years" (viii).

8. To cite a portion of the passage: "His wife was just as old. She had gray hair and was bent double. The two young men were angry. They would not talk to their wives. They drove them away" (*Spoken Word* 38).

9. Grey, the Kiowa-Navajo medicine woman in Momaday's novel, *The Ancient Child*, reminds herself to "be true to the story" (217), thereby sounding a note heard in much contemporary writing.

10. For stories about this tree, see especially Teit, Purdy, and Weisel.

11. Note reflection of novel's first title, "The Hungry Generations." See Purdy for other associations with this title.

12. With other examples, Purdy makes this point about the whole novel, particularly in reference to the same impulse evident in the early draft. See Owens (1989) for another discussion of attention to audience.

13. For further discussion of McNickle's challenge in this regard, see Ruppert's application of Wolfgang Iser's term, "implied reader," in *Narrative Chance*.

14. For interpretation of his meaning for this term, see Todorov's chapter entitled, "Theory of the Utterance."

15. For present purposes I do not discuss roles of Charlot and Rivais, teller and translator. I realize the interaction between Sanders and each of them affects understanding of the larger situation and invites further study. For brief comment on Rivais's relationship to white culture, see Merriam (130).

16. See Todorov (47) for explanation of this term.

17. See Purdy (53) and corresponding footnote for context of McNickle's claim.

18. For a version of "Coyote and the Railroad"—a Coast Salish story about white settlers' monologic tendencies, see Holden (289). The article contains other entertaining stories on the same subject.

19. Holden, for example, shows the presence of this theme in Coast Salish traditional stories, especially from the Transformer cycles. See also Ortiz's "Crossing" for an Acoma account of this idea. It comes as no surprise that the 1992 Festival of North American Native Writers, held in Norman, Oklahoma, was entitled "Returning the Gift."

20. These two brief articulations of painting approaches come from fuller descriptions in Todorov (69).

21. As suggested in this essay's final paragraph, the idea of erasing borders among forms gains importance in tribal fiction.

22. Note Tedlock's point that "What oral narrative usually does with emotions is evoke them rather than describe them directly" (*Spoken Word* 51).

23. Although he does not directly address this story, Owens discusses its major theme of tragic misunderstanding (1985).

24. I intend this phrase to echo Momaday's poem, "Angle of Geese," as well as his statement that one "ought to give himself [*sic*] up to a particular landscape in his experience, to look at it from as many angles as he can" (*Rainy Mountain* 83). This same process appears in parallelisms within native oral narrative.

25. One sees other possible interactions between between McNickle and Sanders insofar as she describes in her book Mrs. Nine Pipes who acts quite generously toward a white partner at a choosing dance; she gives him a blanket and kerchief (68). Paul is one of the two men she names of the four who traveled to St. Louis to retrieve the Blackrobes; Narcisse is the other. She claims these men "sacrificed themselves to a fruitless cause" (107).

26. This insensitivity is echoed by Coast Salish versions of the "Bungling Host" story in which "the 'guest' who visits his neighbors [is] feasting on their hospitality and then failing miserably to reciprocate" (Holden 272).

27. For another, more recent story on this precise point, see Elizabeth Cook-Lynn's "A Visit from Reverend Tileston" in *Talking Leaves*.

28. Hear echoes of Coyote's desperation.

29. In this description, the dynamics of listening are amplified: "Archilde, listening closely, felt something die within him. Some stiffness, some pride, went weak before the old man's bitter simple words" (74).

30. Max does not appreciate what Gerald Vizenor in a recent essay calls "the *creative* power of tribal literature" (224; emphasis added).

31. Cf., an echo in a Zuni story of the beginning: "At the beginning / when the earth was still soft / the first people came out / the ones who had been living in the first room beneath" (*Finding the Center* 225).

32. Cf. Bruchac's *Songs from This Earth on Turtle's Back*.

33. The novel, that genre which Bakhtin says absorbs all others (8–10).

Chapter Five

1. Murray is here pointing out the dangers of the sentimental myth of wholeness and unity prominent in Native American writing. It represents "a nostalgia without any political cutting edge . . . a simplicity which fits neatly into the patterns of literary Romanticism" (88–89).

2. The vexed issue of what Chief Seattle said, and how this speech has come down to us, is discussed by Kaiser. The story of its politicization is in some ways more interesting than what is supposed to have been taken down by Henry Smith. Its historical trackrecord epitomizes the problem of translation as an inadequate recording mode.

3. See, for example, Governor Stevens's speech to Northwest Indians at the council of Medicine Creek in Stevens, I, 457–58, and the assimilationist goals of this council's treaty, I, 454, 459–60. Such speeches are typical of white language and point of view recorded in nineteenth-century frontier history.

4. Again, see the speech of Chief Steachus (Stevens, II, 50), or the account of the Flathead council (II, 81–91), where the future of McNickle's own people was decided.

5. Governor Stevens, for instance, names white interpreters, usually those serving with the military, but never Indians. See Stevens II, 135, where a "faithful half-breed interpreter" is "set" to keep watch on the Nez Perce leader, Looking Glass. A delightful exception is recorded in Stanley Vestal's account of the Medicine Lodge Treaty (1867):

The sensation of the meeting was Mrs. Adams, interpretress for the Arapaho. She appeared in a crimson petticoat, black cloth coat, and a small coquettish velvet hat decorated with a white ostrich feather. The Indians regarded her with great respect, for as one of them said, "I have hunted among the Spaniards and the Red Coats, in the mountains to the west and the forests east of the Missouri River. But I have never seen a bird with feathers like *that*. This woman must be the daughter of a great chief." (*Warpath and Council Fire*. New York: 1948. 121)

Of course, Mrs. Adams may not have been Indian.

6. The Boy does speak metaphorically at least twice, once when he refers to the sheriff as the "man-with-a-star."

Chapter Seven

1. McNickle, *Runner in the Sun.*

2. *Saturday Review of Literature* 13 November 1954:90; *New York Herald Tribune*, "Book Review Section" 14 November 1954:2, 26; *Library Journal* 15 January 1955:2501; *Christian Science Monitor* 11 November 1954:16.

3. McNickle, *The Surrounded.*

4. McNickle, *Wind from An Enemy Sky.*

5. Ibid., 256.

6. Alfonso Ortiz, friend and associate of McNickle in the decade before his death, arranged the transfer of most of McNickle's library to the Navajo Community College at Tsaile, Arizona. Ortiz has told the author that among the collection were most of Campbell's works. During the 1930s and 1940s, Campbell was investigating Native American religions, and it is possible that the two men corresponded. See also Campbell, *The Hero's Journey.*

7. McNickle, *They Came Here First*, 48.

8. McNickle, *Runner*, ix–x. See also Purdy, *Word Ways*, 84–85.

9. McNickle met Houser at the Intermountain Indian School in Brigham City, Utah, in 1950. Houser was teaching art and

McNickle was involved with the BIA's summer school for teachers.

10. Purdy, *Word Ways*, 87.

11. Katherine Spencer, *Mythology and Values*, 33–35.

12. Alfonso Ortiz, "Ritual Drama," 143–44. The opposites Ortiz ascribes to the Pueblos are also an integral part of Navajo cosmology.

13. Paul G. Zolbrod, "When Artifacts Speak," 27–28.

14. McNickle, *Runner*, 61–62.

15. Ibid., 49–50.

16. Ibid., 82–83.

17. Joseph Campbell, *The Hero With A Thousand Faces*.

18. Campbell, *Hero*, 4, 12, 17–19.

19. Ibid., 62.

20. Ibid., 388, also 17–8.

21. Campbell, *Hero*, 30.

22. Ibid., 51.

23. McNickle, *Runner*, 28–37.

24. Campbell, *Hero*, 323–26.

25. Spencer, *Mythology and Values*, 20–28. While a possible lineage for McNickle's story might be found in Spencer's detailed analysis of motifs in this very perceptive monograph, that work did not appear until 1957, several years after publication of *Runner in the Sun*.

26. Campbell, *Hero*, 59.

27. McNickle, *Runner*, 58.

28. Campbell, *Hero*, 71–73; Spencer, *Mythology and Values*, 34.

29. McNickle, *Runner*, 53–54.

30. Campbell, *Hero*, 152–53, 162.

31. Ibid., 55–56.

32. McNickle, *Runner*, 166.

33. Campbell, *Hero*, 36.

34. Ibid., 77–78, 82, 327.

35. Purdy, *Word Ways*, 99.

36. Campbell, *Hero*, 109.

37. Ibid., 193, 196–97.

38. McNickle, *Runner*, 229–31.

39. Campbell, *Hero*, 388–89.

40. Ortiz, "Afterword," in *Runner*, 248.

41. McNickle, *Runner*, x.

42. Ortiz, "Afterword" in *Runner*, 244–45.

1. John Purdy also makes reference to this text in conjunction with *Runner in the Sun* in *Word Ways*, 86.

2. See also Ortiz, Alfonso, "Afterword," in McNickle, *Runner in the Sun*, 238.

3. McNickle, *Runner in the Sun*, vii.

4. Meli, "D'Arcy McNickle," 363.

5. See also Ruppert, *D'Arcy McNickle*, 35.

6. See also Ruppert, *D'Arcy McNickle*, 24.

7. See also Ortiz, "Afterword," in *Runner in the Sun*, 237.

8. Grant, review of *Runner*, 38.

9. Purdy also observes that the novel bridges the gap between the two cultures, *Word Ways*, 85.

10. See also *Word Ways*, in which Purdy observes that "Salt's journey ends in a new story and ceremony that produce the power to promote health" (103).

11. See Purdy's *Word Ways* for more information about these titles.

12. Purdy, *Word Ways*, 86.

13. In *Word Ways*, 86–88, Purdy discusses this idea in conjunction with some of the earlier drafts of the novel.

14. For more information, see Josephy, *The Indian Heritage*, 156–57.

15. Josephy, *Indian Heritage*, 151. Josephy notes that some people think that corn first reached the Anasazi region from the U.S. Southwest; for a more in-depth discussion of the origins of maize farming in Pueblo cultures, see chapter 16 his text.

16. I am indebted to Dr. Jarold Ramsey who made this connection.

17. Josephy, *Indian Heritage*, 158–59.

18. Smith, "Mesa Verde," 734.

19. "The early Spaniards apparently heard the Hopis refer to some of the abandoned settlements as those of Mokis, a Hopi word meaning 'dead,' and, in time, used the name Moki, or Moqui, for the Hopis themselves. Even today, many non-Indians in the Southwest refer to the prehistoric Anasazi peoples as Mokis, although it is known that those Indians were ancestors of the present-day Pueblos," (Josephy, *Indian Heritage*, 160).

20. For more information about the Anasazi and Pueblo Indians, see Josephy, *The Indian Heritage*. For paleoenviron-

mental and archeological data on the Anasazi Indians, see Gumerman, *The Anasazi*.

21. See also Purdy, *Word Ways*, 99.

22. In Pueblo numerology, four is a sacred number; it encompasses the four sacred mountains and the four cardinal directions.

23. See Bierhorst, *Four Masterworks*, for an English translation of the Aztec hero myth.

24. Hunt, "Quetzalcoatl," 93.

25. Quetzalcoatl, who has a human face and the body of a feathered serpent, was "deity of the summer winds" (Hunt 93), and hence, he had a significant effect on maize farming. For more information about the Aztec god Quetzalcoatl, see Hunt, "Quetzacoatl," and Wiley, et al.

26. Chicomecoatl sits on a pedestal overhung with seven rattlesnakes and holds a double ear of corn in one uplifted hand. "The name Chicomecoatl means seven-snakes . . . snakes were a symbol of rain or water," Weatherwax, *Indian Corn*, 229.

27. See 229–34 of Weatherwax, *Indian Corn*, for more information about maize deities.

28. Ramsey, *Reading the Fire*, 153.

29. " 'Retroactive' because, without denying the possibility of authentic prophecy (by which most Indian groups set great store), I think that these texts poignantly suggest that during the Contact era, Western Indians tried to assert the traditional continuity of their disrupted and disordered lives by retroactively fixing upon or inventing prophecies, set in past times, of present calamities" (Ramsey, *Reading the Fire*, 153).

30. See also Purdy, *Word Ways*, 90.

Chapter Nine

1. Larson, *American Indian Fiction*, 67, 95. These themes are further expressed in Owens's Afterword, *Wind from an Enemy Sky*, 259; Owens, "Map of the Mind," 275–283; Owens, "The Red Road to Nowhere," 239–48; Parker, *Singing an Indian Song*, 233–34; and less so in Zachrau, "N. Scott Momaday" 39–56.

2. Ruppert, *D'Arcy McNickle*, 20, 16–17, 38. Although acknowledging the themes of conflict and tragedy, several other scholars appear to take an approach similar to Ruppert; see Ortiz's, afterword to *Runner*, 236–37; Towner's afterword, *The Surrounded*, 304; Purdy, *Word Ways*, 131–32.

3. Purdy, *Word Ways*, xxi–xiv, 104; Larson, *American Indian Fiction*, 78; and Ruppert, *McNickle*, 5.

4. McNickle, *Runner in the Sun*. Subsequent references to and quotations from this novel are from the reprint edition.

5. Birgit Hans, "The Hawk is Hungry," 84–85; William W. Bevis, *Ten Tough Trips*, 92–93; and Parker, *Singing an Indian Song*, 168, who affirms this perspective declaring that the novel "was published in 1954 by Holt, Rinehart and Winston as part of their Land of the Free series for young adults."

6. McNickle, *Runner*, 239.

7. McNickle, "Americans Called Indians," 29; this statement bears comparison with his earlier collaborative work, see Fey and McNickle, *Indians and Other Americans*, 14.

8. McNickle, *Runner*, 241. The European colonial occupation theme with procedures to alienate Indian land is expressed in McNickle, *Native American Tribalism*, 26.

9. The savagism dogma that guided European attitudes toward Indians is explicated in Pearce, *Savagism and Civilization; A Study of the Indian and the American Mind*; for further articulation of this theme, see Sheehan, *Savagism and Civility*. Explication of the illusion that is primitive society theory is given in Adam Kuper, *The Invention of Primitive Society*.

10. McNickle, *Native American Tribalism*, 34, 53, 55–56; Fey and McNickle, *Indians and Other Americans*, 20, 63, 80, 144; and McNickle, *Runner*, 240–41.

11. McNickle, *The Surrounded*, 304–305; McNickle, *Wind*, 259, 237–39; and Ruppert, *McNickle*, 24–25, 32–33.

12. Purdy, *Word Ways*, 84.

13. Parker, *Indian Song*, 143.

14. McNickle, *They Came Here First*, 9.

15. Parker, *Indian Song*, 117.

16. McNickle also rebutts these ethnocentric claims—savagism, primitivism, imperialism—in Fey and McNickle, *Indians*, 14, 17 where he again cites significant accomplishments of Native American civilizations.

17. Parker, *Indian Song*, 168–69.

18. This distinction between myth and legend is given expression in Hultkrantz, *Belief and Worship*, 3–19; and in Overholt and Callicott, *Clothed-in-Fur*.

19. Purdy, *Word Ways*, 85–86.

20. Lee, *Freedom and Culture*, 62.

21. Purdy, *Word Ways*, 84–85, 153, citing McNickle's Field Notebooks, 1 June 1950, McNickle Papers.

22. Plog, "Western Anasazi," and Cordell, "Eastern Anasazi," 108–51.

23. Purdy, *Word Ways*, 86.

24. McNickle, *They Came Here First*, 47, 48, 113.

25. Ibid., 92, 96.

26. Ibid, 77, 86–88.

27. Initiating this mythological reading during my presentation on *Runner* at the 25th Annual Meeting of the Western Literature Association, I must regretfully conclude here without explication of this perspective. Purdy, *Word Ways*, and Parker, *Singing an Indian Song*, have also suggested such a reading.

Chapter Ten

1. The manuscript version of *Wind from an Enemy Sky* is an ambitious undertaking. The wide range of issues advanced does not permit for character development; consequently, even the main characters, Rafferty and Bull, remain flat. The writing is cumbersome and the entire manuscript is disjointed.

2. Two contemporary Native American novelists were John Joseph Mathews and Mourning Dove; their novels are mainly concerned with assimilation. Another Native American novelist publishing during the early decades of the twentieth century was John Milton Oskison; however, Native American themes are only incidental in his fiction.

3. McNickle's diaries indicate that he gave the manuscripts various working titles, among them "The Flight of Feather Boy," "How Anger Died," "Wind from Far Away," and, finally, "Wind from an Enemy Sky." The manuscript version at the Newberry Library in Chicago is untitled but internal evidence suggests that it is one of those called "How Anger Died." I use either "How Anger Died" or the "manuscript verion" to distinguish it from the published version, *Wind from an Enemy Sky*. Page numbers in parentheses refer to "How Anger Died."

4. McNickle worked under John Collier, who put the Indian Reorganization Act into effect, in the Bureau of Indian Affairs. He had an enduring admiration for Collier and his reform work and, on occasion of his death in 1968 wrote a short article for *The Nation*, entitled "John Collier's Vision." In it he mentioned

why his reform idea failed to take firm root, the same reasons that he had anticipated in "How Anger Died":

Because he would not temper the quality of his conceptual grasp, Collier was sometimes dismissed as a visionary, an impractical intellectual. Because he expounded Indian worth, and more particularly, perhaps, because he insisted on extending religious and cultural freedom to Indian groups . . . he was accused of turning the clock back on Indian development and of trying to convert Indians into museum pieces. His detractors constituted a strange medley of unlikely pieces—frustrated land grabbers, special-interest lobbyists, Indian "experts" of various shades of competence, overzealous Bible thumpers, and an occasional part-time Indian who had been discovered in some act of chicanery (719).

Commissioner Eaton is certainly no portrait of John Collier, but Pell exhibits some of the traits that McNickle admired in John Collier.

Chapter Eleven

1. By mediation, I mean an artistic and conceptual standpoint, constantly flexible, which uses the epistemological frameworks of Native American and Western cultural traditions to illuminate and enrich each other. A mediational approach explores how contemporary Native American writers create a dynamic that brings differing cultural codes into confluence to reinforce and recreate the structures of human life—the self, community, spirit, and the world we perceive. For a more detailed discussion, see Ruppert, *Mediation in Contemporary Native American Fiction*.

2. In the use of the term "conversation", Bialostosky is closer to Richard Rorty in *Philosophy and the Mirror of Nature* than Kenneth Burke's use in *The Philosophy of Literature*.

3. A description of the negotiations with the Heye Foundation Museum of the American Indian is published by Roy Meyer in his *The Village Indians of the Upper Missouri*, 205–208. One might even speculate that McNickle modeled Adam Pell on George Heye.

4. McNickle specifically cited *Notes* in his conclusion to *Native American Tribalism* as a pan-tribal political source.

5. This letter is one of many in the D'Arcy McNickle collection at the Newberry Library.

Chapter Twelve

1. Ella Carla Deloria, *Waterlily* (Lincoln: University of Nebraska Press, 1988).

2. Mary Crow Dog's phrase is in *Lakota Woman* (New York: Grove Weidenfeld Press, 1990).

3. For further information on the trauma of the breakup of McNickle's parents' marriage, his own family heritage, and his schooling, read chapter one Purdy, *Word Ways*.

4. James Ruppert, *D'Arcy McNickle*. Western Writers Series. (Boise, Idaho: Boise State University Press, 1988); 31. This booklet gives an excellent summary of McNickle's nonfiction works and provides a good introductory overview on McNickle's life and fiction.

Bibliography

Works by D'Arcy McNickle

"Americans Called Indians," in *North American Indians in Historical Perspective*. Edited by Eleanor Burke Leacock and Nancy Oestreich Lurie. New York: Random House, 1971.

"Anthropology and the Indian Reorganization Act," in *The Uses of Anthropology*, edited by Walter Goldschmidt, 51–60. Washington, D.C.: American Anthropological Association, 1979.

"Clash of Cultures," in *World of the American Indian*, edited by Melville Bell Grosvenor, 311–53. Washington, D.C.: National Geographic Society, 1974.

"Commentary," in *Indian-White Relations: A Persistent Paradox*, edited by Jane F. Smith and Robert Kvasnicka, 251–57. Washington, D.C.: Howard University Press, 1975.

The Hawk is Hungry and Other Stories. Edited by Birgit Hans. Tucson: University of Arizona Press, 1992.

"The Indian in American Society," in *Social Welfare Forum*, 68–77. New York: Columbia University Press, 1955.

Indian Man: A Life of Oliver La Farge. Bloomington: Indiana University Press, 1971.

"The Indian New Deal as Mirror of the Future," in *Political Organization of Native North Americans*, edited by Ernest L. Schusky, 107–19. Washington, D.C.: University Press of America, 1980.

"Indians of North America," in *Encyclopaedia Britannica*, 14th ed. Chicago, 1954.

The Indian Tribes of the United States: Ethnic and Cultural Survival. London: Oxford University Press, 1962.

"John Collier's Vision." *The Nation*, June 1968, 718–19.

Letter to William Gates, 25 March 1934, McNickle Papers, Newberry Library, Chicago.

Native American Tribalism: Indian Survivals and Renewals. London: Oxford University Press, 1973.

"The Right to Choose: A Policy for the Future," in *Captives Within a Free Society: A Review of the American Indian Policy Review Commission*, prepared for the American Indian Policy Review Commission by D'Arcy McNickle, Mary E. Young, and W. Roger Buffalohead. N.p., 1976.

Runner in the Sun: A Story of Indian Maize. New York: Holt, Rinehart and Winston, 1954. Reprint with afterword by Alfonso Ortiz, Albuquerque: University of New Mexico Press, 1987.

"Snowfall." *Common Ground* 4, no. 4 (1944): 75–82.

The Surrounded. New York: Dodd, Mead, 1936. Reprint with an afterword by Lawrence W. Towner, Albuquerque: University of New Mexico Press, 1978.

They Came Here First: The Epic of the American Indian. Philadelphia: J. B. Lippincott Co., 1949.

"They Cast Long Shadows," in *Look to the Mountain Top*, edited by Charles Jones, 19–28. San Jose, Calif.: H. M. Gousha Co., 1972.

Wind from an Enemy Sky. San Francisco: Harper & Row Publishers, 1978. Reprint with an afterword by Louis Owens, Albuquerque: University of New Mexico Press, 1988.

General Bibliography

Adams, James Truslow. *The Epic of America*. Boston: Little, Brown and Company, 1931.

Bakhtin, Mikhail. *The Dialogic Imagination: Four Essays*. Translated by Caryl Emerson and Michael Holquist. Austin: University of Texas Press, 1981.

Barbeau, Marius. *Indian Days in the Canadian Rockies*. Toronto: Macmillan, 1923.

Beers, Henry A. *An Outline Sketch of American Literature*. New York: Chautauqua Press, 1887.

Bevis, William W. *Ten Tough Trips: Montana Writers and the West*. Seattle: University of Washington Press, 1990.

Bialostosky, Don H. "Dialogics as an Art of Discourse in Literary Criticism." *Publications of the Modern Language Association* 101 (1986): 788–97.

Bierhorst, John. *Four Masterworks of American Indian Literature: Quetzalcoatl/The Ritual of Condolence/Cuceb/The Night Chant*. New York: Farrar, Straus, and Giroux, 1974.

Bigart, Robert James. "The Ideal Personality Form Seen in Ten Animal Tales of the Salishan Flathead Indians of Montana." *Plains Anthropology* (1972): 36–43.

Boas, Franz. *Folk-Tales of the Salishan and the Sahaptin Tribes*. New York: American Folklore Society, 1917.

Brandon, William. *The Last Americans*. New York: McGraw-Hill, 1973.

Brinton, Daniel G. *Aboriginal Authors and Their Productions, Especially Those in the Native Languages. A Chapter in the History of Literature*. (1883). Reprint, Chicago: Checagon Press, 1970.

Bronson, Walter C. *A Short History of American Literature*. 1910. Boston, New York, Chicago: D. C. Heath & Co., Publishers, 1919.

Brown, Bill. "Trusting Story and Reading *The Surrounded*." *Studies in American Indian Literatures* 3 (Summer 1991): 22–27.

Bruchac, Joseph. *Songs from This Earth on Turtle's Back: Contemporary American Indian Poetry*. Greenfield Center, N.Y.: The Greenfield Review Press, 1983.

Burke, Kenneth. *The Philosophy of Literary Forms: Studies in Symbolic Action*. Rev. Ed. New York: Vintage Press, 1957.

Campbell, Joseph. *The Hero's Journey: Joseph Campbell on His Life and Work*. Edited and with an introduction by Phil Couseneau. San Francisco: Harper, 1990.

———. *The Hero with A Thousand Faces*. Published for Bollingen Foundation by Princeton University Press, 1949; third printing, 1973.

Cervantes Saavedra, Miguel de. *The Adventures of Don Quixote*. Translated by J. M. Cohen. Baltimore: Penguin Books, 1970.

Clark, Ella E. *Indian Legends from the Northern Rockies*. Norman: University of Oklahoma Press, 1966.

Cordell, Linda S. "Eastern Anasazi," in *Handbook of North American Indians*, Vol. 9, *Southwest*. Edited by Alfonso Ortiz. Smithsonian Institution. Washington, D.C.: U.S. Government Printing Office, 1979.

Dealey, James Quayle. *Sociology: Its Simpler Teachings and Application*. New York, Boston, Chicago: Silver Burdett & Company, 1909.

De Man, Paul. "Conclusions: Walter Benjamin's 'The Task of the Translator.'" *The Resistance to Theory. Theory and History of Literature* 33 (1986): 73–105.

Dickinson, Thomas H. *The Making of American Literature*. New York: The Century Co., 1932.

Dundes. Alan. "Text, Texture and Context." *Southern Folklore Quarterly* 28 (1964): 251–65.

Dunsmore, Roger. "Reflections on *Wind from an Enemy Sky* and 'killing the water.'" *Studies in American Indian Literatures* 11, no. 1 (Winter 1987): 38–56.

Fahey, John. *The Flathead Indians*. Norman: University of Oklahoma Press, 1974.

Fey, Harold E. and D'Arcy McNickle. *Indians and Other Americans: Two Ways of Life Meet* (1959); Revised edition, New York: Harper & Row, 1970.

Foley, John Miles. *Traditional Oral Epic: The Odyssey, Beowulf, and the Serbo-Croatian Return Song*. Berkeley: University of California Press, 1990.

———. *Immanent Art: From Structure to Meaning in Traditional Oral Epic*. Bloomington, Indiana: Indiana University Press, 1991.

Foucault, Michel. *The Order of Things: An Archaeology of the Human Sciences*. New York: Vintage Books, 1973.

Frye, Northrop. *Anatomy of Criticism: Four Essays*. Princeton, N. J.: Princeton University Press, 1957.

Giraudoux, Jean. *Four Plays*. New York: Hill and Wang, Inc., 1989.

Grant, Bruce. Review of *Runner in the Sun*, by D'Arcy McNickle. *Chicago Sunday Tribune*, November 14, 1954: 38.

Gumerman, George J., ed. *The Anasazi in a Changing Environment*. Cambridge and New York: Cambridge University Press, 1988.

Hale, Edward E. *History of the United States*. New York: Chautauqua Press, 1887.

Halleck, Reuben Post. *History of American Literature*. New York, Cincinnati, Chicago: American Book Company, 1911.

Hans, Birgit. "The Hawk is Hungry: An Annotated Anthology of D'Arcy McNickle's Short Fiction," Master's thesis. University of Arizona, 1986.

——. "Re-Visions: An Early Version of *The Surrounded*." *Studies in American Indian Literature* 4, no. 3 (Fall 1992): 181–95.

——. "Surrounded: The Fiction of D'Arcy McNickle." Ph.D. diss. University of Arizona. Ann Arbor: University Microfilms International (1988): 8822423.

Havelock, Eric A. *The Muse Learns to Write: Reflections on Orality and Literacy from Antiquity to the Present*. New Haven: Yale University Press, 1986.

Higginson, Thomas Wentworth and Henry Walcott Boynton. *A Reader's History of American Literature*. Boston: Houghton, Mifflin and Company, 1903.

Hofstadter, Richard. *The American Political Tradition*. New York: Vintage Books, 1948.

Holden, Madronna. "Making All the Crooked Ways Straight: The Satirical Portrait of Whites in Coast Salish Folklore." *Journal of American Folklore* 89 (1976): 271–93.

Horr, David Agee, ed. *Interior Salish and Eastern Washington Indians III*. A Garland Series: American Indian Ethnohistory, Indians of the Northwest. New York: Garland, 1974.

Huberman, Leo. *We, the People*. 1932. Reprint, New York and London: Harper & Brothers Publishers, 1947.

Hultkrantz, Åke. *Belief and Worship in Native North America*. Edited by Christopher Vecsey. Syracuse: Syracuse University Press, 1981.

Hunt, Eva. "Quetzalcoatl." *Encyclopedia Americana*. 1992.

Huntington, Ellsworth. *The Character of Races as Influenced by Physical Environment, Natural Selection and Historical Development*. New York and London: Charles Scribner's Sons, 1925.

Iser, Wolfgang. *The Act of Reading*. Baltimore: Johns Hopkins University Press, 1978.

——. *The Implied Reader: Patterns of Communication in Prose Fiction from Bunyan to Beckett*. Baltimore: Johns Hopkins University Press, 1974.

Jorgensen, Joseph G. *Salish Language and Culture*. Bloomington: Indiana University Press, 1969.

Josephy, Alvin, Jr. *The Indian Heritage of America*. New York: Alfred A. Knopf, 1968.

Kaiser, Rudolph. "Chief Seattle's Speech(es): American Origins and European Reception." *Recovering the Word*. Edited by Brian Swan and Arnold Krupat. Berkeley: University of California Press, 1987, 497–536.

Kuper, Adam. *The Invention of Primitive Society: Transformation of an Illusion*. New York: Routledge, 1988.

La Farge, Oliver. "A Half-Breed Hero." Review of *The Surrounded*, by D'Arcy McNickle. *The Saturday Review*, 14 March 1936.
————. *The Enemy Gods*. Boston: Houghton Mifflin, 1937.

Larson, Charles R. *American Indian Fiction*. Albuquerque: University of New Mexico Press, 1978.

Lee, Dorothy. *Freedom and Culture*. Englewood Cliffs: Prentice-Hall, 1959.

Leslie, Criag, ed. *Talking Leaves: Contemporary Native American Short Stories*. New York: Dell, 1991.

Limón, José E. "Oral Tradition and Poetic Influence: Two Poets from Greater Mexico," in *Redefining American Literary History*. Edited by A. LaVonne Brown Ruoff and Jerry W. Ward, Jr. New York: Modern Language Association, 1990, 124–41.

Lincoln, Kenneth. *Native American Renaissance*. Berkeley: University of California Press, 1983.

Long, William J. *American Literature*. 1913. Boston: Ginn and Company, 1923.

Lukacs, Georg. *The Theory of the Novel*. Cambridge: MIT Press, 1971.

McDermott, Louisa. "Folklore of the Flathead Indians of Idaho: Adventures of Coyote." *Journal of American Folklore* 14 (1901): 240–51.

McLuhan, Marshall. *The Gutenberg Galaxy*. Toronto: University of Toronto Press, 1962.

Meli, Franco. "D'Arcy McNickle: The Indian War that Never Ends, or the Incredible Survival of Tribalism." *Revue français d'etudes americaines* 13 (November 1988): 363–65.

Merriam, Alan P. *Ethnomusicology of the Flathead Indians*. Viking Fund Publication in Anthropology 44. New York: Wenner-Gren Foundation for Anthropological Research, Inc., 1967.

Merriam, Alan P. *Songs and Dances of the Flathead Indians.* Folkways Records FE 4445 (1953).

Momaday, N. Scott. "The Man Made of Words." *Literature of the American Indians: Views and Interpretations.* Edited by Abraham Chapman. New York: New American Library, 1975, 96–110.

———. "The Native Voice." *Columbia Literary History of the United States.* Edited by Emory Elliott. New York: Columbia University Press, 1988, 5–15.

———. *The Way to Rainy Mountain.* Albuquerque: University of New Mexico Press, 1969.

Mourning Dove. *Cogewea, The Half-Blood: A Depiction of the Great Montana Cattle Range.* Boston: Four Seasons, 1927. Reprint. Lincoln: University of Nebraska Press, 1981.

Murray, David. *Forked Tongues.* Bloomington: Indiana University Press, 1991.

Oakes, Priscilla. "The First Generation of Native American Novelists." *Multi-Ethnic Literatures of the United States* 5, no. 1 (1978): 57–65.

Ong, Walter J. *Orality and Literacy: The Technologizing of the Word.* New York: Methuen, 1982.

Ortega y Gasset, José. *Meditations on Hunting.* New York: Charles Scribner's Sons, 1972.

Ortiz, Alfonso, ed. *New Perspectives on the Pueblos.* Albuquerque: University of New Mexico Press, 1972.

———. "Obituary: D'Arcy McNickle, 1904–1977." *American Anthropologist* 81 (1979): 632–36.

———. "Ritual Drama and the Pueblo World View," in *New Perspectives on the Pueblos.* Edited by Alfonso Ortiz. Albuquerque: University of New Mexico Press, 1972, 135–61.

Ortiz, Simon. *Fightin': New and Collected Stories.* 1969. Chicago: Thunder's Mouth Press, 1983.

Overholt, Thomas W., and J. Baird Callicott. *Clothed-in-Fur: An Introduction to an Ojibwa World View.* Washington, D.C.: University Press of America, 1981.

Owens, Louis. "Where the Road Divides: D'Arcy McNickle's *The Surrounded,* Before and After," in *Native American Literatures.* Edited by Laura Coltelli. Pisa: SEU-Pisa, 1989, 133–40.

———. "The 'Map of the Mind': D'Arcy McNickle and the American Indian Novel." *Western American Literature* 19 (1984): 275–83.

———. *Other Destinies: Understanding the American Indian Novel.* Norman: University of Oklahoma Press, 1992.

———. "The Red Road to Nowhere: D'Arcy McNickle's *The Surrounded* and 'The Hungry Generations.' " *American Indian Quarterly* 13, no. 3 (1989): 239–48.

Parker, Dorothy. *Singing an Indian Song: A Biography of D'Arcy McNickle.* Lincoln: University of Nebraska Press, 1992.

Pattee, Fred Lewis. *A History of American Literature with a View to the Fundamental Principles Underlying Its Development: A Text-Book for Schools and Colleges.* New York, Boston, Chicago: Silver, Burdett & Company, 1896.

Pearce, Roy Harvey. *Savagism and Civilization: A Study of the Indian and the American Mind* (1953). Reprint, Berkeley: University of California Press, 1988.

Phinney, Archie. *Nez Perce Texts.* 1934. Columbia University: Contributions to Anthropology 25. Reprint, New York: AMS Press, 1969.

Plog, Fred. "Prehistory: Western Anasazi," in *Handbook of North American Indians,* Vol. 9 *Southwest.* Edited by Alfonso Ortiz. Smithsonian Institution. Washington, D.C.: U. S. Government Printing Office, 1979.

Purdy, John Lloyd. *Word Ways: The Novels of D'Arcy McNickle.* Tucson: University of Arizona Press, 1990.

Ramsey, Jarold. *Reading the Fire: Essays in the Traditional Indian Literatures of the Far West.* Lincoln: University of Nebraska Press, 1983.

Reuter, Edward Byron. *Race Mixture.* New York: McGraw Hill Book Company, Inc., 1931.

Rorty, Richard. *Philosophy and the Mirror of Nature.* Princeton: Princeton University Press, 1979.

Ruppert, James. *D'Arcy McNickle.* Western Writers Series, no. 83, Boise, Idaho: Boise State University, 1988.

———. *Mediation in Contemporary Native American Fiction.* Norman: University of Oklahoma Press, 1995.

———. "Mediation and Multiple Narrative in Contemporary Native American Fiction." *Texas Studies in Literature and Language* 28, no. 2 (Summer 1986): 209–25.

———. "The Quest for Harmony: Ethno-Historical Perspectives in D'Arcy McNickle's Fiction." *Native American Literatures.* Edited by Laura Coltelli. Pisa: Servizio Editoriale Universitario, 1989.

———. Review of *Wordways*. *Studies in American Indian Literatures*. 3 no. 2 (Summer 1991): 75–77.

———. "Textual Perspectives and the Reader in *The Surrounded*," in *Narrative Chance: Postmodern Discourse on Native American Literatures*. Edited by Gerald Vizenor. Albuquerque: University of New Mexico Press, 1989, 91–100.

Sanders, Helen Fitzgerald. *Trails Through Western Woods*. New York: Alice Harriman Co., 1910.

Sandner, Donald. *Navaho Symbols of Healing*. New York: Harcourt Brace Jovanovich, 1979.

Secco, Anne. "Indian Life in the 1930's as Portrayed in *The Surrounded*, a Novel by D'Arcy McNickle." *Revue française d'etudes americaines* 13 (November 1988): 366–68.

Shaffer, Paul. "A Tree Grows in Montana: Indians turn to old ways to meet new challenges." *Utne Reader* (Jan./Feb. 1990): 54–60. Excerpted from *Arete* (April/May 1988).

Sheehan, Bernard W. *Savagism and Civility: Indians and Englishmen in Colonial Virginia*. Cambridge: Cambridge University Press, 1980.

Silko, Leslie Marmon. *Ceremony*. New York: Viking, 1977.

Smith, Jack F. "Mesa Verde National Park." *Encyclopedia Americana*. 1992.

Spencer, Katherine. *Mythology and Values: An Analysis of Navajo Chantway Myths*. Philadelphia: American Folklore Society, 1957.

Stevens, Hazard. *The Life of Isaac Ingalls Stevens*. 2 Vols. Boston: Houghton, 1900.

Tappan, Eva March. *A Short History of America's Literature with Selections from Colonial and Revolutionary Writers*. 1906. Boston, New York, and Chicago: Houghton Mifflin Company, 1907.

Tedlock, Dennis. *Finding the Center: Narrative Poetry of the Zuni Indians*. Lincoln: University of Nebraska Press, 1978.

———. *The Spoken Word and the Work of Interpretation*. Philadelphia: University of Pennsylvania Press, 1983.

Teit, James. "Salishan Tribes of the Western Plateaus." *Annual Report of the Bureau of American Ethnology* 45 (1930): 23–396.

Todorov, Tzvetan. *Mikhail Bakhtin: The Dialogical Principle*. Vol. 13, Theory and History of Literature. Minneapolis: University of Minnesota Press, 1984.

Turney-High, Henry Holbert. *The Flathead Indians of Montana*. Vol. 43, No. 2, Part 2. Memoirs of the Anthropological Association. Menasha, Wisconsin, 1941.

Vizenor, Gerald. "Native American Indian Literature: Critical Metaphors of the Ghost Dance." *World Literature Today* 66, no. 2 (Spring 1992): 223–27.

Weatherwax, Paul. *Indian Corn in Old America*. New York: The Macmillan Company, 1954.

Weisel, George F. "A Flathead Indian Tale." *Journal of American Folklore* 65 (1952): 359–60.

———. "The Ram's Horn Tree and Other Medicine Trees of the Flathead Indians." *Montana Magazine of History* 1, no. 3 (1951): 5–13.

Wiley, Gordon R., William T. Sanders, and John V. Murra. "Pre-Columbian Civilizations." *The New Encyclopedia Britannica Macropedia*. 1991.

Zachrau, Thekla. "N. Scott Momaday: Towards an Indian Identity," *American Indian Culture and Research Journal*, 3, no. 1 (1979): 39–56.

Zolbrod, Paul G. "When Artifacts Speak, What Can They Tell Us?" In *Recovering the Word: Essays on Native American Literature*. Edited by Brian Swann and Arnold Krupat. Berkeley: University of California Press, 1987, 13–40.

Quotations from McNickle's manuscript version of *The Surrounded* and his journals were obtained from the McNickle Collection at The Newberry Library, Chicago.

Alanna Kathleen Brown is a Professor of English at Montana State University. She has focused her work on the life and writings of Mourning Dove. Major recent essays include "Mourning Dove, Trickster Energy, and Assimilation Period Native American Texts," in *Tricksters in Turn-of-the-Century American Literature* (1994); "Looking Through the Glass Darkly: The Editorialized Mourning Dove," in *New Voices in Native American Literary Criticism* (1993); and "The Evolution of Mourning Dove's Coyote Stories," in *Studies in American Indian Literatures* 4, no. 2 and 3 (1992). She teaches and does public presentations on the works of D'Arcy McNickle, which has led her to publish "The Dilemmas for Antoine and the Readers in D'Arcy McNickle's *Wind from an Enemy Sky*," in the *Canadian Multicultural Education Journal* 13, no. 1 (1995), and the essay written for this book.

Bill Brown, a Ph.D. candidate from the State University of New York at Buffalo, lives in Bixby, Oklahoma, and teaches Native American Fiction at Holland Hall School in Tulsa. He has published articles in *The English Journal* and *Studies in American Indian Literatures*.

Lori Lynn Burlingame received a Ph.D. from the University of Rochester, where she taught, as well as researched Native

American literatures under the direction of Jarold Ramsey. She taught as a FIPSE Fellow at St. John Fisher College, and has published an interview with Leslie Marmon Silko in *Bookpress*.

Phillip Doss is currently finishing his dissertation for a Ph.D. in Humanities from the University of Texas at Arlington, focusing on media-specific concepts of textuality. His other publications include "Traditional Theory and Innovative Practice: The Electronic Editor as Post-structuralist Reader," in *The Literary Text in the Digital Age*.

Robley Evans teaches nineteenth- and twentieth-century English literature at Connecticut College. His special interest is American frontier literature and history, and he is writing a monograph on George Bird Grinnell for the Western American Literature series.

Robert Franklin Gish is Director of Ethnic Studies at California Polytechnic State University, San Luis Obispo. He is the author of *Songs of My Hunter Heart: A Western Kinship* (1992), *First Horses: Stories of the New West* (1992), *When Coyote Howls: A Lavaland Fable* (1994), and numerous other books and writings about the American West. He is a member of the Cherokee Nation of Oklahoma.

Birgit Hans was born and raised in Germany and received a Ph.D. in English from the University of Arizona. She is an Assistant Professor in the Indian Studies Department at the University of North Dakota. She has edited a collection of McNickle's short fiction, *The Hawk Is Hungry & Other Stories*, and has published a number of articles on McNickle's work and other subjects. She is currently preparing an edition of McNickle's unpublished early manuscript of *The Surrounded* for publication.

Dorothy Parker received her Ph.D. from the University of New Mexico. She is the author of *Singing an Indian Song: A Biography of D'Arcy McNickle* (1992), and *Phoenix Indian School: The Second Half Century*. She is currently an Associate Professor of History at Eastern New Mexico University.

James Ruppert holds a joint appointment in the English and Alaska Native Studies Departments at the Univesity of Alaska—

Fairbanks, and is past president of the Associaton for the Study of American Indian Literatures. He is the author of numerous articles on oral and written Native American Literature, as well as *D'Arcy McNickle* (1988), and *Mediation in Contemporary Native American Fiction* (1995), published by the University of Oklahoma Press.

Jay Hansford Vest is Assistant Professor of Native American Literature and Cultures in the American Studies Department at Arizona State University West, Phoenix. A 1992 Fulbright Professor in Bamberg, Germany, his is a Native Monacan Indian from Virginia. Concentrating on American Indian cultural studies, comparative mythologies, and environmental ethics, he has published extensively in scholarly journals and anthologies.

Assimilation; Cultural pluralism; Ethnocentrism; Noble Savage

Feather Boy (Thunderbird), 118, 198, 203, 221, 226; power of, 177, 185; as symbol of culture, 94, 100, 179, 181–82, 209–10, 224–25; and Thunderbird story, 172–73, 224–25
Federal anti-poverty programs (1960s), 14, 27
Flathead, 3, 34
Foley, John, 57–58
Foucault, Michel, 54–55

Grepilloux, Father, 79–82, 89–90, 180–81

Hero myth. *See* Campbell, Joseph
Higginson, Thomas Wentworth, 45–48
History, Native American, 21–22, 24–25, 52; in *Runner in the Sun*, 136–37, 140–42, 153–54; in *Wind from an Enemy Sky*, 97. *See also They Came Here First*
Holy One (Salt's mentor), 123, 126–29, 131–32, 144–46
Hopi, 12, 158, 160, 163
"How Anger Died" (manuscript version of *Wind from an Enemy Sky*), 241n.1; BIA in, 172–77, 183–84; ethnocentrism in, 171, 174–81, 183–84;

federal government in, 177–78; spirituality in, 172–73. *See also Wind from an Enemy Sky*
Huberman, Leo, 36–40
"Hungry Generations, The" (manuscript version of *The Surrounded*), 33–35, 38, 41, 44, 51–52, 104. *See also Surrounded, The*
Huntington, Ellsworth, 38, 43

"Indian Civil Service," 3
Indian Man: A Life of Oliver LaFarge, 6
Indian New Deal (Wheeler-Howard Act), 3, 5, 8, 25–27
Indian Personality Study, 10
"Indian problem," 18–19
"Indian Renaissance," 5, 22, 45
Indian Reorganization Act (1934), 6–9, 27, 35, 44, 185–87, 202; in "How Anger Died," 169, 171–72, 175–76, 182, 184
Indian Rights Association, 20
Indians and Other Americans, 6, 140, 200–201
Indians at Work, 4, 7–10
Indian Tribes of the United States, The, 6, 192, 201–202, 204
Iser, Wolfgang, 64, 189, 199, 203–204

Rafferty, Superintendent Toby, 95, 99, 183–84, 196, 210–11, 216–17, 220, 226

Religion, Native American, 7, 11–12, 21, 179–80, 209, 213. *See also* Native American Church

Reuter, Edward Bryan, 43–44

Runner in the Sun: A Story of Indian Maize, 15, 88; early drafts of, 121, 140; harmony restored in, 122; part of Land of the Free series, 120, 138; reciprocity of opposites in, 121–23; retroactive prophecy in, 149, 150, 239n.29; termination in, 136–37, 143, 153, 155; *They Came Here First* as inspiration for, 119–20; vision quest in, 121, 126–35, 145–46. *See also* Campbell, Joseph; Dark Dealer; Holy One; Navajo, mythology in *Runner in the Sun*; Salt; Stereotypes, in *Runner in the Sun*

Ruppert, James, 94, 100, 152, 219

Salish, 34, 56–57, 61–62

Salt, 118–19, 122–23, 126–31, 134–35, 143–44, 150, 153

Sanders, Helen, 69, 74–79. *See also* "Coyote and Flint"

"Savage" Indian, 39–40, 43, 46, 154–55, 164. *See also* Euroamerican perspective

Stereotypes (of Native Americans), 37–38, 44, 136–38, 218; in *Runner in the Sun*, 151, 154–55, 160; transforming of, 157–58, 164, 194. *See also* Euroamerican perspective

Surrounded, The, 5, 9, 53–57, 59–61, 64–67, 64n.16, 69–86, 89–92, 117–18, 180; change in, 82–83; miscommunication in, 66–67, 80–81, 232n.17; story of Big Paul in, 79–82; "Story of Flint" in, 59, 62–63, 82; "Thing That Was To Make Life Easy" in, 62, 82, 85. *See also* Archilde; "Coyote and Flint"; Grepilloux, Father; Catharine

Tappan, Eva March, 46–48

Termination, 12–15, 17–18, 22–23, 192. *See also Runner in the Sun*, termination in

They Came Here First, 6, 12–13, 54, 56, 64–65, 156, 160, 162–64. *See also Runner in the Sun*

Thunderbird. *See* Feather Boy

University of Chicago, 4, 10, 15, 201

University of Colorado, 4, 17

University of Montana, 5

University of Saskatchewan, 4, 23